THE
BATTLE
FOR YOUR
COMPUTER

THE
BATTLE
FOR YOUR
COMPUTER

ISRAEL AND
THE GROWTH OF
THE GLOBAL
CYBER-SECURITY
INDUSTRY

ALON ARVATZ

TRANSLATED FROM HEBREW BY EYLON LEVY

WILEY

Original edition © Sella Meir Inc. 2022. This translation © 2023 John Wiley & Sons, Inc., published under license from Sella Meir Inc.

Published by John Wiley & Sons, Inc., Hoboken, New Jersey.
Published simultaneously in Canada.

For general information on our other products and services or for technical support, please contact our Customer Care Department within the United States at (800) 762-2974, outside the United States at (317) 572-3993 or fax (317) 572-4002.

Wiley also publishes its books in a variety of electronic formats. Some content that appears in print may not be available in electronic formats. For more information about Wiley products, visit our web site at **www.wiley.com**.

Library of Congress Cataloging-in-Publication Data is Available:

ISBN 9781394174157 (Cloth)
ISBN 9781394174164 (ePub)
ISBN 9781394174171 (ePDF)

Cover Design: Wiley
Cover Image: © ElenVD/Getty Images

SKY10051210_071723

Contents

Preface

It was one of the toughest days in my life. I was sitting on the bus, replaying the last two years in my mind. After endless preparations and six grueling months of boot camp, I walked into the military doctor's tiny clinic and was given the news I'd been dreading: I was being kicked out of the Egoz Unit.

With the benefit of hindsight and age, this might not sound like such dramatic news, but as a young guy with his whole future ahead of him, it was the collapse of a dream. I'd dreamed of joining this elite special reconnaissance unit in the Israeli army since I was in high school. But during a shooting exercise, I'd forgotten to use earplugs and got stuck with a nonstop ringing sound in my ears. I did my best to forget about it because, as an Egoz soldier, I'd been told to overcome any difficulty, whether physical or psychological. Right at the start of my service, I'd promised myself that whatever obstacles I faced, I'd cross them and storm the finish line of our training course—but now I started to worry that avoiding treatment might permanently damage my hearing. I went for a checkup and the doctor gave me two heavy blows: first, there was no cure, and second, there was no way I could remain in combat.

After several hours of being thrown around on buses, I got back to base. I'll never forget that moment: my commander ordered me to change into my fatigues immediately and join the platoon for a routine fitness session. I changed and ran to join the exercise, which I'd always been one of the best at: rope climbing. I tried to shimmy up the rope, but I just couldn't lift myself. I tried again and again, but it was no use. Not even my commander shouting in the background—"Arvatz, get on with it!"—could pick me up an inch. I had zero motivation and zero energy because I knew it would be pointless and useless to try: I was on my way out of the unit anyway. I burst into tears.

Little could I guess this painful moment would change my life for the better.

From territorial commando to cybercommando

I was transferred to the Egoz Unit's human resources branch, but I was absolutely convinced I had so much more to give the army somewhere else. After three months of basically driving everyone around me crazy, I was finally transferred, in June 2009, to Unit 8200 in military intelligence.

Unit 8200 is the IDF unit responsible for gathering signals intelligence ("SIGINT") from cell phones, computers, and suchlike. I was still a soldier in uniform, with ranks and commanders, but in many ways I felt like I'd landed in a different army. Until then, military service had been mainly an experience of self-abnegation, endurance, and discipline. But Unit 8200 placed a completely different emphasis. Creativity, initiative, and critical thinking suddenly took center stage. Only one thing stayed the same: the mission was above all else.

What on earth did I have to do with computer technology? In high school I'd decided I had no interest in anything to do with computer science (I cared much more about physics and social activities), but suddenly at the age of 20, I now found myself devoting my every day and night to it. The human fabric at Unit 8200 was also totally unlike anything I'd known. When I arrived at the unit, I got assigned to Michal—who now lives in Silicon Valley as the CMO of a major startup—and she helped me fill the gaps in my knowledge because I hadn't gone through a proper training course before joining. What struck me immediately about Michal, like all the soldiers in the unit, was not only her extraordinary intelligence, but also her incredible passion for technology and for every new opportunity she could create to gather high-quality intel. I stuck my head in my books, but it all felt so strange to me.

Back then, Unit 8200 was under the command of Brig. Gen. Nadav Zafrir. Unlike his predecessors, he had not climbed up the unit's ranks, but rather came from the special command forces. Zafrir has always been a charismatic leader, a visionary and creative thinker. I once took part in a meeting he chaired and I pitched him one of our ideas. His sharp mind, attention to detail, and vision were striking. Maybe it was thanks to the refreshing perspective that he brought to the unit after gaining most of his military experience in other units, but he understood that in order to remain the tip of the spear of intelligence technology, 8200 would have to undergo a strategic shift.

Besides embracing new modern management methodologies, such as ways to measure the quality of intelligence, Zafrir redefined the unit's focus. Instead of intercepting telephone traffic and digital communications, we pivoted to focus much more on cybertechnologies and intelligence derived from active cyberoperations. We understood that since cyberspace was developing at a dizzying speed—more and more information transferred between computers was no longer "open" and vulnerable to interception, but sent in encrypted form, and sometimes never left computers at all—we urgently needed to shore up our ability to scoop intelligence from there.

This strategic shift set the course of the rest of my training and military service, and probably also my personal future. I became a researcher of computer networks and how they are used, and I learned more and more about cyberattacks and about how to defend against them. I understood that, unlike the picture I had in my head, cybersecurity was not all about sitting in front of a computer and writing lines of code from morning to night. It was a fascinating world of technology, offensive operations, and defensive action, open only to those who were willing to dedicate themselves to studying it in depth. It was a field I didn't think suited me at all when I was in high school, but it soon turned out to be one of the most captivating worlds that I could choose to work in.

A wonder called Stuxnet

In 2010, in the middle of my military service, the world witnessed one of the most significant cyberevents in history: the Stuxnet cyberattack. Stuxnet was a computer worm (a secret program used to penetrate computers) that was launched to hijack and remotely control software developed by Siemens—a program that operated industrial systems, including centrifuges. The worm was able to wriggle between computers plugged into the same network, and at each computer it reached, it checked whether it had this Siemens program on it. If it could not detect it, it left the computer untouched and spread onward. As soon as Stuxnet reached a computer with the right program, it kicked into action: it extracted the list of industrial machinery that the program could operate, identified the centrifuges, and sabotaged their operations to make them spin furiously, far beyond the recommended settings. Stuxnet arrived in disguise: as the centrifuges spun out of control and heated up, Stuxnet made sure that everything would look normal on the operations manager's computer screen.

Stuxnet was discovered by researchers from cybersecurity companies in June 2010, and by July, the worm's existence was public knowledge. In August 2010, the security company Symantec reported that around 60% of Stuxnet-infected computers were in Iran, suggesting that Iran was the target of an attack by the worm's developers. Only then did the scope of the damage at Iran's nuclear facilities come to light; according to estimates, thousands of Iranian centrifuges had been permanently destroyed. The worm astonished cybersecurity researchers, who scrambled to investigate it and its spread.

The experts were also astonished by the technology *behind* Stuxnet. Whoever had programed it had identified no fewer than four security flaws in the operating systems of the computers that controlled the centrifuges, and the worm had exploited them to glide between computers without getting any authorization to access them and without getting caught. Exploitable vulnerabilities (a subject we explore later in the book) are a rare commodity in the cyberworld. Such vulnerabilities can sell for millions of dollars on the black market, and an attack exploiting *four* different vulnerabilities is almost unheard of. Moreover, the computers that this worm attacked were equipped with antivirus programs, but none of them managed to detect Stuxnet because it had camouflaged itself to look like an inoffensive, legitimate program.

The researchers' conclusion was unambiguous: Stuxnet was a weapon created by a state actor to attack the Iranian nuclear program. Such capabilities could only have been the work of many years of research by some of the world's finest cybersecurity experts. Stuxnet could only have been developed by a state actor with major cyberabilities and extensive resources. It was assumed that the United States and Israel, which were already known as supremely capable cybersuperpowers, were behind the attack on Iran. Stuxnet was simply the next stage of an international conflict that had now spilled into cyberspace. Instead of sending troops to Iran by land, air, or sea, a state had launched a computer program to destroy large swaths of its nuclear program. Whereas in 1981, Israel sent warplanes to Iraq to destroy its nuclear reactor, thirty years later, a bunch of people sat at their computers in an air-conditioned room and dispatched a computer program to do essentially the same thing in Iran. Years later, according to media reports, U.S. officials confirmed that Stuxnet had been developed by researchers from the United States and Israel.

Stuxnet left me with my jaw on the floor, and it was all anyone talked about in the hallways of Unit 8200. It was a stunning feat, practically science fiction, far more staggering than any cyberattack I had ever known or heard about. Stuxnet was not the first cyberattack by a state actor, but it was the first to use such high-level technologies and the first to destroy industrial machinery on such a massive scale. It also made the penny drop, for me and for many others, that cyberspace was now a fully fledged new domain of warfare.

Birth of an entrepreneur

After I finished my army service, I started studying law and accounting at Tel Aviv University, where I met my future business partner, Guy Nizan. We discovered that we both came from cybersecurity backgrounds—and cared much more about entrepreneurship than our studies. I brought my experience from reconnaissance cyberattacks at Unit 8200. Guy had served in a unit responsible for defending the Israeli military from cyberattacks and already had experience as a professional consultant for organizations that wanted to keep themselves safe. Opening a cybersecurity company was a natural step for us.

After a failed attempt to launch a cybersecurity consultancy for organizations in Africa, we spotted another opportunity. During a vacation at the Sea of Galilee, Guy started chatting with a family on holiday there. They got to the subject of Guy's cybersecurity experience, and the parents said how important it was for them to give their children early exposure to the cyberworld. Guy didn't wait around, and on the drive home he phoned me and said, "Arvatz, I've got an idea for our next business. We'll set up a company to teach cybersecurity to kids." As the more realistic partner, still reeling from the failure of our previous company, I was skeptical. "I'm with you," I told him, "but I won't believe in an idea till I see the bank's cleared the first client's check!"

We worked hard. We built a course and created promotional materials, and this time, we saw results immediately. There was incredible demand for our content from schools, pupils, and parents, and we cashed in our first check quicker than expected. We realized that we'd put our finger on a real need, and that was how we founded Cyberschool. We sold dozens of courses and workshops for young people, mainly in Israel and the United States, and two years after founding the company, having taught computer technology and cybersecurity to hundreds of students, we sold the firm. Straightaway, we linked up with Gal Ben-David, one of my old Unit 8200 comrades. We had run a few projects together and had great chemistry. On the day I got out of Unit 8200, I went up to him and said, "Just you see, one day we'll do something together." He laughed. He still had three years of military service ahead of him, and starting a company wasn't even on the horizon for him. But then, a few months after he got out of the army, the three of us founded IntSights.

By founding IntSights, we boarded the roller coaster known as a "startup." We started a journey of setbacks, tensions, and sleepless nights, along with loads of achievements that filled us with pride. Along the way, we were joined by many investors, who believed in us and trusted us with their money, and by many talented and dedicated employees, who kept pushing our company forward. Within six years, IntSights had hundreds of clients all around the world and employed some 200 people, including over 100 in Israel itself. At this point, we decided that it would be best for IntSights to become part of a cyber-security company selling a bigger range of products, and we sold the business to Rapid7, an American company, for $350 million.

Being an entrepreneur, at least in the first few years, means being in full-time survival mode. I felt like I owned every success, and every failure was my fault. But looking back, there were undoubtedly many major factors that contributed to our success, and the supportive environment for innovation and cybersecurity in Israel deserves full credit. My partners and I met many cyberentrepreneurs along the way who had taken a similar path to us and generously shared advice from their own experiences. Specialist cybersecurity investors pushed us ahead. Israeli clients who loved adopting new cybertechnologies streamed our way, and we made countless new connections with distributors and clients, thanks to Israelis with expertise in the field. We were also helped by Israel's global reputation for cybersecurity, in terms of both the sheer number of startups developing software to protect organizations from cyberattacks and in terms of its ability to export expert consultants. This opened up plenty of doors for us, and gave us tons of credit from both clients and the market.

I owe thanks to the closest people around me for joining me on this journey: to Smadar, my wife and life partner, for her unwavering support throughout the whole writing and innovation process, and especially for all the evenings and weekends when I was away from home and she took over everything that had to be done; to my dear parents, to whom I owe everything; to Guy Nizan and Gal Ben-David, my partners on this business journey, who held me tight in moments of crisis and deserve full credit for so much of what I've learned and many of my successes. I thank the "reading forum" that gave me priceless words of advice: Ami Even, Liran Gabbay, Meital Levi, Eti Arvatz, Dana Eldar, Guy Finkelstein, Gideon Klugman, Gal Genut, and Amir Hozez. I also want to thank Rapid7 for allowing me to focus on writing this book while still working at the company.

Running throughout this book is my astonishment at the colossal global success of the Israeli cyberindustry, along with recognition of the State of Israel's major contributions to my own personal success. I wrote this book to explore the roots of the cyberindustry's success and to take a glimpse at what the future holds for the State of Israel and its people in this field. I am sure that it will interest colleagues in the cyberindustry, but I wrote it in a friendly and accessible way to make it enjoyable for all readers. Section 1 provides a general introduction, suitable also for readers who are not personally familiar with the industry, and then I hope you will all enjoy diving into the book and learning more about one of the most fascinating and important fields in modern-day Israel—and the whole world.

Acknowledgments

I owe an enormous debt of thanks to the people interviewed in this book. They all generously dedicated their time to me, sharing with me their experience and insights in confidence. For understandable reasons, some of these interviewees asked to remain anonymous and so are not shown. The others are listed chronologically, by the years they entered the Israeli cybersecurity industry.

Brig. Gen. (Res.) Isaac Ben-Israel
Director, Blavatnik Interdisciplinary Cyber Research Center, Tel Aviv University

Gil Shwed
Founder and CEO, Check Point

Shlomo Kramer
Founder and CEO, Cato Networks

Brig. Gen. (Res.) Pinhas Buchris
Former commander, Unit 81 and Unit 8200

Gili Raanan
Founder and Managing Partner, Cyberstarts

Alon Cohen
Founder and CEO, nsKnox

Amichai Shulman
Co-founder, Imperva

Mickey Boodaei
Founder and CEO, Transmit Security

Michal Braverman-Blumenstyk
General Manager, Israel Research & Development Center at Microsoft; CTO, Microsoft Security division

Nir Zuk
Founder and CTO, Palo Alto Networks

Emmanuel Benzaquen
CEO, Checkmarx

Esti Peshin
General Manager, Cyber Division at the Israel Aerospace Industries

Shalev Hulio
Founder, NSO Group; Founder and CEO of Dream Security

Israel Grimberg
Managing Partner, Team 8

Ofer Schreiber
Senior Partner, YL Ventures

Sagi Bar
Founder and CEO, Cyber Education Center

Michael Shaulov
Founder and CEO, Fireblocks

Kobi Samboursky
Co-founder and Managing Partner, Glilot Capital Partners

Lior Div
Founder and CEO, Cybereason

Assaf Rappaport
Founder and CEO, Wiz

Brig. Gen. (Res.) Ehud Schneerson
Former commander, Unit 8200; Founder and CEO, Paragon

Eyal Benishti
Founder and CEO, Ironscales

Ofer Bin-Nun
Founder and CEO, Talon

Liron Tancman
CEO, Rezilion

Dan Amiga
Founder and CTO, Island

Aviv Gafni
Founder and Managing Partner, Hyperwise Ventures

Barak Perelman
Founder and CEO, Indegy

Yevgeny Dibrov and Nadir Izrael
Founders, Armis Security

Hed Kovetz
Founder and CEO, Silverfort

Shira Kaplan
Founder and CEO, Cyverse Capital

Sagi Dagan
Executive VP for Growth and Policy, Israel Innovation Authority

Nir Falevich
Former Cybersecurity Sector Lead, Start-Up Nation Central

Tony Velleca
Founder and CEO, CyberProof

Jay Leek
Founder and Managing Partner, SYN Ventures

Alon Kantor
Founder and CEO, Toka

Ron Reinfeld
CFO, Morphisec

Noa Zilberman
Co-Founder, Odo Security

Gal Glickman
Founder and CEO, Insanet

Brig. Gen. "Y."
Commander, Unit 8200

Amitai Ziv
Tech Reporter, Tech12

Dino Boukouris
Founder, Momentum Cyber

Richard Stiennon
Founder and CEO, IT-Harvest

SECTION 1

What Is Cybersecurity?

CHAPTER 1

The New Gold— Cybersecurity 101

December 23, 2015, was just another typical winter's day in the Ivano-Frankivsk Oblast of western Ukraine. It was late afternoon, near the end of a normal working day at the Prykarpattyaoblenergo power station, which supplies electricity to local residents. One of the maintenance workers took a quick glance at a screen, and for a moment, it looked like a ghost had taken over his computer: the cursor started moving around by itself, and windows started popping open without anyone touching the computer or the keyboard.[1]

It was immediately clear that the mouse wasn't just glitching: someone was moving it on purpose. The cursor started clicking on the programs that controlled the electric circuit breakers and opened them, to interrupt the flow of electricity. The consequences were clear: for every circuit breaker that was opened, thousands of people lost power at home, at the height of winter. The maintenance worker threw himself at the computer, trying to seize control of the cursor— but it was no use. The computer didn't respond. And then suddenly, the computer was locked and the password was changed, so that he could not log in at all. In the end, the electricity supply was cut off at around 30 substations, and hundreds of thousands of Ukrainians were left without power.

For six dark, frozen hours, the electricity company's technicians labored to get electricity flowing to people's homes again. In normal circumstances, they would have been able to take control of the substations' computer systems and work on them remotely, but whoever was behind the attack on the main power station had also scrambled the software that allowed the technicians to work on them remotely, so they had to physically visit every single one of the dozens of substations and fix all the damage by hand. It would take over a year for Ukraine to finish replacing all the damaged components and for all the power stations in the district to return to normal operations.

The attackers did not stop at causing major disruption to Ukraine's electricity supply. They wanted to keep the electricity cut off for as long as possible. At the same time as paralyzing the substations, therefore, they launched another assault: a telephony denial-of-service attack. They unleashed a blitz of automated phone calls to the electricity company's customer service center to block incoming calls from customers phoning to report problems.

This was a well-planned attack, which combined the remote hijacking of computers with the destruction of systems and tactical diversions. The result was that over 200,000 Ukrainians had their electricity cut off at the peak of winter and the power company's operations were disrupted for months on end.

Even though the incident affected tens of thousands of homes, none of the actions that caused it took place in the physical world. If you had walked around this Ukrainian electricity company's power station on the day of the attack, you would not have seen anyone breaking into the facility or hitting the "off" switch. The attackers accessed the company's computers by implanting them with malware— malicious software. The orders to open the circuit breakers were sent remotely, over the internet, and the substations were destroyed with code sent from the electricity company's own computers. In other words—this whole story unfolded in cyberspace, but it had dramatic effects on the physical world.

Cyberspace is the virtual space that is created by connecting computers around the world to each other via the internet or smaller networks. Just as every house has an address, which can be used to deliver mail, on the internet, every computer has an address that other computers can use to send it information. This ability to send and receive information creates a platform that facilitates all the other actions we perform every single day from our computers or cell phones: buying or selling goods, interacting on social media, building all sorts of creative projects, and so on.

Computers have been a part of our lives for nearly 100 years, but cyberspace, the realm in which computers are all interconnected and send each other information, emerged only in the late 1960s. Until then, the only way to connect two computers was to physically connect them with a networking cable. Bob Taylor was a computer scientist at the Advanced Research Project Agency (ARPA, later DARPA) at the U.S. Department of Defense, the agency that led information technology research. For his job, Taylor had three computers, which he used to communicate with three different research institutions. Whenever he wanted to make contact with one of them, he had to switch to working from the computer connected to that specific one. Taylor thought there had to be a way to connect all these computers to each other, so that he could use just one computer to communicate with the rest. The idea of ARPANET, a network of computers capable of communicating with each other, was born.[2]

ARPANET entered development. By October 1969, researchers had managed to send part of the word *login* from a computer at University of California, Los Angeles (UCLA) to a computer at Stanford University, and by November of that year, a network of four computers had been created. ARPANET would soon be connected to a similar network in the United Kingdom, and together, they would become the internet we know today, which connects computers and networks from all around the world into a single network through which they can communicate with each other. Users quickly understood that the internet let them do so much more than just communicate, and this new network became a platform for information sharing, commerce, and creative projects.

The word *cyber* comes from the Greek *kybernetes*, which has its root in the word meaning "govern" or "navigate." But unlike other spaces that you might navigate—land, air, and sea—in cyberspace, the physical and geographic space between any two computers has practically zero significance. Every computer connected to the internet can, in a matter of seconds, receive information from any computer located on the other side of planet Earth.

This platform, connecting computers all over the world and erasing geographic distance, has sparked one of the most dramatic revolutions in human history, accelerating globalization even further. Whereas the Industrial Revolution made it possible for people to reach faraway countries in a matter of hours, the Cyber Revolution now makes it possible to meet virtually with anyone else, anywhere in the world, in a matter of seconds. Whereas the former technological breakthrough let people send each other messages using Morse Code on large and cumbersome machines, this newer breakthrough has made all of us walk around with sophisticated gadgets in our pockets, capable of sending all sorts of messages to anyone else on the planet with a similar device.

But the Cyber Revolution goes much further than any particular technological invention: it has made the developed world redefine what it considers the most valuable commodity on the planet, and it isn't gold.

It's the new gold.

The battle over data

Throughout history, certain commodities have always been considered especially valuable. Whoever controlled them, their extraction, and their trade routes controlled the world, and they drove countless conflicts and wars. In the Middle Ages, it was spices: demand was high because meat was salted for preservation, making its taste difficult to bear without seasoning. Supply was low because spices were grown mainly in Asia, and transporting them, whether by land or by sea, was a long and dangerous business. Gold has always been considered valuable. Originally used to make jewelry and other luxuries, it later became a means of exchange; during the Industrial Revolution, when it was discovered that petroleum could be refined and used to power vehicles, petroleum came to be known as "black gold." The richest man in history, John Rockefeller, made his fortune thanks to his control of the petroleum market and his discovery of cheaper and more efficient means of refining it. In later years, states that controlled oil reserves would gain extraordinary geopolitical power.

The Cyber Revolution has created a new kind of gold: data. Many of today's cyberattacks are connected to the dramatic ascendancy of data.

In late 2020, Iranian hackers managed to pull off a cyberattack against Shirbit, an Israeli insurance company. In a major security breach, scans of customers' ID cards, credit card details, personal medical information, and lots of other data leaked into hands that were, according to assessments, Iranian. Shirbit put out a statement confirming a "data leakage incident"—a vague description that might have covered anything from the minor theft of some documents to a massive hack. Having won several government contracts, Shirbit provided insurance for many public sector workers, whose details were now in hostile hands. The damage was twofold: besides the blow to Israeli national morale, knowing that foreign hackers could breach databases with intimate information about state employees, this information was vulnerable to exploitation in the wrong hands. It would be easy for criminals to impersonate the people whose details had leaked, or else to exploit information about their personal needs (specifically, their health) to contact them and offer them "services," like new insurance programs, charge them—and then disappear.

The hackers initially demanded a ransom of $50 in Bitcoin—around $1 million—to not release this data, but after 24 hours, they doubled it to $100 in Bitcoin. When their demand was ignored, the ransom kept shooting up, hitting $200 in Bitcoin within a week. The insurance firm decided not to pay the ransom, apparently assuming that it could not trust the hackers not to publicize the stolen materials anyway. There are organized hacker groups in the world that operate like real businesses and invest in their reputations for "trustworthiness," such that whoever coughs up really does get "protection" for their data. In the attack on Shirbit, however, that didn't seem to be the case.

Israel's National Cyber Bureau—the national authority responsible for providing cybersecurity for Israel's critical infrastructure—was involved in this incident, and it is safe to assume that its officials instructed Shirbit not to cooperate with the hackers. Whereas Shirbit ended 2019 with profits of 26 million NIS, in 2020, its profits crashed to less than one million NIS. The attack on Shirbit caused shockwaves in the Israeli economy.

As the CPO of IntSights at the time, I received calls from dozens of desperate customers. They knew that Shirbit held lots of data about them, including contracts and confidential information about shared clients, and they understood that the hack had exposed sensitive information that was theirs, too. They saw us, an intelligence provider, as the right address to work out how much commercial damage this incident had exposed them to. Among the clients knocking on our door were other insurance firms that worked with Shirbit and other banks that feared that customers who had insurance policies with Shirbit had shared their bank account details with it—details that had now leaked.

We opened an operations room at IntSights and manually pored over the leaked files, searching for information that belonged to our clients. The incident made clear to us not only the importance of top-notch cyberdefense, but also our need as a company to keep developing technologically. In the long run, the Shirbit hack pushed us to develop new technologies that would analyze information leaked in ransomware attacks and find files belonging to our customers. As in every highly publicized cyberincident, our customers quickly understood that our most basic data could be a powerful weapon in the wrong hands.

Gold on the cloud

Until not long ago, we (or our parents) wrote documents, letters, and accounts by hand, without any easy way to edit them, and they took up lots of space in our homes and offices. Computers, however, let us type up documents quickly and conveniently, with memory drives that can store thousands of files. Thanks to the ability to search for text and easily classify files, it is easy to find a specific string of text in a pile of documents.

One of the major changes caused by the accelerated development of computing was that people realized that it was much easier to create and store information digitally than by other means. Computers have thus become humanity's main storage space for personal and commercial data—from documents to images, correspondence, games, shopping, and more. Over 92% of households in the United States now own at least one computer.[3]

This process was accelerated in several stages, as the internet became accessible to all. In the first stage, the internet allowed for anyone to open a website and upload information accessible to anyone surfing the internet. This shifted lots of information that used to travel through newspapers or billboards to cyberspace. The invention of email led many people to abandon postal services and start sending all their correspondence digitally. In the second stage, websites started letting visitors upload their own content. This process was very limited at first, with forums that let internet users publish and reply to messages, but this gained major momentum when social media networks entered the scene and Facebook was opened up to the general public in 2006.

The next leap in the Cyber Revolution came with the development of cloud computing, which pushed internet users to upload their data to servers connected to the internet instead of storing them on their own devices. A server is a computer that is not designed for human use, but rather provides services needed to store vast amounts of information in a single place. The world of computers is divided into servers and terminals, connected through home or organizational networks or through the internet itself. Servers store all kinds of information that is available online. They are usually physically located on server farms all around the world, and as long as there is an internet connection between them and our own computers, information can be extracted from them in seconds. When you enter a news site, for example, you are effectively going to a server and asking it for information from the site you want to reach, and your web browser—your gateway to the internet—opens up that information for you in a readable format.

But your browser can also offer you so much more. Actions that we used to perform *on* our computers, like creating documents, sending emails, or saving files, can now be done *using* our computers; not on *them*, but on the cloud. The cloud stores the software that runs these operations and saves them, and it also helps to relieve pressure on computers' processing capacity. But its biggest advantage has to do with software updates: providers no longer have to worry that their software might not work on particular computers, and end users no longer have to bother installing software updates because providers can simply update their programs and send the upgraded versions straight to the cloud, without them ever needing to reach the end users' personal devices.

The story of one of the pioneers of cloud computing begins with Drew Houston, a student at the Massachusetts Institute of Technology (MIT). During college, he found himself having to write and edit the same documents on many different computers. The problem was that he kept forgetting his USB drive with all his files. To solve this problem, instead of starting over with every file from scratch, he started emailing himself the latest documents, so that all he had to do was download them onto the right computer. But as he started working on more and more documents, it became increasingly hard to keep track of all his documents and the latest versions in all these emails.

The straw that broke the camel's back came when his computer charger caught fire one day and completely destroyed his hard drive, erasing all his documents without any backups.[4] Houston looked around for a good solution but couldn't find anything decent, and so he decided that it was time to develop his own solution: he saved all his files on a main computer, which was connected to the internet, and then whichever computer he sat down to work from, he was able to "pull" the latest files from this device and work on them. Having revised the files, he saved the latest version back on the main computer. This way, the latest version would always be available online, so that even if the computer he was working on was destroyed—everything would still be backed up.

Houston realized that he was not the only one grappling with this problem and he set up a company to provide a similar solution to anyone who needed it: a massive virtual box for documents, where anyone could drop files. Dropbox was born. It went public in 2018, with a market valuation of $8.2 billion.

Like Dropbox, the market was soon filled with companies based on the idea that everyone's computer files could be saved on servers connected to the internet, collectively known as the "cloud," instead of on personal computers. This makes the latest versions of files accessible from any computer with an internet connection, so that if your personal device breaks down and all your files get erased, everything will still be saved on the cloud.

The world soon came to understand the advantages of cloud storage, and Dropbox was confronted with challengers, such as Google Drive and OneDrive. There soon developed other services, such as Amazon Web Services and Google Cloud, that let software developers save and run their programs on the cloud. Photos can also be saved on the cloud, with services such as Google Photos. In short, people have started transferring more and more of their information from their personal devices to cyberspace.

As this trend intensified, people began to understand the immense potential of access to this data. The technological units of the Israel Defense Forces (IDF), where I served at the time, also understood that intelligence material was increasingly stored there and that getting a hold of it would require a whole different kind of effort.

If you know what someone likes eating and wearing, what their political opinions are, and who their families are, you can start finding patterns, managing massive reams of data, and running countless social experiments. This ability allows the companies that control this data to analyze and predict human activity better than ever before. It is easier to target advertising or offer services based on a seller's "familiarity" with a buyer's habits. Data about preferences and opinions—content that people post online regularly—is worth *a lot* of money to advertisers. Information contained in commercial files uploaded to Dropbox or similar services may be highly sensitive and deal with a company's business plans. Such data, which can include sensitive financial details, such as credit card numbers, is worth buckets of money to competitors. For this reason, the more personal and commercial information exists in cyberspace, the greater the demand for security solutions to keep this information safe. The dependency on these solutions is only deepening, and individuals and companies are increasingly willing to pay top dollar for them.

The result of this whole process is that the value of data is constantly rising. Advertisers are willing to pay huge sums for precise information about customers to sell them products more easily. Private individuals and companies are willing to pay up to store their files conveniently. During the Industrial Revolution, coal and petroleum powered trains, generated electricity, and fueled factories, but now during the Cyber Revolution, it is data and the quest for it that drives companies to develop services to store and easily access data, which then make them some of the world's biggest and most successful companies. As of 2022, for example, four of the five most valuable companies in the world sell products that include services for users to upload and store their information online. Google's stated mission, as one of the biggest technology giants of all time, is to organize the world's information and make it universally accessible.

Data has become the "digital gold." And just as pirates used to hunt real gold, the pirates of the modern world—hackers—are hunting this digital gold. Any information that they can steal, they sell to the highest bidder in the black market of cyberspace: the dark web, which we explore in Chapter 4.

Corporations have started to make a fortune from selling this information to advertisers and other third parties, and so in the name of privacy and people's ownership rights over their own data, many democratic states have started passing laws to curb the exploitation of this data. Companies are legally required to take strict steps to prevent their customers' personal data from leaking, and they risk getting slapped with fines if they negligently fail to protect it. Shirbit, the Israeli insurance company, was fined nearly 11 million NIS (around $3 million) by Israeli authorities for breaching regulations.

One of the best known laws in this regard is the Global Data Protection Regulation, or GDPR, which came into force in the European Union in 2018 and imposes fines and data protection standards on corporations that store user data. The biggest-ever fine for violations of the GDPR was imposed on Amazon by the EU regulation in Luxembourg. Amazon was accused of exploiting its users' personal data without consent to show them targeted ads and was fined €746 million. The EU regulation in Ireland slapped another massive fine on Instagram.

Having exposed the email addresses and phone numbers of its platform's underage users, Instagram was fined €405 million.[5] The messaging giant WhatsApp also entered the list of history's biggest GDPR fines when it too was penalized the amount of €225 million by the regulation in Ireland after being accused of not providing its clients transparent information about the information traffic between its platform and other Facebook subsidiaries.[6]

But unlike what you might expect, regulation has not cooled the market. On the contrary. This modern gold rush has generated vast amounts of gold, and unlike other precious materials, where rising supplies meant falling prices, this bonanza of digital gold has caused prices to *rise*, precisely because information is more valuable when there is more of it. It can be squeezed for more and more value, stored in more advanced ways, and analyzed with new techniques to extract more and more benefit from it, move it around, and use it in ways that can practically breach walls, cripple power stations, and topple states. A gold rush has given way to a rush to control as much data as possible.

The Internet of Things

In 2015, Andy Greenberg stepped into his white Jeep Cherokee and started driving through St. Louis. After a short drive, he boarded the freeway and sped up to 110 kmph. Suddenly, as Greenberg gripped the steering wheel with both hands, the AC switched itself on and started running. The radio started blaring, and no matter what buttons he hit, he couldn't turn it off or down. The wipers started swishing, and Greenberg couldn't see anything but cleaning fluid covering his windshield. And then finally, his gearbox was disabled. He repeatedly slammed his foot on the brakes, but it was no use. Greenberg had to swerve off the road, straight into a ditch.

Throughout all this time, two security researchers, Chris Valasek and Charlie Miller, were sitting in Charlie's living room with their laptops. Greenberg's Cherokee was connected to the internet through the cell phone network, and Valasek and Miller managed to hack the car remotely, send it orders, and gain full control of the vehicle. They hijacked not only the AC and multimedia system, but also the engine, the door locks, the steering wheel, and the brakes.

Luckily for Greenberg, he was in the loop on the experiment. Valasek and Miller were security researchers and had no intention to hurt him, only to illustrate the dangers of connecting vehicles to the internet and to raise public awareness by having *Wired*, the technology magazine where he worked as a reporter, cover the experiment.[7] Nowadays, vehicles are increasingly being manufactured with internet connections and with computers that control their many functions, such as the ignition, the gears, and the brakes. This system allows for vehicles to be sent software updates over the internet.

These information researchers proved that not just personal computers, but any other machine with computing capabilities and an internet connection could be hijacked remotely. The global trend today is to add computing capabilities and internet connectivity to an increasing range of products—fridges, home lighting, traffic lights, and even satellites—creating what is called the "Internet of Things," or IoT.

The IoT lets users remotely gather information about their devices' components and operate them. For example, if your home AC unit is connected to cyberspace, it can send you information about the temperature at home and let you operate it from your smartphone. In effect, this whole shift began when the first telephone was connected to cyberspace. It might sound almost trivial nowadays, but the idea of the smartphone—of which Apple's iPhone is the flagship product—is to add computing capabilities to a telephone, so that it can perform almost any task you might run on a computer, including tasks that require an internet connection. What the car experiment in St. Louis proved was that any device that connects to cyberspace exposes itself to cyberattacks.

What the Internet of Things means is not only that many more devices can be connected to the internet, but that this connection creates a reciprocal relationship between all connected devices. They can all transfer information to each other, analyze it, and follow any instructions it contains. A smartphone, for example, can operate a vacuum cleaner; a camera can send information to a computer or the cloud. This shift has been so revolutionary that some claim that the Internet of Things is the next revolution after the Industrial Revolution and the Cyber Revolution. But whether this is a brand-new revolution or simply an outgrowth of the Cyber Revolution, nobody can deny that our lives will look different once everything around us is interconnected and able to communicate, and we can operate any device by tapping the screens of the phones in our pockets. Imagine a fridge sending your phone an alert when you run out of milk, a public toilet that sends a signal when it needs a deep clean, or a wardrobe that uses a daily weather briefing from your phone to recommend an outfit.

But the most sensational benefits offered by this new technology come hand-in-hand with their most alarming dangers. If a traffic light system is connected to the internet, then sophisticated hackers can plug in, play around with its sequences, and cause an accident. If home cameras are connected to the internet, then strangers can also connect to them. In our work at IntSights, we saw a dramatic rise, starting in 2017, in darknet forums where hackers were interested in hacking objects connected to the IoT—especially cameras.

As this modern gold rush produces more and more gold, it is becoming increasingly urgent to shield it from bandits. The need to protect our many devices from getting breached has become essential and impossible to ignore.

CHAPTER 2

The Keyboard War—How Global Militaries Exploited the New Domain

After the attack on the Ukrainian electricity company, with which Chapter 1 began, Ukraine was quick to accuse Russia of leaving 200,000 of its people without power for hours on a freezing winter's day. Experts agreed that the evidence pointed to Russia, which made sense in the context of its relations with Ukraine. This book was completed as the war in Ukraine still raged with full force, and nobody could predict when and how it might end. One thing, however, is clear: for years now, cyberspace has been a domain of war between Russia and Ukraine, just like the other traditional domains of war.

Humanity's most familiar domain has always been land. That is where humans have always lived, settled down, evolved, and fought their wars. But early in its development, humanity also discovered the sea as another important domain through which people and goods could be moved. Maritime warfare—whether organized or as piracy— intensified as a result. The invention of the airplane by Wilbur and Orville Wright in 1903 created another brand-new domain of human activity, which was swiftly harnessed for warfare.

Cyberspace confronts humanity with a challenge similar to the challenges posed by land, air, and sea. On the one hand, human living standards are soaring beyond all recognition, just as the discovery of the traditional domains opened up new opportunities, but at the same time, humanity has also become exposed to countless new dangers. Criminals have begun to spot the commercial potential of cyberattacks, and this new form of crime has spiraled.

In 2013, government infrastructure in South Korea was targeted in two major cyberattacks: the first was in March and paralyzed three media channels and two banks for several hours; the second followed in June, hacking the website of the presidential office and nearly 70 other government sites.[1] The U.S. cybersecurity firm McAfee, which investigated the first (March) incident, concluded that the attack was the grand finale of a long and covert espionage campaign aimed at obtaining military information about South Korea and the United States. The clues pointed to a group of hackers from North Korea.

In December 2015, the month of the cyberattack against the Ukrainian electricity company, the conflict between Ukraine and Russia was in full swing. In February 2014, Russian soldiers had seized control of key positions in the Crimean Peninsula in Ukrainian territory. Soon after that, Russia held a referendum among the residents of the peninsula (which was strongly condemned as illegal), and after the vote showed overwhelming support for "rejoining Russia," Moscow officially annexed Crimea.[2] In November 2015, about a month before the cyberattack on the power station, pro-Ukrainian activists blew up power lines carrying electricity from mainland Ukraine to the Crimean Peninsula and blocked the electricity company's technicians from accessing the damaged pylons in order to delay their repair. More than 1.6 million residents of Crimea were left without power, and some even without water or internet.[3] It looked like Russia, with its cyberattack on the Ukrainian power grid, was trying to send a message: *if you attack our electricity infrastructure, then we'll attack your power supplies, too.*

But this was not the full picture. Cyberresearchers pointed out that Russia might have been motivated by more than the sabotage of the power lines and the damage it caused the Crimean Peninsula. Executing such a cyberattack would have taken months of preparations, including planning, gathering advance intelligence, penetrating the relevant computer network, and "roaming" around that network until the hackers found the command center computer that controlled the power stations that were ultimately crippled. Researchers believe that the planning for the attack started in May 2014, if not earlier: not long after Russia's original invasion of the Crimean Peninsula and over a year before the Ukrainian sabotage of the power lines.[4] The power lines were probably just the pretext for the Russians to exploit their access to the Ukrainian electricity company and to shut down power to hundreds of thousands of Ukrainians as part of their international conflict.

Since Russia's invasion of Ukraine on February 24, 2022, cyberspace has served as a fully-fledged theater of war, waged in tandem with ground offensives. Russia has launched attacks to gather intelligence, but mainly to damage infrastructure in the hopes of destroying it (with some success), and especially the infrastructure of energy, telecoms, media, and finance companies as well as government bodies. Experts estimate that the damage to Ukrainian cyberspace has been fairly limited and that, paradoxically, Ukraine has bounced back from attacks relatively quickly precisely because it is *not* a developed country, like the United States, which has a much higher rate of Internet of Things (IoT) connectivity. Some of Ukraine's primary systems, such as critical infrastructure in chemical plants, hospitals, networks, and traffic light grids, are still operated manually. With many home appliances, such as electric lights or insulin pumps, not yet connected to the IoT, it is definitely not the most "advanced" situation, but it does give Ukraine partial protection from hackers.[5]

Ukraine is not alone. Russia is probably the world's most active state cyberattacker, and groups of Russian hackers regularly attack a range of targets. In 2007, after Estonia decided to move a memorial to Soviet soldiers from the heart of its capital, Tallinn, to a less central location, major unrest erupted in the streets because of stiff resistance from ethnic Russians. The disturbances coincided with cyberattacks on banks, media outlets, and government ministries, including DDoS (distributed denial-of-service) attacks bombarding servers with simultaneous messages from thousands of computers to make them collapse. An investigation into the attacks pointed to computers in Russian territory, but Russia has always refused to cooperate with any inquiry. Other groups of Russian hackers were probably responsible for hacking a central computer at a water facility in Florida in 2021 and boosting the amount of sodium hydroxide in the water: an attack that, had it gone undetected, would have spelled catastrophe. The same year, hackers also entered the computer controlling the Colonial Pipeline, the biggest petroleum pipeline in the United States, and crippled it until the company paid a $4.4 million ransom in Bitcoin.

Russia is not alone: many states are harnessing cyberspace for warfare against their enemies. Besides Russia, cybersuperpower status is also attributed to the United States, China, Britain, and Israel, among others,[6] but official cyberwarfare entities exist in more than 70 states worldwide.[7] The difference between states with "normal" cyberabilities and cybersuperpowers is mainly in their ability to detect vulnerabilities and in the breadth of their cyberwarfare ambitions. Cyberwarfare capabilities are no longer "nice to haves," but tools that nations realize they *must* have in their arsenals, or else they will find themselves in a position of significant inferiority relative to countries that can hijack their most critical infrastructure without any means of fighting back.

In 2010, the United States established its U.S. Cyber Command as the military body responsible for coordinating the activities of the other branches of the military in cyberspace. The U.S. Cyber Command is responsible not only for providing cyberdefense, but also for "providing support to combatant commanders"[8] as part of a strategic conception that sees warfare in cyberspace as an integral part of wars waged in other domains, and in some respects, even a preferable form of warfare to these traditional ones.

Why? First, cyberspace makes it possible to attack targets without risking human lives. Stuxnet, the computer worm that damaged centrifuges in Iran, is a classic example. By way of comparison, in its efforts to sabotage the Iranian nuclear program, Israel is reported to have carried out assassinations of scientists involved in nuclear weapons development. The most striking assassination was that of Mohsen Fakhrizadeh, one of the architects of the Iranian nuclear program, near Tehran in November 2020.[9] The machine gun that shot Fakhrizadeh dead was operated remotely, but its assembly and positioning required people to risk their lives on the ground. The advantage of an attack like Stuxnet for Israel or the United States, in terms of the ability to keep their agents safe, is obvious. In this respect, this mode of attack is similar to certain uses of airspace, like the U.S. assassination of the commander of Iran's Quds Force, Qasem Soleimani, on January 3, 2020. The assassination was carried out using unmanned aerial vehicles, avoiding the risk that forces on the ground would have faced if a land route had been chosen for the mission.

Second, in many cases, cyberattacks let attackers remain anonymous. When soldiers or weapons are sent into enemy territory, it is relatively easy to work out which country the attack is coming from. In the case of cyberattacks, however, computers are often breached so quietly that the victim has no idea.

Moreover, attackers can also conceal their identities by using special technologies, such as proxy servers: online computers that serve as a buffer and intermediary between other computers and the internet. Let's say I want to access Wikipedia. Instead of going straight to **Wikipedia.org** and asking for a particular page, my computer can access a proxy server, tell it that it wants to receive information from Wikipedia, and get it to make the request and pass on the information. In none of this process are any details that might identify my computer disclosed to Wikipedia because the proxy server acts like a buffer between us. This is an extremely valuable option in cyberwarfare, especially when the attacking state is afraid of a counterattack or some other response, such as international economic and political sanctions. The attack on the Ukrainian electricity company is a good example because even today, nobody can say with 100% certainty that Russia was indeed behind it.

A third advantage of cyberwarfare is cost. Countries that want to buy "Made in USA" F-35 fighter jets, in order to fight in the aerial domain, must pay over $100 million for each plane. In the maritime domain, the cost of a Sa'ar 5-class corvette, of the sort used by the Israeli Navy, can also reach $100 million, and a German Dolphin-class submarine will set you back $500 million. In the land domain, a country that wants to buy a British Challenger 2 tank will have to cough up more than $7 million per tank—and will have to buy a whole fleet. It will also have to invest millions of dollars in maintenance for each tank.

In contrast, in order to execute a cyberattack, all a state needs is a few computers and a few servers, at a cost of no more than a few tens of thousands of dollars. For cyberattacks like those pulled off in Ukraine and Iran, a state has to buy computers in order to write the malware's code and a few internet-compatible servers in order to send instructions to malware once it has found its way to the target computer. With a very small upfront payment, therefore, it is possible to wreak enormous damage, such as the damage that set Iran's nuclear program back by several years. These computers and servers do not reflect the full cost because states must also invest money and effort in finding and training the skilled manpower to execute such an attack, but still, the sums are nowhere close to the cost of a fighter jet, a tank, or any other advanced weapon.

Fourth, cyberwarfare blurs the boundaries between the home front and the real front, making it possible to strike deep inside enemy territory, hitting civilian areas and even underground bunkers. In this respect, too, cyberspace resembles airspace, which opened up the possibility of direct attacks on the home front and turned entire countries into battlegrounds. Cyberattacks do not involve bombings from above, but rather penetrations from within: every device is exposed to cyberattacks, and virtually all military or civilian infrastructure relies on machinery that can be hacked this way.

Attacks on strategic infrastructure are only one form of cyberwarfare. Nations also use cyberspace on a massive scale for a whole other purpose: espionage.

The new Trojan horse

The basis for cyberespionage is the wholescale transfer of information to cyberspace, as we have seen. Increasing amounts of information are being stored on computers. Information that used to be written down and saved on paper or in books has long since been moved to word processing programs or similar software and stored digitally. Likewise, communications that used to be conducted through letters or over the phone now take place online. The internet processes vast amounts of information every day, including text, images, voice recordings, and more. This trend, the migration of information from pages and phones to cyberspace, has also had a profound effect on international espionage.

As long as the information that states want to obtain from their enemies exists on paper, they have to physically send spies to photograph or snatch it. When conversations take place over the phone, states must physically wiretap the phone line to eavesdrop on a call. When enemy soldiers communicate over radio devices, spies need gadgets near those troops' location in order to pick up on what they are saying. But as soon as information is located on computers and sent over the internet, none of these physical workarounds close to the enemy's location are needed. Enemy computers can be hacked remotely, scooping up all the information they store, and attackers with more advanced tools can convert enemy computers or telephones into spying devices in their own right.

In 2009, Lockheed Martin, one of the U.S. Defense Department's major contractors, reported a breach of its computer network in 2007–2008. The hackers seem to have gotten in through access given to an external contractor, using Trojan horse technology: malware designed to steal information, but which looks like normal software, giving naïve computer users no reason to suspect it will harm them. As soon as this malware was installed on Lockheed Martin's computers, the hackers managed to breach even computers that were not connected to the network. They stole highly sensitive information about the F-35 project, the Defense Department's most expensive weapons development program, worth some $300 *billion*. U.S. government officials said that the attack had apparently come from China, but without providing clear proof.[10]

Over the next decade, China produced several versions of the Chengdu J-20, a fifth-generation stealth aircraft similar to the American F-35. There are suspicious similarities between the models' electro-optical and other systems, and experts reasoned that the ability of the Chinese to copy the American designs was probably connected to the Lockheed Martin breach. In 2015, these suspicions became even better grounded, when some of the documents leaked by former NSA employee Edward Snowden confirmed that F-35 blueprints had, indeed, been stolen by the Chinese. Thus, instead of pouring gargantuan sums into the development of their own advanced fighter jets, the Chinese simply invested a small sum to hack American computers and steal plans that had already enjoyed such massive American capital investments.[11]

Blueprint thefts also occurred before the cyber era. The design of Israel's Nesher fighter jet, the forerunner of the Kfir aircraft—which served the Israeli Air Force for some 20 years—was based on France's Mirage 5. The French warplane was developed in cooperation with Israel, but a few days before the outbreak of the 1967 Six-Day War, French President Charles de Gaulle imposed a weapons embargo on Israel. A Swiss engineer smuggled blueprints of the engine to Israel (and served a prison sentence for it)—and the Israeli Aircraft Industries developed the Nesher. Putting aside the sheer human audacity behind the development of the Nesher jet, the technological shift is stunning: whereas in the 1960s, 10 tons of physical documents were smuggled from France to Israel, by the time of the theft of the F-35 schematics, such a heist could be pulled off entirely digitally. The costs, the risks, and the dependence on outside actors have all dropped significantly.

Cyberattacks have become one of the most important methods of espionage in international conflicts. By stealing information about weapons development programs, states can bring their weapon technologies up to speed without having to invest resources in research and development. Espionage can also give states a much better understanding of their rivals' weapons systems, helping them defend themselves much more effectively. Cyberattacks allow states to obtain sensitive information on their enemies in so many fields, from strategic plans to operational military programs to armament levels and more. Offensive cybercapabilities, harnessed for espionage purposes, open the door not only to sensitive information—but also to intelligence superiority.

Nevertheless, effective espionage does not necessarily require exposing covert plans or other secret strategic information: in March 2019, in the run-up to Israel's elections, Israeli media revealed that the personal cell phone of the main opposition leader, former Israel Defense Forces (IDF) chief of staff Benny Gantz, had been hacked— apparently by Iranians.

A minor political storm erupted in Israel as people demanded to know whether Gantz, potentially Israel's next prime minister, might be vulnerable to extortion by the hackers. After all, access to his phone meant access to all his text messages and emails, photos he had taken, and phone calls he had made. Besides the psychological impact of an enemy state breaching the personal device of a former military chief and candidate for prime minister, the hack raised concerns that someone might try to blackmail Gantz by threatening to leak personal photographs or any other sensitive information. Fortunately, no such thing happened, but the looming threat reminded many of another hacking episode, also during an election campaign, halfway around the world.

Hacking public opinion

The 2016 U.S. presidential election was especially stormy. Democratic candidate Hillary Clinton was running against Donald Trump, the Republican candidate known for his brash and provocative style. Both parties' campaigns were considered particularly negative, and polarization in America seemed to have reached a historic high. This polarization was not limited to the politicians; it seeped into social media and resulted in extreme and violent rhetoric. Hillary Clinton was the favorite throughout the race, but it ended with Trump's shocking victory.

Behind the scenes of the candidates' high-profile campaigns, there was action in cyberspace. Throughout the whole race, Democratic strongholds and Clinton campaign officials came under repeated cyberattacks. Trojan horses were planted on party officials' computers, which then sent documents and emails from them straight to the attackers. The leaked files contained sensitive information about the Democratic National Committee, which was supposed to be neutral in the presidential primaries, but had, in fact, promoted Hillary Clinton over her rival Bernie Sanders. The leak also exposed the Democratic Party's fundraising methods, which looked more like a well-oiled machine for squeezing money out of donors based on psychological profiling than the conduct of a genuine nonprofit organization. These documents and correspondences were published online and caused immense embarrassment to the Democratic Party and to Hillary Clinton during the election against Trump. In December 2016, around a month after the election, the U.S. Department of Homeland Security and the FBI published a report revealing that these attacks against the Democratic Party had come from Russian intelligence agencies.[12]

In January 2017, the Office of the Director of National Intelligence published a report that claimed with "high confidence" that Russian President Vladimir Putin had ordered a wide-scale campaign to promote Donald Trump's candidacy.[13] The report concluded that Putin not only wanted to undermine American democracy in general; he also believed that Clinton would take a harder line against Russia and therefore wanted to thwart her election to the Presidency. It also concluded that the cyberattacks against the Democrats and the online leak of embarrassing materials were part of the same campaign to harm Clinton's popularity. The report also revealed that Russia had employed trolls, people hired to fuel antagonism and discord. They had opened thousands of fake profiles pretending to belong to Americans, which they used to promote pro-Trump events.

This was not Russia's first campaign to influence American public opinion during a presidential election. During the Cold War, the Soviet Union had employed agents and promoted articles in the media to sway elections. But what once had to be done through physical newspapers, with real people on the ground, can now be done with the click of a mouse, thousands of miles away.

States under attack were the first to realize that if offensive warfare had migrated to cyberspace, then cyberdefense would have to develop there, too. Any state that possesses digital assets that it cannot protect is in serious danger.

CHAPTER 3

"Hello, It's Me, a Nigerian Prince"— New Crime

Albert Gonzalez was born to a Cuban immigrant family in the United States. He was a good boy, who helped his father run his business and studied hard at school in Miami, Florida, where he was branded a "computer geek." But nobody could imagine what would soon come of him. The big twist in his life came when the computer his parents bought him when he was 12 caught a virus. The young Gonzalez was bummed, but also intensely curious: how could computers be protected from viruses? Why would anyone infect them with viruses in the first place? Soon enough, Albert developed an obsession for computers and went from being a friendly boy who enjoyed helping others to a socially challenged introvert. By the age of 14, Gonzalez had managed to obtain credit card details on the dark web and use them to buy video games, music albums, and shoes, and even to link up with hackers who had breached NASA computers.[1]

In time, Gonzalez joined a group calling itself the ShadowCrew, which stole credit card details and other personal information—and sold them. In 2002, the group set up **shadowcrew.com** as a platform for selling this stolen data, along with a forum for cybercrime professionals to consult with each other and even share documents teaching others how to steal credit card details. Gonzalez was arrested by the Federal Bureau of Investigation (FBI) and became an informant, helping the bureau gather information and reach the criminals active on the website. His assistance ultimately led to mass convictions and the platform's closure in October 2004.

But for Gonzalez, this was only the beginning. In 2006, with 10 other partners, he started traveling around Miami with his laptop, hunting for passwordless Wi-Fi networks. He managed to enter the networks of TJX, the conglomerate that owns retail giants such as T.J. Maxx and Marshalls. As soon as he was able to connect his computer to the company's Wi-Fi network, he installed a program on its computers that scooped up customers' credit card details and sent them to him. In this way, he managed to steal over 40 million credit card numbers, the biggest-ever bounty in any cyberheist.[2] Gonzalez did not stop there, and in 2009, he broke into payment processing supplier Heartland Payment Systems and several other companies, stealing the details of over 160 million credit cards. With this, he smashed his own record for the world's biggest credit card heist, and his new record has never been broken. He did so by hacking computers that processed customers' payments and sucking details out of them. Heartland lost over $200 million in fines and compensation to its customers.

Unsurprisingly, Gonzalez's business allowed him to lead a hedonistic life. He used the stolen details to forge credit cards, make withdrawals from cash machines, and buy anything he wanted—all at other people's expense. Eventually, he was arrested at a hotel in Miami. In raids on his parents' house and other assets he owned, police confiscated $1.6 million in cash.[3] He was charged immediately and sentenced to 20 years behind bars. Gonzalez became one of the world's most famous cybercriminals, and his story reflects that of many others who grew up as normal kids, except in cyberspace, and spotted the "commercial" potential of stealing other people's money.

Modern crime has effectively undergone the same shift as warfare: humanity has always cared about amassing private property and assets, and there have always been bandits and thieves who have coveted this wealth and tried to steal it. Organized crime was active in cities, in villages, and on roads, and in time, it also ventured out to sea. Bandits on sea and land usually stole valuable goods and commodities until money became the main means of exchange and they pivoted to robbing banks, vaults, and vans transporting cash.

The Cyber Revolution brings together both key elements of this process: digital goods or digital property and digital money. We all have valuable digital documents and products that we are willing to pay a high price to protect, while the banking system has converted our money from coins and banknotes to digits on a screen. Moreover, not only have our assets and money migrated to cyberspace; so have our money transfers and payments. We can buy physical products, such as clothes and homeware, without seeing or touching them outside the digital world and without even touching real money. After we punch out our credit card details, our money is transferred to stores entirely digitally. Every day, over 1.3 billion payments are made with credit cards all around the world, and more than 20% of transactions between consumers and businesses are online.[4] In such an enormous system, with millions of machines—computers, terminals, networks, and programs—the possibilities facing hackers grow every day. Albert Gonzalez got 20 years behind bars, but cybercrime is still undeniably an enormous temptation for many others.

Fraud

Credit card theft is just one of a wealth of options available to criminals to perpetrate cyberfrauds. In March 2017, Lithuanian police arrested a man by the name of Evaldas Rimasauskas, and thus, ended the ongoing heist of $120 million from mega-corporations Facebook and Google: a robbery pulled off by email.[5]

The plan was simple, but its scope was staggering. Rimasauskas had opened a company in Lithuania called Quanta: the same name as a Taiwanese manufacturer that did business with Facebook and Google. After incorporating his company, he got to work: he sent emails to Google and Facebook employees with fake Quanta invoices. They assumed these were invoices from their Taiwanese supplier and didn't suspect anything. In 2013–2015, these firms' employees transferred millions of dollars into the accounts of the Lithuanian company. Rimasauskas quickly funneled the money away to other bank accounts around the world, including in Cyprus, Hungary, Slovakia, Hong Kong, and his native Lithuania. He was eventually arrested, sentenced to five years in prison, and ordered to pay restitution, but his actions showed that nobody is immune to phishing attacks, even seemingly simple ones that do not require advanced cyberknowledge, like fake invoices sent by email.[6]

Phishing attacks are attacks in which criminals impersonate someone else or a company in order to fleece their naïve victims. Phishing attackers do not directly attack their victims' computers, but rather make them believe that they are dealing with legitimate actors and that it is safe to send them money or sensitive information. In Facebook and Google's case, emails were sent from someone pretending to be one of their legitimate suppliers, asking for payment for services, but such attacks can also be carried out via SMS ("smishing") or over the phone (voice phishing, or "vishing"). Such attacks can be carried out to convince victims to hand over not only money, but also secret information, such as passwords or credit card numbers. These are also called social engineering attacks because they seek to "engineer" their victims' behavior, rather than exploiting vulnerabilities in computers in order to hack them.

Extortion

On Friday, May 12, 2017, a message started popping up on around 230,000 computer screens in 150 countries. "Oops, your files have been encrypted!" it announced, demanding the payment of $300 in Bitcoin if users wanted their files back. The attackers threatened to double the ransom if it was not paid within three days. It was one of the biggest ransomware attacks of all time, and it was carried out with a computer worm called WannaCry.

The worm exploited a breach in Microsoft's Windows operating system. It later turned out the National Security Agency (NSA) had already detected it, but had apparently chosen to use it for its own ends instead of reporting it to Microsoft. The existence of this breach had leaked before the attack, and Microsoft had quickly sent out a security update, but not all computers had installed the patch in time, either because they were too old or because network managers had not understood the importance of downloading the update. WannaCry exploited this breach to lock computer files and spread to other computers plugged into the same network, and the worm spread at a dizzying pace, creating one of the worst cybersecurity crises to date: British hospitals were forced to suspend operations, car factories were crippled, and the overall damage from the attack was estimated at between hundreds of millions and billions of dollars.[7]

Experts warned users not to pay the ransom because there was no proof anyone had coughed up and got their files back. But the attackers still received payments from 430 victims, totaling $110,000.[8] The attack was stopped only after a computer security researcher called

Marcus Hutchins discovered a "kill switch" encoded in the worm, and successfully exploited it to slow down the attack and eventually eliminate it.

Who was behind the attack? The ransom messages were written by people fluent in Chinese with a solid grasp of English. An examination of the code suggested that the computers on which it was written used a Korean font and were set to North Korea's time zone, UTC+9. Taken together, this raised suspicions that the attackers belonged to the Lazarus Group of hackers backed by North Korea, which was suspected of being behind other famous attacks, such as the attack on Sony's computers in 2014 and the Bangladesh Bank cyberheist of 2016. In December 2017, these suspicions became official, when the United States and allies publicly accused North Korea of being behind the WannaCry attack. On September 6, 2018, the FBI issued an arrest warrant for Park Jin Hyok, a programmer who worked for a North Korean government company and was linked to WannaCry and other attacks attributed to the Lazarus Group.[9]

At the time, we at IntSights already had close to 100 customers, and without exception, they all wanted to know how they were supposed to respond. Since I was responsible for the firm's intelligence services, I had to deliver the goods. Straight after the WannaCry attack, we sent a guide to all our customers explaining how to protect themselves against such attacks. We stressed the importance of regularly updating their Windows operating systems in order to block the vulnerability that the worm was using. We also provided information about other technical details that could be blocked, such as the specific characteristics of the file carrying the ransomware, in order to stop their computers from getting infected. Luckily, we recognized the hallmarks of ransomware attacks and we were able to defend against them.

The first recorded ransomware attack in history was in December 1989. Twenty thousand floppy disks were sent to attendees at a World Health Organization conference on AIDS. People who inserted the disks into their computers found them locked a few days later, with a message on their screens demanding they send $189 to a P.O. Box in Panama or their information would be erased. Some panicked users erased their hard drives, and several research institutes and medical centers lost years of work. The attacker, an evolutionary biologist called Dr. Joseph Popp, was quickly snatched after authorities tracked down his P.O. Box. His precise motivations, and whether he had any co-conspirators, are still unknown. Popp's idea, to deny access to computer files by encrypting them and demanding a ransom to decrypt and release them, was revolutionary at the time. It has since been refined and repeated countless times.

In 2020, ransomware attacks moved up a notch. Attackers started not only encrypting their victims' information, like before, but also stealing it and threatening to publish it online for everyone to see unless they paid a ransom. This escalation turned up the heat on the targeted companies, which feared that sensitive information such as business plans and customer data would be leaked online, causing them commercial and reputational damage. From the attackers' perspective, the venture undoubtedly paid off: in 2020, the average payment per company for each ransomware attack jumped from $100,000 to $150,000. The highest payment ever made to ransomware attackers—$40 million—was by an American insurance firm.[10] Ransomware attacks have therefore become an exceptionally profitable source of income for attackers, and their popularity is only rising. Attackers have become even more sophisticated and have added new elements to pressure their victims into paying the ransom, such as crippling their websites or even actively inviting news sites to report on these incidents.

On October 13, 2021, in one of the worst ransomware attacks that Israel has ever known, the Hillel Yaffe Medical Center in Hadera was attacked, and all its files—including its backup files—were encrypted.[11] I live a 10-minute drive away from Hillel Yaffe. It was my go-to hospital for emergencies, and I know many people who work there. A few hours after the attack, I got a startled phone call from a friend who works there, who said I was the only "cyber guy" he knew and asked me to help him make sense of what had happened. "Everything's malfunctioned," he told me. "There are no computers. We've switched to working with paper until we can go back to normal."

The damage was immense: doctors were unable to access patients' medical files, and many machines became inoperable. Nearly all elective surgeries were canceled, and new patients were sent to other hospitals for several weeks after the attack.[12] The motivation for the attack was not political but financial, and the attackers belonged to a (probably Chinese) group called DeepBlueMagic.[13]

Ransomware attacks are not the only form of cyberextortion. Cybercriminals understand that individuals and companies are growing increasingly dependent on information stored on computers and on other digital platforms, such as websites, apps, and even social media profiles, and they are exploiting their ability to steal or attack them in order to extort their victims.

On June 10, 2014, the servers of Feedly (a news aggregator app) and Evernote (a note-taking and task management app) came under ferocious distributed denial-of-service attacks.[14] The attackers demanded a ransom in exchange for calling off the attacks. The companies refused to pay, and after a few hours of interrupted services, they managed to stop the attacks—but there was nothing to stop future attempts to extort them by attacking them again.

The many stories about cyberattacks demonstrate that cybercriminals do not fit a single profile. They might be state actors, trying to secure revenue for their countries (and harm their enemies along the way) or private individuals working alone or as groups in pursuit of profit. Albert Gonzalez is an example of a highly technologically sophisticated hacker—who managed to hack the computer networks of major corporations, reach their most sensitive devices, and steal vast quantities of credit card details—but there are also cases that require much less technological savvy, like that of Lithuania's Rimasauskas, who only opened an email account and pretended to be an Asian company.

Although cyberattacks are widely thought of as "technological" attacks that work by attacking computers, most cybercrimes are, in fact, based on exploiting human weaknesses. In many cases, cyberfraudsters rely on impersonations or establish trust with their victims in order to make them perform actions like transferring money or handing over passwords and credit card details. Cyberextortion attacks also exploit human psychology to pressure victims into paying the ransom. By threatening to publicly release sensitive information or blocking access to valuable digital assets, cyberattacks threaten to force individuals and companies to pay hundreds of millions of dollars. If they want to be successful, cybercriminals need to have as good a grasp of human psychology as of the technology behind the internet and computers.

Hacktivism

As I write these words, Iran is being swept by a major wave of protests after a young woman was beaten to death for allegedly not wearing a hijab as required. All across Iran, masses of people have been protesting against the oppressive regime, women have been tearing off their hijabs, and hundreds have been killed in clashes with regime forces. This image of a civil protest against a violent regime is nothing new, but since the internet revolution, the idea that it is not even necessary to take to the streets to resist abuses of power has gained steam. This idea has given rise to groups of hacker-activists—or in one word, *hacktivists*—the most famous and influential of which is Anonymous. Anonymous is not just an organized group of hackers with set members; it is an *idea* based on a desire to unite and fight injustices arising from the use of excessive power and use cyberattacks to promote a particular ideology.

In 2011, after the Arab Spring erupted in Tunisia, Anonymous activists launched intensive online activities supporting the regime's opponents. They distributed a guide explaining to citizens how to maintain their anonymity online and how to protect their computers from regime monitoring.[15] In addition, Anonymous activists all around the world shared images and videos from Tunisia and launched a DDoS attack on government websites. The same activity was then repeated in other countries: Algeria, Egypt, Libya, and more.

The advantages of cyberwarfare were already apparent in the cyberactivism of the Arab Spring: cyberspace allowed people to protest without going out in the streets and risking their lives or even exposing themselves at all because all activity was online—and anonymous. In cyberspace, it is possible to attack distant targets or share information between cities or states in less than a second, so even activists outside a nation's borders can join the effort. And most importantly, cyberspace makes it possible to attack important government internet targets, thus piling even more pressure on governments in addition to all the pressure arising from protests in the streets.

But are these hacktivists brave groups of freedom fighters or just anarchists? It is relatively easy for us to identify with groups like Anonymous in the case of what we see as justified protests, like popular uprisings against violent dictatorships, but the dilemma becomes more acute when we consider Anonymous's dogged battle against Scientology. This organization—part-religion, part-cult—has come under heavy criticism over the years because of its closed nature and allegations about the exploitation of its members' money. In January 2008, a video was uploaded on YouTube showing the actor Tom Cruise having what looked like a manic fit and talking about his love for the Church of Scientology. The church demanded that YouTube remove the video, claiming that it had been misleadingly edited, and threatened to sue websites that shared it.[16] Activists from Anonymous responded with physical protests all around the world, but mostly by attacking Scientology websites and distributing the phone and fax numbers of Scientology churches. In order to explain itself, Anonymous published a message of its own on YouTube in a video called "A Message to Scientology," in which it said that "Anonymous has decided that your organization should be destroyed for the good of your followers or the good of mankind and for the benefit and for our own enjoyment."

The question in this case is not whether Scientology is a legitimate religion or a dangerous cult, but whether we want to leave the treatment of such organizations in the hands of anonymous groups of hackers. This was a clear case of people taking the law into their own hands, and it would have been wrong for world governments to just let them carry out cyberattacks. Some extreme injustices might justify such pushback, and we might see cyberattacks that pose no threat to human life or uninvolved persons as a reasonable form of protest—but in the same breath, cyberweapons that are used to hack computers must be treated as weapons, or at least as tools used for vandalism. These are not exactly tools that any state wants to encourage its citizens to use as they wish. Either way, what is becoming clear beyond doubt is that criminal cyberspace is alive and kicking—but it cannot survive without a vital resource: money.

CHAPTER 4

The New Money— Catalysts of Cybercrime

W hat do criminals care about most: money, honor, or revenge? The real answer is: not getting caught. Criminals who know that they will get caught for committing a crime simply won't commit it. What is true of criminals, in general, is also true of cybercriminals: there is nothing they care about more than anonymity.

Technological developments since the new millennium have given rise to new tools to achieve online anonymity. Two technologies have been especially significant: the dark web, which allows for anonymous activity online, and Bitcoin, which allows for cash transfers without the mediation of a bank.

The dark web

One day in 2017 at IntSights, we discovered that someone, using a false identity, was offering the personal details of the customers of one of our major clients for sale on the dark web. We investigated his activity on the dark web and managed to connect it to a Turkish Facebook account that belonged to an employee at that company. He had exploited the dark web to make a few thousand dollars on the side, and when we showed the proof to his employer, the company sued him and he was, of course, fired and forced to pay damages.

In February 2019, it was reported that Dream Market, a site on the dark web, had put up for sale 620 million user accounts from several sites, including MyFitnessPal and MyHeritage.[1] The accounts, which contained users' personal information, emails, and passwords, were obtained in a series of cyberattacks by hackers who identified themselves on the dark web as GnosticPlayers. This group of mostly French members was one of the most productive in its field: according to analysis by Night Lion Security, a consultancy and information security service, between January 2017 and June 2020, the group was responsible for 42% of all noncredit card related data breaches, amassing the login details of more than two billion website accounts.[2]

The dark web is a network that exists inside the internet we all know, the one you can access from any home internet network. What makes it distinct is that it supports websites that can only be accessed using special software that totally anonymizes all internet activity. This means that any content that dark web users want to see is transferred in an encrypted format, and so are their addresses, such that if law enforcement agencies find information passing through it, they have no way of knowing what exactly is being sent and who is receiving it. The anonymity that the dark web offers internet users is attractive to cybercriminals, who use it to hawk credit card details and other stolen information, share information with other hackers, buy "how-to manuals" for cybercrimes, and more. The dark web also "hosts" other forms of illegal activity, including arms and narcotics trades and child pornography.

Perhaps surprisingly, the dark web did not begin its life in the service of cybercrime, but rather as a project of the U.S. Navy's research lab, built with the aim of hiding American intelligence agencies' online activities. The project was called "The Onion Router," or "Tor" for short, and in 2004, the technology was released to the general public. The developers understood that, paradoxically, mass use of the network would allow intelligence agents to communicate through it secretly, just as agents blend more easily into a crowd.

Some two years later, a nonprofit organization was established with the aim of developing and upgrading the Tor network to allow for internet browsing unmonitored by the authorities, in the interests of freedom of speech and the right to privacy. Tor is not the only network on the dark web, but it is the largest and most important one, and the most prominent example of what the dark web does: the encryption of information and concealment of users' identifying characteristics.

Despite its negative associations, the Tor network also has hugely positive consequences, letting individuals in totalitarian regimes share news and access censored information. The BBC, for example, has developed a Tor version of its site, letting it report news to Russia and Ukraine in wartime. It is not for nothing that Tor is supported by human rights organizations. Nevertheless, studies show that most websites on Tor are used for illicit activities, such as cybercrime and narcotics deals.[3]

As you might expect, there is a lively debate around the world about Tor's practical and moral value. Having regularly surfed the dark web over the past decade, I have no doubt that the damage it causes far outweighs any benefits. Tor hosts far more sites dedicated to hacking, narcotics, child pornography, and other harmful business than positive sites. That said, for ideological reasons, I always prefer to fight the "agents of evil" who exploit the platform—and that can be done, through a common international effort—than to fight the platform itself, which still has some good qualities. Our role is to make sure that we are cultivating the good guys and stopping the bad guys, instead of throwing the baby out with the bathwater and harming freedom of expression precisely where it is needed most. Moreover, it is not clear how effective any war against this platform would be because if Tor closed down, another network would replace it. Even if the dark web shut down, anyone who wanted to preserve anonymity would switch to Telegram or similar platforms. In the end, "agents of evil" will find a way to continue their work.

The dark web's impact on the scope of cybercrime has undoubtedly been immense. It is one of this industry's main catalysts because it allows cybercriminals to rake in higher profits while lowering the entry barriers to cybercrime, and thus, letting more people join the circle of criminality.

In June 2015, LinkedIn was hacked and many of its user passwords were stolen. Four years later, 117 million LinkedIn passwords stolen in this breach were put up for sale on the dark web for $2,200.[4] Over those four years, the hacker had probably used these passwords to hack accounts and steal money, and when this course ran dry, he decided to turn to the dark web, sell the information, and make another buck from the attack. He felt comfortable doing all this on the dark web, of course, because it guaranteed anonymity.

The dark web contains forums and e-commerce websites that operate just like Amazon or eBay on the regular internet, except that they exist to support illicit trades. Cybercriminals use these websites to hawk their wares, and the most sophisticated ones even sell genuine cyberweapons, such as malware and knowledge of vulnerabilities that can be exploited to plant such malicious software in computers and steal information from them.

Some cybercriminals go even further and sell their own hacking services. Want to make a website crash with a DDoS attack but have no idea where to start? All you've got to do is visit the website of a hacker who offers this service, pay them, and they'll do the work for you. Similarly, there are countless other hacking services being offered for sale on the dark web. In effect, the dark web allows people with insufficient technological knowledge and not even that much money to execute cyberattacks. If people want to make a purchase with a stolen credit card, all they need to do is to enter the dark web and buy this stolen information for a few dollars. This extra way to make money boosts the incentives for cybercriminals to commit even more cybercrime and hack even more computers. As we have seen, it also invites more people to join the circle of cybercrime by making the information and tools needed for cybercrimes accessible to even those without advanced technological know-how.

Bitcoin

On October 2, 2013, U.S. law enforcement agents raided a public library in San Francisco and arrested Ross Ulbricht, born in 1984 in Houston, Texas, who was the man behind the darknet website Silk Road. Ulbricht stood accused of money laundering, conspiracy to commit computer hacking, and conspiracy to distribute narcotics. He was convicted and sentenced to two life sentences plus 40 more years in prison, with no option of parole, and every appeal or request for a pardon was rejected.

Silk Road, deliberately named for the historic East-West trade route, was groundbreaking: it was like eBay, but a version that cracked some of the basic problems that had made it difficult for black market actors to trade reliably and trust that they would not be ripped off—a widespread problem on a network where most users were criminals. The site provided ratings for buyers and sellers, making it possible to trust traders with a good score, as well as a reliable payments system, on which payments were not sent directly to sellers, but were held by the system until buyers confirmed that their goods had arrived. The website boomed, allowing the sale of narcotics and so much more. From the perspective of its libertarian founder, the website served his free market ideology, and indeed it banned the trade of anything intended to cause "harm or fraud," like child pornography, stolen credit card details, hit jobs, and arms. Other dark web sites would have to fill that gap.

The Silk Road website was preceded by another website, called The Farmer's Market, which had its own oversight and credibility systems, but also had a major drawback: payments had to be conducted through platforms such as PayPal or Western Union, letting law enforcement agencies track down merchants and their customers. Silk Road was the first to use the new digital currency Bitcoin. The currency's unique selling point, that it protects its users' anonymity, made the website a paradise for black market merchants and other criminals. In addition to Silk Road, and even after the site was shut by the FBI, other websites popped up based on transactions in Bitcoin, the currency that has transformed the online black market beyond recognition.

Bitcoin is a cryptocurrency invented in 2008 by "Satoshi Nakamoto," a pseudonym for an unknown individual or group of people. The idea was to let people send each other money without relying on a central financial institution to mediate the transfer, while making sure to charge one account and credit another. In practice, anyone can install a "Bitcoin wallet" on their computer and use it to store files that represent Bitcoins. You don't need to prove your identity to download the program. The blockchain technology behind this cryptocurrency lets people send Bitcoin to each other in a way that reveals to all Bitcoin users in the world that this virtual money has exchanged hands.

Unlike opening a bank account, installing a Bitcoin wallet on your computer does not require any identifying details, such as a name or Social Security number. Anyone can conduct a Bitcoin transfer using the wallet's number without sharing any identifying details about the parties involved.

Bitcoin addresses two major problems that have bothered purveyors of illegal goods: it is anonymous, and thus, eliminates dark web merchants' fears of getting caught, and it is not controlled by any central institution that might limit transfers or shut down a bank account. Bitcoin was exactly what darknet commerce needed to take off. In March 2013, over 10,000 products were offered for sale on Silk Road. In March 2015, black markets based on the same idea were offering close to 70,000 products for sale. Since then, this black market has only expanded, and as of 2021, it is valued at $2.1 billion.

Besides illicit trades, Bitcoin has had a major impact on ransomware attacks, as we have already seen in the case of the WannaCry attack.

The story of Joseph Popp, the mastermind of the world's first ransomware attack, highlights a major problem in the ransomware business model: how can attackers get their ransom money without getting caught? Bitcoin provides an almost perfect solution to this problem. Instead of opening a bank account and providing ID, ransomware attackers can simply open Bitcoin wallets and ask their victims to send them Bitcoin in exchange for decrypting their files. This allows attackers to get their money without identifying themselves, thus dramatically reducing the risk of getting caught. Bitcoin has made ransomware attacks especially popular for cybercriminals and their preferred way of making money.

***

Most cyberattacks that we hear about are committed by individuals who want to make money or promote a certain ideology, usually in the name of freedom and privacy. But many states are also active in this field, aiming to promote their geopolitical or security interests, and they are usually highly sophisticated, armed with very advanced technologies, and able to wage protracted campaigns.

Cyberthreats from states are called "advanced persistent threats," or APTs. These threats require potential victims to build massive defensive walls, capable of holding firm in the long run, and to understand that threats will catch up with them sooner or later. Given the combination of cybercriminals' growing political interests, there is hardly any person, business, or state body in the world that is not vulnerable to cyberattacks. It is therefore only natural that in recent decades, the tech world has mobilized to address the most urgent and rewarding challenge in the industry: making cyberspace safe.

SECTION 2
Cybernation

CHAPTER 5

The Pioneer—The Story of Check Point

Unit 8200 has produced several legends, who even years after leaving, are still talked about with reverence there. They have become symbols of daring, professionalism, and creativity—examples of extraordinarily talented people who realized their full potential. I met some of them when I started writing this book, to hear firsthand from them about how they had taken off, what drove them, and what it takes to turn a small startup into a global company. I often went to interview them with a racing heartbeat, knowing I was going to meet people who had blazed the trail I was taking—as a soldier, entrepreneur, and investor. One of these trailblazers, if not the first among them, was Gil Shwed.

In the spirit of those early post-COVID days, I met with Shwed on Zoom. His personal assistant booked me in for half an hour and warned me to stick to the schedule. I got the message. Shwed's time, as the Nasdaq's longest-serving CEO, was precious. But Shwed was a talker, and he patiently spelled out for me his many reinventions and explained how he saw the world, and he even gave me an extra half-hour. Behind him, on my screen, I could see his first product in its original cardboard packaging. We chatted and I tried to get a sense from him about what he had learned about the fields of cybersecurity and innovation since the days when he was a young man who knew he was going to change the world.

Aged 22 and fresh out of the army, back in 1991, Shwed knew that he was sitting on a product with real potential. Shwed had lived and breathed computers since he was a kid: as a teenager, he had worked at computer labs while studying computer science, and he took this knowledge and understanding to Unit 8200. During his service, he was tasked with finding a solution to a particular technological problem: how to connect two separate top-secret networks, such that nobody using either of the networks could access the other without authorization. Unable to find a satisfactory commercial solution to the problem, Shwed decided to develop his own solution: technology that would monitor everything entering the network, which could then also control who could enter that network—and who could not. This technology had the potential to be extremely useful in the civilian world, but there was little use for it back then, and he assumed—and hoped—that its day would come. He started working at a hi-tech company called Optrotech (later Orbotech) and waited.

What Shwed could not imagine was that when his opportunity came, the business he would found with his old army buddy, Shlomo Kramer, and a colleague from Oprotech, Marius Nacht, would become one of the world's biggest companies in its field, employing thousands of people in offices across 70 cities around the globe, and serving as an incubator and model for the entire Israeli cybersecurity industry. Nor did Shwed think that this rare wonder would survive for another 30 years and that he'd still be heading and running it. He definitely couldn't imagine that, one day, dozens of entrepreneurs and thousands of engineers would gain their professional experience at his firm.

Before cyber was fully cyber

To understand Shwed's position in the Israeli cybersecurity industry, we've got to take a few steps back. When Shwed was still in the army, in 1987, Yuval Rakavy and Omri Mann, computer science students at the Hebrew University in Jerusalem, spotted an unfamiliar virus. The virus, soon dubbed the "Jerusalem Virus" because of where it was discovered, harmed Rakavy's computer and other devices on campus on a Friday, the thirteenth of the month. Nobody had any idea where it had come from. In fact, no one even knew that computers could catch viruses! Together, with two childhood friends, brothers Eli and Nir Barkat (a future mayor of Jerusalem), the pair developed antivirus software to protect their computers from the Jerusalem Virus, and in time, also from other viruses. Together, the four guys founded a company and called it BRM, using the initials of their three surnames: Barkat, Rakavy, and Mann. The company started selling its antivirus program and soon signed contracts and some impressive distribution agreements to sell its software overseas.

Israel was buzzing with antivirus companies at the time. Besides BRM, there was also Carmel, which developed Turbo Antivirus, which Microsoft used to protect its own operating systems at the time; IRIS, another software company that spotted an opportunity to create its own program; and Eliashim Antivirus, which developed the eSafe antivirus software. These companies all sold their software internationally, and Israel gained a global reputation in the field.

But the Israeli antivirus scene did not survive long, as these companies were overtaken by other global firms, such as McAfee and Symantec. Aladdin, an Israeli company, bought IRIS's antivirus software in 1992, and in 1998, it acquired most of Eliashim's operations for $23 million in a part-cash, part-stock deal. In 2002, Aladdin stopped selling the eSafe Antivirus to private customers.[1] IRIS was sold to CA, a global corporation, for $4 million in 1999,[2] and Carmel slowly withered after Microsoft suddenly abandoned a contract it had signed with it. Its contract with Symantec also went nowhere.[3] The promising Israeli market faded in the face of global competition.

When Shwed finished his IDF service, he discovered there was no real demand for the technology he had developed. The internet was still in its infancy: it was a network that served mostly academic and military institutions, and nobody needed to protect internal company networks. But all this started to change in late 1992. More and more companies started connecting to the internet, and the World Wide Web, which allowed anyone with an internet connection to surf other organizations' websites, took off. In 1993, Shwed realized that the internet was about to transform our lives and that the conditions were ripe for a company that would sell technology to protect companies from the threats lurking in this new domain. He picked up the phone to Kramer and Nacht and said, "It's time." His big idea, which he had kept on the back burner, was ready to become a commercial product—and the Israeli firewall was born.

Without any capital or office space, and with only their own computers, the three young entrepreneurs set about building a brand-new system. They commandeered Kramer's grandmother's apartment, sitting there for a whole year to write code for their product, which they decided to call Firewall-1. They gave their new company the military-sounding name "Check Point" because their product was effectively an observation post that would monitor everyone entering a network and check whether they had authorization to enter.

A firewall is a technology that sits at the "gateway" connecting two networks, such as between the internet and a company's internal network, and blocks free passage between them. This ensures that data transferred between a company's computers cannot spill out. Check Point did not invent the idea of a firewall; in fact, Kramer recalls, one of the first things that Shwed did in his investigation before launching Check Point was to subscribe to a mailing list for firewall managers.[4] But what Check Point proposed was a simple, easily installable product—and that made all the difference. The company entered the market at the right time and offered the most effective product. Business managers spooked by the threat of hackers penetrating their networks were desperate for a product to keep them out and specifically for one that was easy to operate. That was exactly what Check Point offered.

When I talk to Gil Shwed, his pride in those early days and his sense of enduring gratitude are still striking, even 30 years later. "For a company to succeed," he says, "it needs an outstanding product, an outstanding market, and excellent people. Check Point had all three elements from day one. Some of it was luck, and some of it was just us sitting and waiting for an opportunity. We had an idea that waited patiently for two years till it got implemented."

"It was obvious we needed a simple product, for two reasons," says Shwed. "Both because that's what network managers were looking for, and because the best market for Israeli entrepreneurs, right from the start, is the United States. The product had to be something the company's staff wouldn't have to spend ages fiddling around with the installation and support at the clients' offices." A disk sent in the post, with simple installation instructions—that's what Check Point was cooking up in Kramer's grandma's apartment.

"I remember our mission statement as entrepreneurs," Kramer tells me. "We wanted a business that would give us a livelihood, something that would be ours—not exactly the definition of a startup. That's why we aimed for a very simple product, which we could just send people and they could use it."

I met Kramer in his office in the Azrieli Sarona Tower, Tel Aviv's most prestigious skyscraper. From his corner office on the 45th floor, the view is simply breathtaking. Kramer is an extremely busy man—that's obvious immediately—and it's impossible not to be impressed with his inexhaustible energies, as he keeps setting up more and more companies.

Shwed, Kramer, and Nacht's role model was an American company called Pure Software, which had developed a simple solution to prevent memory leaks. Reed Hastings, one of Pure Software's founders, would go on to found another, more successful company a few years later: Netflix. "There was no ecosystem, there were no conditions, there was no horizon," Kramer recalls. "So we decided to build a solution that could fit in a single disk, and it worked."

At a certain point, it dawned on the young founders that they would need money, after all, to buy servers and equipment or even to fly to the United States and pitch their product. With their first product in hand, they started searching for an investor. Several firms, including Aladdin and BRM, were intrigued by their innovative new company. After some hesitation, the friends decided to accept BRM's offer to invest $250,000 in Check Point in exchange for half of its stock. Such a small investment in a startup now looks ridiculous, by any metric, but back then, it was more than enough. The deal was signed, and BRM's investment soon proved wildly successful: after just a few years, the investors cashed out for tens of millions of dollars—not a bad return for the couple of hundred thousand dollars they'd invested. But those returns would have been so much higher if they had waited before cashing in because Check Point's value kept skyrocketing, and in November 2022, it hit $16.9 billion.

Shwed and Kramer received a demonstration of their product's importance almost immediately. In 1993, they took their product to BRM to show them how it worked on their system. "It wasn't even a product," Shwed once said. "It was a first prototype. And we weren't actually even connected to the internet."[6] Within 5 or 10 minutes of installing the program, Shwed got an alert that someone was trying to hack the network. Shwed suspected it might have been a bug in the system because, after all, what were the chances they'd catch a break-in while installing their first pseudo-product? But all the data and IP addresses looked genuine.

Back then, few people in Israel were connected to the internet, and the team managed to track down the source of the breach and gave the company a ring. "Who's trying to hack our network from your company?" Shwed asked his contact. Nobody there had a clue what he was talking about, but they invited him to come and check. After a brief investigation, he called the police, and within two weeks, they arrested two young men who had exploited a breach in Israel's emerging internet network that had given them access to every company with an internet connection in the country. The three founders couldn't have

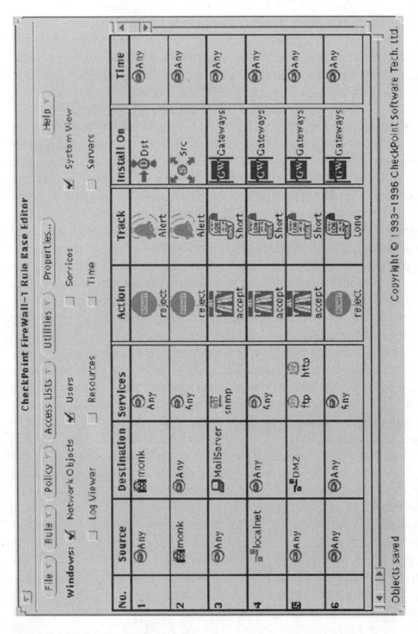

FireWall-1's early interface[5]

asked for a better demonstration of why their system was vital and addressed a tangible need.

The moment they understood that Check Point was going to be something special came after they met a representative of Sun Microsystems, a major player in networks and workstations at the time. Its information systems manager visited Israel in early 1994. Using Shwed's connections with the company's Israeli representative, A.M.T. Computing, the founders managed to rope him in for a demonstration of their new system. In a tiny office, using physical slides, the trio—Check Point's only employees at that point—sat down in front of a senior executive from one of the global market's biggest software giants and ran a simulation of their firewall on a Sun Microsystems workstation.

The executive was impressed. "If your product really does everything you say," he said, "then I'll want to buy installation licenses for the product and I'll advise SunSoft [Sun's software branch] to distribute it."

"That was like an atom bomb," Kramer recalls. "He left the room, and that was the moment we understood we had something serious. We'd gone from 0 to a 100, just like that. Before that, who even wanted to talk to us? And now we were about to close a deal with an international software giant."

Even before the deal with Sun was signed, Shwed was sent to the United States to build ties with its management and explore other avenues for distributing their firewall. Shwed's cofounders had set him a strict target: not to return to Israel without deals worth at least $1 million. In late April 1994, Shwed happened to hear that the Networld Interop trade show would be taking place in Las Vegas at the start of May. "Why don't you pitch your product there?" suggested someone at one of the companies he was talking to. Shwed convinced Kramer and Nacht to piggyback another company's stall and to be ready within 10 days, and the three of them flew out to Las Vegas and pitched their firewall at the expo, with few props, and without even a press release. Check Point's product was the right thing at the right time. Firewalls were a hot topic because of the recent release of a popular academic book on the subject,[7] and Interop's founder had recently given an interview stressing the importance of firewalls for security as companies opened up to the internet.[8]

The new company's stall attracted a lot of attention at the trade show, impressing Sun's executives, who could see the interest that

Check Point's firewall was exciting. Check Point's firewall won the coveted Best of the Show award, and that, Shwed tells me, was the moment they realized they were not just three guys from Israel, but in the same league as major tech companies.

Sun kept its word and paid $300,000 for the software licenses, which had cost no more than $250,000 to develop. "In that instant, we became profitable, and that's been the case ever since," Kramer says. Only after the contract with Sun was signed did Check Point start hiring more employees. The first engineer it hired was tasked with building a system to receive email orders from Sun and send back software licenses. One of the engineers hired at this initial stage was a fresh veteran of Unit 8200 named Nir Zuk. He was put in charge of developing Check Point's firewall, and later, also its VPN (virtual private network). Check Point would soon sign contracts with HP and other tech giants before, finally in 1996, going public on Wall Street, where it raised $67 million.

Despite being the first Israeli cybersecurity company to succeed on a global scale, Check Point continued to maintain not only its R&D center, but also its headquarters in Israel, including its senior executives, marketing teams, salespeople, financial managers, and human resources teams. Check Point became the undisputed symbol of the incredible growth of not only Israel's cybersecurity industry, but of its entire hi-tech sector.

As we wrap up our conversation, Gil Shwed's eyes twinkle: "We were the first ones who showed that success was possible."

CHAPTER 6

The Love Letter That Leaked—From Personal Security to Systems Security

"I won't invest in ideas or products, I'll invest in people. Ideas are overvalued, and people are undervalued. My experience tells me that when I meet an entrepreneur, it doesn't matter what they've got for me on day one; in two months, everything'll look different, so why should I waste energy on what's just a temporary stage of a project's life cycle? I prefer to leverage my time as an investor to understand the element that isn't going to change dramatically, and that's the people I see in front of me."

With these words, Gili Raanan describes the experience that he had built up on his long road from rookie entrepreneur to serial investor. Raanan was serving in Unit 8200 just as Check Point's success started to excite the Israeli market. The idea of a firewall to protect against unwanted intrusions ignited people's imagination, and there were many other ways to put it into practice. Several Israeli entrepreneurs decided to take up the gauntlet, and in the first decade of the new millennium, the Israeli cybersecurity industry shifted gears: from an era dominated by one successful company—Check Point—it moved into an era in which former employees of this company and other entrepreneurs started discovering this field and its immense potential for new ventures.

Sanctum: Firewalls for browsers

"Nowadays when entrepreneurs complain about aggressive competition in the market," Raanan tells me, "I say to them: wait till you see the kind of competition I had in Unit 8200, with Shwed, Kramer, and Zuk." Raanan enlisted in Unit 8200 in 1987, alongside Gil Shwed, Shlomo Kramer, and Nir Zuk. During his service, he won the prestigious Israel Defense Prize for a top-secret project that he had worked on, and he left the unit in 1996—"unfortunately, three years after the guys who got out before me built the firewall." Asking himself what he wanted to do, he explored this new network called the internet. "At that time, there was a new and subversive project called HTTP, a new browser called Netscape was taking off, and websites ending with .com were sprouting all over the network really quickly," he recalls.

Indeed, this was exactly when HTTP technology started taking off and getting used all around the world. Hypertext Transfer Protocol (HTTP) was an exciting way to transfer data—text, media, and links—between pages. This was the basic technology underpinning the ability to surf websites, which made it possible for a website's content to be transferred from its server directly to any user's computer. The original version of HTTP was invented in 1991, but only in 1997 was its most stable version released. New browsers entering the scene at the time, such as Netscape (which would soon be defeated in the "browser war" by Microsoft's Internet Explorer), were now able to receive data, decipher it, and present it as customized web pages for users.

Raanan realized that Check Point's solution was no good for defending websites against attacks launched by hackers who operated by sending data to websites through browsers. Check Point's firewall filtered access to networks through their ports, the computer "gates" that can be opened or closed. But the port that allows access to website content through browsers (known as Port 80) had to be left open for users to be able to surf the web, and a different solution had to be found to guard this entry-point, too. "We decided to be Check Point for applications," says Raanan, and he can take credit for inventing the first firewall capable of protecting applications accessed through web browsers.

This new firewall was developed by Sanctum, the company that Raanan cofounded in 1997 with Eran Reshef, who left after a short while. They raised their initial capital—$2 million—from Eli Bar, a former commander of Unit 8200 and general manager of Mofet, an investment fund. The fund wrote them a check before they even had a properly hashed-out idea, based only on confidence in their abilities. "Everything was very premature," Raanan recalls, "it was a crazy playing field." They split into teams within the company, with each team working on a different idea. One team invented CAPTCHA, the technology that shows internet users distorted letters and numbers to check they're human. Another team developed a capability to run several operating systems on the same computer, and yet another built a firewall for applications.

CAPTCHA proved extremely effective in blocking access to bots—programs that execute automatic operations on the internet—and in stopping computer systems from being exploited, and after a few months, the founders decided to ditch all their other projects and focus just on this one. Raanan and his friends went to Israeli organizations that already had websites and offered to run penetration tests ("pen tests") on them. One of them was the Israeli branch of Motorola, which operated Mirs Network's website, where people could type in their usernames and passwords, and get invoices. Sanctum's team sat one Thursday night at Motorola's offices in Tel Aviv and managed to hack Motorola's customer website. "That night, we made one of the most important breakthroughs in the field of information security to date," says Raanan.

The sorts of security systems used at the time had a problem: their policies were predefined. They could be programmed, for example, to reject requests featuring one million characters, or to block requests to access networks as the manager. But since all applications are different, taken together, they could potentially perform an infinite number of operations, and the question was how to design an information security policy capable of filtering all these applications. Sanctum's team understood that it had to work backward: it could treat each website that reached users like a policy page, and instead of specifying what was *not* allowed—it would specify what *was*. For example, on a menu page with four options, these would be the only options that users would be allowed to access; any other action would be prohibited.

The moment that Sanctum's team conceived this idea, it seemed so simple and logical. Raanan knew that he had to be careful. At Check Point, Nir Zuk was responsible for its firewall product, and Raanan knew him from their Unit 8200 days as an aggressive and especially clever character. If Sanctum told anyone what they were doing and how they were doing it, Nir Zuk would have no trouble copying their concept and taking it to market himself. Raanan decided to play up his story and make his product sound more complicated than it was. "That's a lesson I still teach entrepreneurs. Because the problem's not about technology; it's the concept. And as soon as they realize how it works, other talented people can implement it. I camouflaged our solution in order not to give away how it really functioned. And it worked."

"You idiot!"

Sanctum started to take off, and in its next investment round, it secured funding from the U.S. investment fund Sequoia Capital. The founders started looking for customers in the United States, and one of the first clients they approached was the world's first online bank, **X.com**, through the mediation of someone on the board of directors of both Sequoia and the bank. **X.com** was founded by Elon Musk and later merged with another company to become PayPal. Sanctum's team opened an account with the bank and after pulling an all-nighter, managed to get $1 million dollars that they didn't have to appear in their account. This security breach impressed **X.com**'s executives, who wanted to sign a $400,000 contract with them. Raanan was overjoyed. He emailed this go-between on the bank's board and excitedly told him about the breach they had found and the deal that was in the works. The next morning, he received a furious email from Elon Musk. The board member, it turned out, had forwarded Gili Raanan's email to Musk, writing: "Elon, forgive Gili for his arrogant Israeli style, but it looks like you've got a security problem." Musk wrote back to Raanan: "You idiot! Who gave you permission to tell one of my board members about a security flaw? I'm never doing business with you again."

That was how their first deal in the United States went down the toilet.

In late 1999, Sanctum received a takeover bid from Symantec for $100 million. Sequoia Capital's advisors told the founders that this was an amazing deal, but they wanted more and negotiated hard. The price jumped to $200 million, then $300 million, and finally $350 million. Sanctum's executives were already planning what to do with this massive windfall, but then the dot-com bubble burst, the stock markets crashed, and the deal was off. Sanctum found itself in the lurch, and Raanan decided to move to the United States to try to stabilize the business. Things settled down after immense difficulties, but Raanan left Sanctum in 2003. In 2004, it merged with Watchfire in a stock-for-stock deal worth no more than $50 million, the total amount invested in the business in its three investment rounds. In 2007, it was bought out by IBM.

"I left that experience battered and bruised," Raanan recalls. "We wanted to build a huge company, and we raised so much money from major funds, but we hit the ceiling just as forcefully as we then crashed on the ground." In 2003, Raanan founded a new company, nLayers, and took a different route. He was its sole owner and he raised very little capital, just $9 million across its entire lifetime. nLayers offered automatic mapping for organizations' applications and hardware, based on a technological concept similar to Sanctum's: "I pulled the same trick as many entrepreneurs: staying with the same technology but changing its commercial purpose and users." nLayers was sold to EMC in 2006 for $50 million, and Gili Raanan went out into the venture capital world, where he would soon become a major player in the Israeli cybersecurity scene.

Imperva: A firewall for websites

In 2000, the Israeli cyberindustry was hit by a minor earthquake when Shlomo Kramer decided to quit Check Point. The newspapers reported friction between the founders. Looking back, Shwed and Kramer prefer not to talk about what happened, and in my conversations with both of them, it's clear that they still have enormous respect for each other. After seven intensive years as an entrepreneur, Kramer founded his own venture capital fund. One day, another Israeli investor sent two young entrepreneurs, Amichai Shulman and Mickey Boodaei, to pick his brain about their idea for a database technology startup. The duo turned to him after ditching an earlier idea, which "nobody wanted to put money in," Shulman tells me. Their latest idea also received insulting offers, but one of the funds they applied to sent them Kramer's way. "He sat there at ease, with a billiard table in his office, and thought our idea was absolute bull," Shulman recalls. But Kramer, it would soon turn out, did not forget the two talented young men who had shown up in his office.

Shulman and Boodaei had met a few years earlier when Shulman was Boodaei's commander at Matzov, the Center of Encryption and Information Security, a unit in what would become the Israeli military's C4I Corps. Matzov was founded to provide encryption solutions for military communications, and soon after it was established, it was given official responsibility for information security in the IDF.

Serving alongside them, doing reserves duty, was Nissim Bar-El, who in 1986 had founded ComSec, a pioneering company in the field of information security consulting. Shulman saw Bar-El as a role model, and he had no doubts that he would work for him after completing his service.

Boodaei had other dreams. Around two months before his release from the army, he approached Shulman and suggested they cofound a startup with much greater global and commercial potential. "Amichai's one of the smartest guys I've ever met," Boodaei tells me, "but I had to invest a lot into convincing him to set out on this adventure." Shulman and Boodaei were also at different stages of their lives: Boodaei was young and single, while Shulman was married and had a young daughter.

They decided, therefore, to work in stages and take a safer route. "In the army, we both specialized in the same field: application security," says Boodaei. "There was a vacuum in this area. In just 15 minutes, we could dismantle any application we touched." They worked as external consultants for ComSec and even founded their own service company, all the while still developing their own idea for an application security product.

The year 2001 was traumatic for the global economy and especially for the hi-tech industry. It was the year when the world tipped into recession after the dot-com bubble burst and sank the tech industry. The sudden takeoff of the internet in the 1990s had attracted huge numbers of entrepreneurs to the field—too many, as the bursting of the bubble and the collapse of these businesses proved. The world economy got dragged down and took any appetite for new startups among entrepreneurs and investors down with it. Kramer understood that despite the collapse of so many companies, websites were not going anywhere and that over time, there would only be more of them. Businesses would provide services such as banking and online shopping, and these services would need security. Back at Check Point, he had built a firewall to stop hostile actors from entering organizations' computers; now, he was setting his mind to building a firewall to stop hackers from stealing information from internet services. When he started searching for partners, he already knew whom to turn to.

"Near the end of 2001, suddenly Shlomo Kramer popped up," Shulman recalls. "He called me and said, 'Do you fancy doing something together?'" Shulman and Boodaei, who had been waiting for such an opportunity, grabbed it. It's not every day you get an offer to launch a startup with a Check Point founder. It was the perfect partnership: they brought their cybersecurity experience from their time as consultants, and Kramer brought his in-depth understanding of the gap in the market and the initial capital. The division of labor was clear: Kramer would be the CEO, Shulman would lead the technology side, and Boodaei would handle the customer-facing business side. Their company, initially called WebCohort and later renamed Imperva, hit the ground running.

Thanks to Kramer's connections, they were able to raise funding quickly from Accel, one of the leading American investment funds. From the outset, it was clear to the three of them that the Israeli market was too small to rely on if they wanted to build a major company. They set up their HQ in California, and Kramer commuted between Israel and California for a decade.

Imperva targeted the same market as Sanctum, Gili Raanan's company. They both wanted to protect websites and build firewalls that could block cyberattacks committed through web browsers. From Raanan's perspective, it was a stark picture: Imperva had done exactly what he had feared Nir Zuk would do. Sanctum, he claims, had hired Shulman as a penetration tester, and he took his knowledge of its product to go and build a better version of his own.

Imperva's founders see things differently. "Our exposure to customers as service providers helped us understand the problems with the products they were trying to bring into the market," Boodaei says. "Sanctum was trying to solve things in a way that made no technological sense. We defined things differently." Shulman argues that they knew about Sanctum's product through customers from their service company before Imperva, and that at Sanctum, they had worked on a different product altogether. He, too, emphasizes his product's technological edge: "We analyzed all the communications with the website, used that to learn what counts as legitimate access and what doesn't, and then we could detect anomalies and block suspicious activity."

Imperva did not skyrocket immediately like Check Point. Its customers did not understand the importance of the company's solution and feared that Imperva's firewall would slow down their websites' loading time. For two years, the trio waged a war of survival and fought for every customer, but then, something began to change. General attitudes toward firewalls shifted, the misgivings dissipated, and Imperva rode a wave of new clients and deals. In 2011, Imperva became the third Israeli cyberfirm to go public on Wall Street, after Check Point and Radware (for which, at the time, cybersecurity was only one aspect of its product range, which focused on internet traffic). In 2022, Imperva's market value hit $2 billion.

At a certain point, Boodaei decided it was time to leave Imperva and founded a new company. Kramer introduced him to his future partner: Rakesh Loonkar, Nir Zuk's partner at OneSecure. Kramer knew Loonkar through Nir Zuk, who had made the connection between them. In 2006, Boodaei and Loonkar founded cybersecurity company Trusteer, which received investment from, yet again, Kramer. The Boston-based company provided banks with technology that detected Trojan horses trying to penetrate their computers and steal money from people's accounts. Over the years, Trusteer raised just $10 million from Kramer and VC funds, and in 2013, it was sold to IBM for $800 million in cash, a staggering and practically unprecedented eighty-fold return.

Boodaei recalls that IBM was setting up its own information security division and was looking for companies to buy. "We were number six or seven on their list, but their acquisition attempts failed because the companies were demanding too much money. Since we were bottom of the list, they were really stressed to seal a deal by the time they got to us. We weren't pressed to sell, so we were able to get extremely good conditions, including that Rakesh and I could leave the company after just three months, and that's what happened."

The man who walked away

"Check Point's a company that has always prioritized profits over investments in technology. That's cool, but it's not for me." That's how Nir Zuk starts presenting the topic when I meet him at Palo Alto Networks' offices in Tel Aviv's Alon Towers, known as the "cyber towers" because of the concentration of tech firms between their walls. We sat down in a small boardroom. Zuk is a matter-of-fact kind of character, who cuts straight to the chase. He keeps it brief, wearing jeans and a T-shirt, because despite living many years in the United States, he's still an Israeli to the core.

Zuk's first computer was the Dragon 64 that his parents bought him for his bar mitzvah, and he used it to teach himself to code and even invented some of the world's first computer viruses. In an interview in 2004, he revealed that he had studied electronics in high school "because I couldn't stand academic subjects. I was always a practical kind of guy and had no patience for the humanities. In fifth grade, my friend got his first computer, a Spectrum Z80. I loved it, and I've been into computers ever since." Living near the Weizmann Institute of Science, he had access to local science clubs and the institute's advanced computers. "By tenth grade, I was writing commercial software, which I managed to sell to lawyers. I was a computer whiz."[1]

As we have seen, Nir Zuk served in Unit 8200, met Shwed and Kramer there, and became the first development manager of Check Point's firewall. But soon enough, Zuk would become one of Check Point's main competitors, and he enjoyed publicly taunting his former employer.

In the beginning, Zuk was given free rein at Check Point, and product development was an exciting adventure. "Officially, my role was senior engineer, but in practice, I did so much more than that. I wrote a large part of the product." But he was disappointed by what came next. In 1997, he was sent to the United States to establish the company's next development center, where he built the team that would work on developing its next product, FloodGate. But Check Point neglected this product. Years later, Zuk claimed that the Israeli engineers preferred focusing on existing products and fixing bugs, and were furious that someone else was enjoying himself in the United States and building new products. "I'm not kidding you, that was the reason!" he said in an interview with *Computerworld* in 2010.[2] Zuk understood that Check Point saw its firewall and VPN products as enough of a cash cow and that the company wasn't in the mood for new innovations; eventually, he decided to quit.

Zuk left Check Point in 1999, and the next year, he founded OneSecure, which offered the first "anti-penetration system" of its kind in the world: a facility that would sit behind firewalls and complement them, checking all the traffic going through them. OneSecure was acquired by NetScreen in 2002 for $45 million. NetScreen itself was snapped up two years later by Juniper Networks for $4 billion. Zuk worked as an executive for both of these companies, seeing himself already as a competitor to Check Point and driving around California with the license plate CHKPKLR: "Check Point Killer."[3] He would later reveal in an interview that this was NetScreen's marketing department's idea, but in any case, it took a character like Zuk to pull it off.[4] But Zuk would ultimately be disappointed that Juniper failed to advance his technological vision far enough or put up a proper fight against Check Point.

In 2005, Zuk founded Palo Alto Networks, which started off with the dream of consolidating everything that the cybersecurity industry was doing into a single, comprehensive solution. "It didn't make sense that more and more cyber companies were popping up, and every organization had to pick from hundreds of existing products,"

Zuk says. "That kind of situation exists only in the cyber market, and it's an anomaly." One of Palo Alto's investors was none other than Shlomo Kramer.[5]

Kramer continued his provocations against Check Point at his new company, announcing that he planned to overtake it. One of many examples came in March 2013, when the consulting firm Gartner crowned Palo Alto a leader in technological innovation. Palo Alto took out a massive billboard over the Ayalon Highway, which cuts through Tel Aviv, near Check Point's HQ, with the provocative text: "You've just overtaken Check Point. So have we!"[6]

This high-profile rivalry, Zuk says in answer to my question, was deliberate and based on a paradoxical, topsy-turvy kind of thinking: these provocations were supposed to make Check Point and Juniper think that their new competitor was not serious, a dog with lots of bark but no bite. "What we did was to disrupt the market," he explains. "When you're an existing company and a new company comes along and tries to disrupt the market, you don't have long to react. But our competitors dozed off, and some of that was the result of our marketing efforts. They thought we were just making noise, that we were out for revenge. That was our conscious strategy: be a lion and look like a small, harmless puppy." Moreover, Zuk reveals, this deliberate competition made Check Point and Juniper unwittingly do Palo Alto's marketing for it. "They used to go to customers and try to convince them not to buy from us. These customers then came to us and told us that only thanks to them had they even heard of us."

Palo Alto was founded as a U.S. company. "We decided from the get-go that this would be an American firm because I was living in the United States. If I'd been living in Israel, maybe I'd have done it in Israel," says Zuk, but he emphasizes that it's much harder to build a company on such a scale in Israel. "There's nobody in Israel who's ever run a company of the size of Palo Alto. These companies just don't exist in Israel and they never have. Even if it's an Israeli company, the management's got to sit in the United States. Israel's got great developers, but it's really hard to find good product people, and it's even harder to find good senior managers: CEOs, chief marketing officers, or even chief finance officers. There's nobody in Israel with experience on that scale. Israeli companies don't manage to grow beyond a certain size."

Nevertheless, when Zuk set up the company's second development center, it was decided to build it in Israel, because of the country's high concentration of talented engineers. Palo Alto acquired many Israeli companies and gained a reputation for being willing to fork out for companies it wanted to buy. Zuk himself returned to Israel in 2021, taking advantage of the new flexible workplace arrangements made possible by the COVID-19 pandemic.

Palo Alto kept its promise, and by 2015, it overtook Check Point in terms of market value, although not yet in profitability. In 2021, Palo Alto completed its revenge when it pushed Check Point out of the prestigious Nasdaq 100 Index, and in 2022, the company reached a market value of $50–$60 billion—compared with Check Point's $15–$19 billion—making it the world's biggest cybersecurity company. As of 2022, Palo Alto employs 12,000 around the world, double the size of Check Point's workforce. Zuk hasn't killed off Check Point, but he has definitely overtaken it in several important metrics.

The love letter that leaked: CyberArk and the digital wallet

"Check Point called the field 'data security.' I'm the first one in the industry who started calling it 'cybersecurity,'" Alon Cohen, the founder of CyberArk, tells me. Cohen played soccer for Hapoel Jerusalem in his youth, and when he enlisted in the Israeli army, he was sent to Mamram, the military's Center of Computing and Information Systems. In May 1999, Cohen and a high school friend, Udi Mokady, founded CyberArk.

The story had a romantic background. During his service, Cohen was responsible for information security at what was the biggest computing center in Israel at the time. "I had a fling with a female soldier, and I wrote her a love letter, which I saved on the computer," Cohen recalls. "One day, I found out that all my comrades from my old unit had copies. I was stunned. I looked into what had happened, and it turned out a soldier had hacked the army's central computer and found my letter there. He thought it was hilarious, so he printed copies and gave them to all his buddies. It was a scandal. If you couldn't feel safe about the information you stored on the military's network, which was meant to be one of the most secure networks in the world, there was something seriously wrong with the world of information security. That was when I sat down and started thinking about how to solve this problem."

Cohen's eureka moment came when he was in Nepal during a post-army trip—a rite of passage for many Israelis, who go hiking in India or South America after finishing their mandatory service. There, in the middle of a challenging trek, the penny dropped: "Just as in the physical world, if you've got something sensitive, like a love letter, you wouldn't try to turn your whole house into a fortress and then just leave it in the kitchen. You'd put it somewhere completely secure, like a safe." The same applied to the virtual world: the solution was a virtual safe for information. The answer was to invent a secure system within a secure system for data that was not supposed to be open to anyone with access to the network. For two years, Cohen sat in his basement and designed this virtual safe: a place that would be impossible to hack, and which would store valuable information that would be inaccessible even to users with authorization to access the network where it was found.

One year after founding CyberArk, in 2000, Cohen and Mokady decided to move to the United States and build its HQ in Newton, a suburb of Boston. "If you hear why we went to Boston, you'll die of laughter," Cohen tells me with a grin. "When we started, I brought in Udi our CEO and Orit our marketing manager to run our stateside operations. Udi had a family and wanted to live in Boston; Orit was still single and wanted to live in New York. I couldn't tell the two cities apart and couldn't make my mind up, so I told them I'd think about it over the weekend and then we'd decide.

"On Thursday I saw my wife watching TV—some show with pretty streets and nice houses and a cool kind of neighborhood. I asked her, 'Where's it set?' and she said, 'Boston.' It was *Ally McBeal*. After the weekend, I picked up the phone to Udi and told him, 'We're going to Boston.'"

After we stop laughing, Cohen wants to make something clear: the choice between Boston and New York might have been random, but his choice of the East Coast was entirely professional. The time difference and flight times made much more sense for working with Israelis than the industrial hubs on the West Coast.

Now that they had a new HQ and a finished product, CyberArk looked for a way to implement it: where could they place this virtual vault? They decided to develop several applications for this safe, launch them, and see which sold the best. They developed, for example, a vault for legal documents and another for HR information. Two of the most successful vaults were an inter-organizational safe, which allowed different organizations to share information between them securely, and a password vault, to store the passwords of users who had access to many computers in the same organization. When it became clear that CyberArk would have to focus on a single product, it picked the password vault. "Its success, starting around 2003, was incredible. It sold like hotcakes," Cohen says.

The password vault was soon upgraded into an entire user management tool, which let organizations monitor network users' identities, to prevent anyone from exploiting their authorizations. Its sales numbers started taking off in 2003, but the urgent need for it became clear only a decade later, during the Snowden incident.

Edward Snowden, like another roughly 1,000 employees of the U.S. National Security Agency (NSA), had access to its servers as a system manager, letting him reach any files he wanted without any real oversight. He managed to collect and leak tens of thousands of documents from the NSA's computer network, exposing the agency's mass surveillance programs on U.S. citizens. The leak showed just how important it was for organizations to protect themselves from their own employees, and not just from external threats, and how urgent it was for access to valuable resources to be supervised and secured. CyberArk undoubtedly benefited from this growing awareness.

CyberArk's password vault was a global success, but in Israel, it was the inter-organizational safe that did the best: nearly every bank, insurance company, and government organization used it to share information, and CyberArk signed massive deals. At one point, Cohen considered opening two separate sales organizations, to sell the two different products, "but I didn't have the courage. Everyone's telling you it's impossible to establish two companies inside another company when you're a startup. But what we saw was that our salespeople abroad were having an easier time selling the story of the password vault. It was simple, it was easy to understand, and that's what sold." They had to pick a direction, but it wasn't easy. The global market eventually won out, when in 2021, CyberArk announced that it would stop supporting inter-organizational safes, and the Israeli market had to start looking for alternatives.

Despite having gone through rough patches, CyberArk is one of the Israeli cybersecurity industry's most iconic success stories, and in 2022, it reached a market value of $6.3 billion, with over 5,300 employees and more than 7,500 clients in 110 countries all around the globe.

Cyber: A booming market

Sanctum, Imperva, Trusteer, Palo Alto, and CyberArk were just some of the growing number of Israeli companies specializing in information security in the 2000s, making the whole world of cybersecurity grow. Super-investors such as Kramer and other Check Point graduates and entrepreneurs inspired by the company massively increased the size of the market, in terms of both the number of firms and the sums invested in them. Investments at the time came from VC funds; the main target market was and remains the United States.

Besides the high proportion of companies closing down or selling for cheap, many other small Israeli cybersecurity companies managed to balloon to massive dimensions and become unicorns (achieving a value of $1 billion) or go public on the stock market. Two high-profile examples were Varonis Systems, which was founded in 2005, went public on the NASDAQ in 2014, and has over 2,000 employees; and Checkmarx, a code security company that was founded in 2006, was sold in 2020 for $1.15 billion, and has a workforce of over 1,000.

These dizzying success stories were the main drivers behind one of the biggest changes of the 2000s: the transformation of Israel's status in the global cybersecurity industry. The early millennium was not particularly kind to the cybersecurity market, and especially not to the Israeli market. Besides the major crises of the 2002 dot-com bubble burst and the 2008 financial crash, which hurt the entire market, Israeli companies also had to deal with the bleak security situation in Israel. The Second Intifada—a wave of terror attacks, and especially suicide bombings, in the early 2000s—and the 2006 Second Lebanon War spooked Israeli cybercompanies' customers, who feared for their stability, and only toward the end of the decade did the tide begin to turn.

New winds started blowing, but some Israeli companies had already made it big before the millennium. Cohen and Mokady, like many fellow cybersecurity entrepreneurs, had models: Cohen mentions two other companies besides Check Point that he considered "examples in the field of security." Check Point went public in the same year as Memco Software, founded by two Mamram veterans in 1990, which raised $50 million. In 1999, Memco merged with the American firm Platinum in a $550 million deal, and the united company was sold immediately to the global corporation CA for $3.5 billion. The same year, software company New Dimension was sold to the U.S.-based BMC for $675 million—the biggest-ever deal involving an Israeli company at the time. "These three companies," Cohen concludes, "gave everyone the feeling that you could conquer the world from Israel."

CHAPTER 7

From Security to Defense—The Cyber "Iron Dome"

L ior Div was 18 years old when he was sent on one of the IDF's most top-secret and cutting-edge training programs. The year was 1996, and Lior was an exceptionally talented young man with an amazing knack for technology. "I used to do things like playing around with the new cellular networks in Israel, trying to ride them so I could eavesdrop on conversations," he tells me. In the army, he had wanted to go to fighter pilot school ("I wanted to be the best of the best, and what's better than a fighter pilot?"), but medical reasons kept him out of this coveted course, and instead, he was sent to Unit 8200.

The unit was working on a new project, for which it was trying to find the most capable candidates in the country. Out of the 1,000 people who started the course, 500 survived the first stage, and of those, 400 dropped out in the next stage. By the end, only 20 special candidates were invited to join Unit 8200. Only the four candidates who displayed the best abilities got into the new course. Lior Div was one of them.

Div was a pioneer of cyberintelligence long before it had that name. He was sent to officers' school and then joined a very small clique of officers who were given the mission of understanding how exactly this new world of cybersecurity worked. Together, they worked on special projects for which he was awarded a citation by the chief of military intelligence and another prestigious prize.

After six years of military service, Div went to study computer science. After a short while, he decided to found his own cybersecurity

company, which would focus on the sorts of things he had specialized in as an officer and would advise companies on how to deal with
emerging cyberthreats. There was just one problem: none of his
potential clients understood what he wanted from them. "I came from
a world with very deep knowledge of how this world works, and the
clients I pitched to simply didn't understand that these sorts of things
were going on," he says. "It was a consultancy that nobody wanted to
consult with."

The turning point of 2010

In the 1990s, four cybersecurity companies came out of Israel. In the
following decade, there were 80 more. In the decade after that, starting
in 2010, Israel produced no fewer than 416 cybersecurity companies.
Only some of them made a significant splash: 25% of them no longer
existed by 2022, and even among the companies that got acquired, not
all made a successful exit. Centrex, for example, founded in 2011 by
veterans of Check Point and the IDF's technological units, raised
$6 million but was sold in November 2015 for just $125,000. Similarly,
the information security company Nyotron, which was founded in 2006
and received $46 million in investments, was sold in 2021 in a stock
deal worth just $15.6 million. But still, this was undoubtedly a period
of incredible growth for Israeli cybersecurity, with the industry's best
entrepreneurs creating mountains out of nothing time and again.

What explains the sudden emergence of these hundreds of cybersecurity companies? In 2010, the world witnessed the start of a chain
of events that led to a rise in global awareness about cybersecurity:
that was when the Stuxnet worm, which had crippled thousands of
Iranian centrifuges, suddenly made headlines. Then a series of other
cyberattacks around the world were exposed, stunning information
security experts—most importantly, China's involvement in the theft
of the F-35 jet plans from a Lockheed Martin subcontractor. The need
for upgraded cyberdefense measures became clearer and more urgent
than ever, and the "founding fathers" of the Israeli cyberindustry,
including its most prolific entrepreneurs, continued working overtime.

Using their money from the sale of Trusteer to IBM in 2013,
Boodaei and Loonkar founded a new business, called Transmit Security. Transmit offered technology to skip the need to keep typing passwords by using biometrical identification instead. In just a few years,

Transmit was declared a "double unicorn": a company with a market value of over $2 billion. In June 2021, Transmit raised $543 million, based on a market valuation of $2.2 billion.

Gur Schatz, who had worked at Imperva from day one, founded a new company in 2009 called Incapsula, in which Imperva had a controlling stake. The company specialized in using cloud services to protect websites, including against DDoS attacks. In 2014, the rest of Incapsula's shares were snapped up by Imperva, and it became a subsidiary of its parent company, but Schatz had already tasted life as an entrepreneur—and he had an appetite for more.

Shlomo Kramer left Imperva in late 2014, and early the next year, he joined Gur Schatz in founding Cato Networks. Cato created a whole new category of cybersecurity, for which the consulting firm Gartner invented the name "Secure Access Service Edge" (SASE) in 2019. Whereas at Check Point, Kramer and his friends had developed a simple firewall to protect basic networks, and at Imperva, they took cybersecurity up a notch to secure internet services, now at Cato, they created a wholly secure, cloud-based network to replace a range of other services that used to be bought separately. This network brings together all of a business's activities, including remote access for employees. Cato also managed to become a double unicorn: in 2021, it raised $532 million, based on a market valuation of $2.5 billion.

In 2015, three Unit 8200 veterans founded Snyk, another successful startup. The three entrepreneurs—Guy Podjarny, Assaf Hefetz, and Danny Grander—identified a system-wide problem in the software industry: every line of code ever written could potentially contain vulnerabilities that hackers might exploit. Code was often based on other software packages, and any vulnerabilities they contained could also expose this new code. Snyk offers a service that scans software packages and flags vulnerabilities, relieving software developers of a heavy burden and boosting their security against hackers. In January 2020, Snyk reached unicorn status, having raised $150 million, based on a market valuation of $1 billion, but it didn't stop there. In September 2021, it raised another $300 million, with a market valuation of $8.5 billion.

Besides Snyk, another Israeli company founded in 2015 was Armis Security, which developed IoT security solutions. One of its founders is Yevgeny Dibrov, a veteran of Unit 81, where he first met Assaf Rappaport. Rappaport hired Dibrov as his first employee at Adallom, which we will expand on soon. When Adallom got acquired, Dibrov exercised his options and turned to founding his own startup with an old army and college friend, Nadir Izrael, and Tomer Schwartz, who left them after a while. Venture capital funds and angel investors poured tens of millions of dollars into Armis, and their investments paid off: in early 2020, Armis was acquired by private investment fund Insight Partners for $1.1 billion, and in November 2021, the company raised another $300 million based on a market valuation of $3.4 billion.

In the past, entrepreneurs tried to hide the fact that they were Israeli, and in the early 2000s, Israel's image started stabilizing—and these businesses' "Israeliness" was now a selling point in its own right.

Paradigm shift

In January 2011, Lockheed Martin published a report identifying some major changes in the field of cyberdefense, and this key document soon overhauled the information security world.[1] The report spoke of *Advanced Persistent Threats* (APTs), which emanated not from amateur hackers looking for "open doors" to squeeze through, but from central, dominant, sophisticated, and dynamic actors willing to invest time and resources in patiently waiting for ill-gotten gains. "Finally," says Div, "the word *attacker* entered the professional jargon." What spies already knew from up close—that the world is full of stubborn and sophisticated attackers who need to be given a taste of their own medicine, and for whom there are no immediate, one-off solutions— became public knowledge.

"The paradigm of information security was simple: there's a problem, you find the solution to the problem, the problem goes away," says Div, describing the old world. "Take firewalls, for example: the problem was that there was no door, so people could enter without permission. Build a door, solve the problem. But in the cyberdefense world, that equation doesn't work. People realize there's no absolute solution. Problems will always keep sprouting up, so you need a defense system that's constantly updating itself and developing." This, Div says, is where the concept of ongoing cyberdefense services—Security as a Service (SaaS) enters the picture. It dawned on people that there was no such thing as a "fire and forget" solution: organizations had to continuously pay for services that were constantly being updated, because attackers would always change and become more sophisticated with time.

Lockheed Martin's January 2011 report called out the traditional assumption that cyberattacks should only be responded to after a breach has already taken place and malware has entered a computer. The cybersecurity world began to realize that it had to identify threats at a much earlier stage—as early as when attackers gathered information on potential targets, or when potentially threatening malware already existed somewhere on the internet, even if it had not yet reached the target computer.

The Lockheed Martin report called out another problematic assumption: that all breaches were necessarily caused by fixable security flaws. In practice, the researchers showed, cyberattackers often exploit unknown vulnerabilities or previously unfamiliar tools, so these attacks are not always necessarily avoidable, nor is there always a way to fix these flaws when they are identified.

Lockheed Martin proposed pivoting to a more complex paradigm, based on obtainable intelligence about attackers and their capabilities. It created a model called the "Cyber Kill Chain," a concept borrowed from the military world to describe the stages of an armed attack: identifying a target, tracking its precise location, monitoring its movement, launching a payload at it, and so on. Lockheed Martin's new model featured stages such as *reconnaissance,* gathering information on a target before an attack; *weaponization,* the development of malware; and *exploitation* of a system's vulnerabilities—all in an attempt to cut off an attack at every stage of this chain as early as possible. This model allowed organizations to create frameworks to ensure that they had the right tools and capabilities to deal with every stage of potential attacks.

Despite this tectonic shift in the world of cybersecurity, change came slowly and painfully. For the whole of 2011, Div and his partners Yossi Naar and Yonatan Streim-Amit passionately debated whether they should quit their clandestine consultancy business and launch their own startup, to address these new challenges. Eventually, the die was cast: they would leave their old world behind and build a brand-new company. On January 1, 2012, they founded Cybereason, which aimed to transform the existing conception of cyberdefense and detect attackers even before they could cause any harm.

"It wasn't long after the Stuxnet attack," Div recalls. "We sat down to talk about what it meant to defend an organization when it gets attacked with such force. We knew the world of cyberattacks very well, but how do you cope with such an attacker? That was a question we cared about the most, and we started running sessions and thinking with Yossi about these things. When we started out, we sat on Yossi's sofa at home and tried to hash out a concept. At a certain point, after many attempts, we ended up with the concept of Malops. It basically says, instead of looking for malware, let's look for attackers instead. If we can detect that an attack on an organization is underway, we'll be able to catch it before it causes any harm." In many respects, Div says, the Malops paradigm is like the Iron Dome: the Israeli missile defense system that was developed to deal with rockets fired by Palestinian terrorists in the Gaza Strip by blowing them out of the sky before they can reach civilian areas. "You realize they've managed to launch rockets, but if you can prevent any damage, you've thwarted the whole incident. You take advantage of the time lag between the attack itself and the harm it's expected to cause."

From inertia to growth

Even though it had been a year since the discovery of Stuxnet and Lockheed Martin's major report, and although the market was now aware of these new threats, Cybereason was struggling to raise funds. Its potential clients agreed with Div that there was a problem, but they thought the solution had to come from the government, not the market. The Israeli funds that Cybereason's founders turned to did not treat them seriously. "You've already got Check Point and Palo Alto," they were told. "The problem's been solved. Why do you think you understand things better than the massive players already in the market?" No matter how stubbornly Div and his friends tried to explain that the cyberworld had changed and that new kinds of solutions were needed, they were struggling to communicate their top-secret and intimate knowledge about the world that attackers operated in. The responses drove them to despair.

Nor were they able to raise any money in the United States. The market, it seemed, did not yet really understand the need for this new kind of defense or the young men's ability, with their profound knowledge of the world of cyberattackers, to provide it. One of the funds even sent a private investigator to check whether they were who they claimed to be. But eventually, a few Israeli angel investors—Eyal Shavit, Yigal Yaacobi, and Zohar Gilon—gave them their trust and invested around $500,000 in them. It wasn't a huge sum, but at least it was something to help them start building their product, and as Div says, "It really helps at the beginning to have people who believe in you."

It would be fair to see Cybereason as the next generation of antivirus technology. In the old world, viruses were often developed by amateur hackers or attackers who were not hunting for a specific computer network, but rather spread a wide net over the internet. Traditional antivirus technology was based on a game of cat and mouse, with antivirus software always playing defense: its job was to spot malware, log its characteristics into a database, and then block it. Cyberattackers then tweaked their viruses to outflank these defense mechanisms, but after a while this change was also detected and fed into the antivirus system, and so forth. In the brave new world of APTs, a generation of much more sophisticated attackers, this would no longer be enough.

Cybereason invented technology that would defend endpoints, just like old antivirus programs, but in a completely different way. Its underlying code would have to handle rapid adaptations made by attackers and the malware they were using, so Cybereason's system uses artificial intelligence capable of studying attackers' behavior and tools, allowing it to confront similar threats, even the sorts that have never actually been seen anywhere else before.

Antivirus products used to detect viruses and then try to block them. Cybereason pivoted in a different direction. Its product switched from targeting malware to the attackers themselves, with the aim of tracking every stage of their operations: how they penetrated organizations, what their malware had done before, what it did afterward, and so on, letting Cybereason's security teams gain a deeper understanding of threats and totally uproot them. What cybersecurity had been doing before, Div explains, was to "search for guns, not terrorists." Cybereason invested in developing tech to hunt the terrorists.

In 2013, Cybereason secured its first investment from the CRV venture capital fund in Boston. It set up its headquarters in the same city and started pitching to the American market. "Back then, this was still a very niche market," Div attests. "The hype came later." And when the hype arrived, around 2015, investments started flooding in. The market began to understand this brave new world, and Cybereason completed a strategic fundraising round with $25 million, led by the American VC fund Spark Capital. "For three years, we sat and built the technology. We hardly sold anything. But in 2015, we massively picked up the tempo, and in less than five years we reached annual returning revenues [ARR, in the industrial jargon] of $100 million."

Div will never forget one of the major incidents they handled, right at the outset, after a preliminary meeting with a massive Asian corporation in 2015. On their way back to Boston, Div received a phone call from the firm's chief innovation officer, who cut straight to the chase: "It was wonderful meeting you. I think we're under attack. How can you help?" Cybereason didn't skip a beat. "We started, on our first attempt, remotely installing our tech on 50,000 endpoints. We'd never come close to something on that scale before. We tried to understand what was happening to their network, but everything was silent. After a week of silence, we asked them, 'Are you sure you've connected all the areas you think are infected?' and they said there was still one network to go. We plugged it in—and saw that's where they were really under attack. At that stage, we started tracking the attacker and reached a point where we could actually name them. The attackers had messed up their code, so we could see the comments they were writing and the people's names. We traced it to a group of government-affiliated hackers in China. We also saw that the attackers had not released any information yet and that we were able to contain the incident without the company suffering any damage. That was the first time we managed to demonstrate our system's power on such a massive scale."

Cybereason now has nearly 1,000 employees, and its products are sold in 50 countries to thousands of clients, from governments and the world's most familiar brands to small businesses. In July 2021, Cybereason raised $275 million from the Liberty Strategic Capital Fund, sending its value upward of $3 billion.

Cybereason was not operating in a vacuum. The most successful company in its field was CrowdStrike, an American firm founded in 2011. CrowdStrike grew at record speed, and as of writing, it is one of the world's three biggest cybersecurity companies. In November 2021, CrowdStrike reached a market valuation of $64 billion, although it has since plummeted, hitting $28 billion toward the end of 2022.

Another major player in this category is SentinelOne, an Israeli company, established in 2013 by Tomer Weingarten and his good friend from second grade, Almog Cohen. Unlike Lior Div and most of the Israeli cybersecurity world, Weingarten and Cohen did not rise up through the IDF's technological units. Since they were kids, they had been interested in opening up computers, playing around with hardware and software, and trying their hand at hacking. After completing his military service, Cohen joined Check Point and worked there for seven years, rising to become its innovation manager. Weingarten established a startup in another field, which monitored posts online to track evolving sentiments toward companies, and which he eventually sold to a public market research company. Eventually, Weingarten and Cohen joined forces to establish a firm that would introduce to the market a new conception of cyberdefense for endpoints.

Like Cybereason, SentinelOne also received a chilly reception. The cyberdefense market for personal computers was controlled at the time by major actors such as Symantec and McAfee, which had already been in the field for over 20 years. "When we said, 'antivirus alternative,' people thought we'd dropped off the moon," Weingarten recalled in a media interview.[2]

And like Cybereason, it also took SentinelOne many years to begin to grow, raise funds, and sell on a major scale. But eventually, it reached impressive achievements. In June 2021, it hit $160 million in annual revenues and went public on the Nasdaq, based on a market valuation of $9 billion. On its first trading day, it broke records and hit a valuation of $12 billion, more than any cybersecurity firm before it had been valued at the moment of its IPO.

CrowdStrike, SentinelOne, and Cybereason are engaged in fierce competition over the next generation of the cyberdefense market for PCs. All three companies operate R&D centers in Israel and compete for the same talent. CrowdStrike is still the leading player, but in an age when it is clear that cyberattacks will only become more sophisticated, these companies will continue shaping the market for years to come. As Div says, reflecting back: "The world understands that lines of code are so much more powerful than anyone could have imagined."

CHAPTER 8

The Best Defense— "Daddy, What Do You Do?"

In mid-December 2013, business managers at the retail mega-chain Target were busy managing the busiest sales season of the year, just before Christmas. Suddenly, they got an urgent phone call from the U.S. Department of Justice. "You've got a problem," said the voice on the line. "It looks like your customers' personal data has leaked online, and hackers are using them." On various sites across the dark web, Target's customers' details were being offered for sale, including their credit card numbers, at $5–$7 a pop.

Target's shocked management tried feverishly to locate the breach and fix it, while trying to keep the embarrassing news under wraps. That attempt failed. On December 18, the independent journalist Brian Krebs broke the story. His report caused an uproar in the media, and the next day, Target was forced to admit that tens of millions of its customers' credit card details had indeed been exposed and stolen. Target's sales started to plummet, exactly at peak sales season. In a desperate attempt to regain his customers' trust, Target CEO Greg Steinhafel announced a 10% discount for all customers. It was no use. The company's profits collapsed, in the middle of the holiday season, by 46%.

The scandal did not die down. It turned out that the hackers had stolen no fewer than 40 million credit card details and the personal data of 70 million customers. The company lost not only missed sales revenues' by February 2014, it had lost a staggering $200 million from the hack, including through damages, regulatory fines, and other costs. Target was subjected to dozens of civil suits, and the overall damage from the breach was estimated at billions of dollars. The uproar reached the U.S. Senate, which launched its own investigation. On May 5, 2014, Target's CEO announced his resignation.

The Target data breach caused shockwaves in the global business world, making it a high-water mark in terms of attitudes to cybersecurity. Before this incident, there had been awareness about cyberthreats, but they had always been considered relatively minor. With this data breach, the subject shot to the top of every CEO's inbox. Cybersecurity became one of the major concerns of any company director: nobody wanted to be the next Greg Steinhafel.

How did the breach happen? The Senate investigative committee used Lockheed Martin's "Cyber Kill Chain" model to analyze it. For its own part, Target made sure to install FireEye's cyberdefense system, but the hackers were still able to use a phishing attack to trick an employee at one of its subcontractors to download a malicious file onto his computer. This Trojan horse sat there and monitored the network until it found access passwords for Target's network, after which it injected another piece of malware, purchased on the dark web for a few thousand dollars, onto the company's servers. FireEye's system raised red flags when it saw the malware in action, but Target's employees ignored the alerts. The malware lingered on Target's servers, from November to mid-December, scooping up credit card details and beaming them back to the hackers, somewhere in Eastern Europe. The hackers quickly sold them on the dark web, for an estimated $200–$250 million.

The Target data breach was a high-profile incident, but not a one-off. In 2013, the U.S. cybersecurity firm Mandiant published a report exposing APT1, one of the most active and dangerous hacker groups in the field of Advanced Persistent Threats. APT1 had deployed advanced spyware against 150 victims over seven years. Its operations were tracked down to Shanghai, exactly where the Chinese military's Unit 61398, a cyberwarfare force, is also based. Mandiant showed how APT1 had systematically stolen hundreds of terabytes of data from 141 companies since 2006, exposing over 3,000 features that could be used to improve cyberdefenses against this group. In 2014, CyberESI revealed that APT1 had hacked the Israeli security firms Elisra, Israel Aerospace Industries, and Rafael Advanced Defense Systems, and had stolen information related to the Iron Dome project and the Arrow 3 anti-ballistic missile system. The report on APT1 demonstrated that intelligence on hackers could be both in-depth and hugely significant for defending organizations, and it inspired the creation of intelligence-sharing groups within the cyberdefense community.

If Israel's cybersecurity pioneers needed to convince customers that there was a problem, by 2014 nobody needed a lecture on the importance of intelligence. But the sheer quantities of intelligence being generated every day were enormous, and organizations were struggling to make sense of it and focus only on the most relevant intel. That's when I understood: it's my turn.

The birth of an idea

As previously mentioned, my friend Guy Nizan and I first founded Cyberschool, a company that would teach cybersecurity to children. We ran courses, workshops, and summer camps for youth in Israel and the United States, with the aim of getting them to understand the field. Despite the sense of purpose and the scope of our activities, we still wanted to set up a technological startup that would achieve a global reach and influence. That had been my dream since I was young, ever since I visited the hi-tech company where my dad worked, all the way through my military service in Unit 8200 and my studies at Tel Aviv University.

While working at Cyberschool, Nizan also moonlighted as a cyber-security advisor for banks and financial bodies in Israel. He discovered that they were all desperate for targeted and precise intelligence to identify specific threats against them. This was just a few years after the launch of the darknet site Silk Road, which as we have seen, was a kind of eBay for illicit trades. Silk Road marked the start of massive activities by hackers on the dark web, alongside the rise of online information-sharing platforms, which were used to share and sell stolen information. This was also when social media platforms started taking off, as well as smartphone app stores, which provided fertile ground for fake profiles and apps to impersonate others and steal personal data. Taken together, these developments flooded the dark web with enormous quantities of stolen information and activities by hackers tied to specific organizations. Tracking them and catching them early would make it possible to thwart attacks before they got underway. If, for example, hackers shared stolen passwords on the dark web, catching them in time would allow targeted organizations to switch passwords before they could be exploited to penetrate employees' accounts.

It was obvious that organizations had to gather intelligence about threats against them, but the solution was convoluted. The only possibility at the time was to gather and analyze information manually. As an observer and consumer of intelligence material, Nizan understood that there was no way anyone or any team could constantly monitor hundreds, or indeed thousands, of relevant sources on the open part of the internet and on the dark web. As a result, they could only have partial coverage of their sources, and security teams were almost always too late to address threats. Moreover, whenever intelligence reports were published with fresh findings, they came in the form of Word documents or PDF files, from which it was tricky to extract all the relevant information to deal with the incidents being reported. Nizan understood the difficulties facing security teams—and the opportunity to create a system that would monitor, 24/7, every place on the internet where hackers were active, and would report on incidents in real time.

Nizan shared this idea with me and suggested we set out on a journey together to build a cyberintelligence company, one that would use algorithms to locate threats against companies. As a military intelligence veteran, I had lots of questions, but the idea made sense. It would undoubtedly be a challenge—I was already married and had a small kid—but I knew my dream was to found a tech startup, and if such an opportunity presented itself to me, I would grab it with both hands. Neither of us had a background in software development, so we understood that we'd need to hire a permanent tech team. It wasn't hard to find one. I reached out to Gal Ben-David, who had served with me in Unit 8200, and he agreed to join us. Off we went. Our startup was founded in 2015, under the name IntSights, a fusion of "intelligence" and "insights."

We reasoned that there was a genuine need for the solution we had in mind, but in order to understand the market in depth, we started conducting a round of meetings with industry professionals. Their responses were shockingly chilly. One famous investor in the Israeli cybersecurity industry threw us out of his office, claiming that similar solutions already existed. We pitched the idea to several major Israeli organizations, including Teva Pharmaceuticals and Bank Yahav, and although they liked the sound of our service, they were willing to pay much less for it than we needed. We turned to a globally renowned cybersecurity expert, and he told us in no uncertain terms that the problem we were trying to solve simply didn't interest anyone. Our initial enthusiasm gave way to despair and thoughts about whether the direction we had chosen was even the right one. We decided to stop and brainstorm some other ideas.

After meeting up many more times, trying to come up with better ideas—with no success—we decided to give our original idea another shot: a system that would supply intelligence about threats targeted directly against our clients. We took the lukewarm feedback from our clients into account. We decided to expand our vision and aim to give every client a complete map of the threats targeting it: fake profiles and apps using their company logo, phishing sites, stolen passwords, stolen data offered for sale, and more. We also decided that besides intelligence, we would supply tools for responding to and addressing these threats: our system would not only detect phishing sites, but would take them off the internet; it would not only locate fraudulent apps, but would take action to remove them from app stores; instead of taking a step back, we decided to go for a much more ambitious vision—a vision of a one-stop shop.

Luckily for us, soon after that, we met up with Yonatan Gad, a distributor of cybersecurity solutions to European companies. We pitched him our idea, and he immediately spotted the potential and understood that the organizations he was working with needed such a solution. Through Yonatan, we reached our first clients in Europe and Glilot Capital Partners, our first investors, who invested $2 million in us.

In time, as IntSights' growth really accelerated, we understood just how radical our innovation was: yes, there already existed similar solutions to ours in the market, but they were either very niche and covered only a small range of possible scenarios, or their systems required huge budgets and manpower. Our novelty was that we leveraged cutting-edge technology for a solution that was both comprehensive and easy to operate. The payback for major organizations was obvious, but smaller organizations could also capitalize on the intel that our technology would find. Within a year, we hit $1 million in annual sales; within two, we reached an impressive $4 million. IntSights was now a success story.

Rise and fall

One of the first clients we met with was the Noble Group, which works in supply chains of goods destined for the energy and industrial sectors. It was 2015, and its information security manager was based in

London. The company was suffering from phishing attacks at the time and asked us whether we could help. We didn't have a readymade plan to supply intelligence about phishing attacks, but said, "Sure, we can do that!" We got to work.

We noticed that the Noble Group's attackers were buying domain names that looked a lot like the company's real domain, and they were using them to send malicious emails. This allowed them to impersonate Noble Group employees and try to trick its *real* employees into sending them money. Imagine an employee suddenly getting a personal email from his boss, instructing him to make an urgent transfer from the company's accounts to a supplier—and he doesn't notice that the email came from CEO@N0ble-Group.net, for example, with a zero replacing the letter "o." The moment we cracked the problem, we were able to offer a rapid solution. Within a couple of days, we had developed a system that would warn us whenever someone registered a domain similar to Noble's one, letting us send an alert to our client's system.

It was an immediate hit. Noble was extremely impressed with our ability to put together a solution in such a short time and decided to buy our product. The order came through on the same day we signed our first investment deal with Glilot Capital, and it was one of the sweetest days of my life. We continued feverishly upgrading our product: we replaced the initial user interface with a more advanced and comfortable layout, and we kept adding new intelligence sources for our clients. Later, we also developed an autonomous system to detect phishing domains and alert our clients directly, without any involvement from us. Our clients loved it, and orders kept growing.

But it wasn't all smooth sailing. There were countless challenges, setbacks, and of course, also mistakes.

In November 2018, I was on vacation in Rome with my wife. We were strolling down a pretty alleyway, licking gelato, when my phone rang and Nizan's name popped up on the screen. "Alon, we've got a one-off opportunity, you've got to come back to Israel," he said. One of the world's major credit card companies was embarking on a massive project, which we assessed to be worth millions of dollars, to provide information about cyberthreats to companies it worked with. We had the necessary technology, but our product didn't provide exactly what they were expecting. It was clear to us that to win this contract, we would have to harness all our resources and make an intense push. So I had to make a sharp U-turn. From Rome, I was supposed to fly to Amsterdam, and from there, to Dallas to attend our annual event with our clients.

I had spent months organizing these events, but now I was looking for flights back to Israel.

The day after landing back, I went to the office early and gathered all our senior managers in the country to brainstorm how we could bridge the gaps and win this contract. Having mapped out everything we could do in a reasonable timeframe, we assembled all our Israel-based employees. With everyone standing in the middle of our open space office, I explained how massive this opportunity was and said that sometimes there are opportunities you've just got to grab, even if it means temporarily deviating from your company's strategy. We divvied up the tasks among everyone and got to work. We launched a period of a few weeks of intensive work to put our plan into practice, and there was hardly a single employee who wasn't involved in the effort.

Having presented our results to the credit card company, we understood there were still a few gaps to plug. The feedback was positive, but we sensed that they were looking for something slightly different and preferred products that other companies would find easier to supply. In the end, after a nerve-racking wait for a final answer, we got turned down.

The next day, we assembled all our employees again in our open space. This time, the mood was not one of excitement, but of a missed opportunity. Not only had we diverted massive resources away from our primary product toward a project that did not serve our existing customers, but all our efforts had gone down the drain. I stood in front of our employees and explained all this, without hiding my personal disappointment. I thanked them for throwing themselves into the work, something we didn't take for granted at all, and I explained that that's how startups work: there are lots of successes, but also no few failures.

It was, without a doubt, one of my biggest disappointments at IntSights. Hindsight is 20/20, but I couldn't avoid regretting the mistake we had made by choosing to go for this project—a project for which we didn't have the right product in the first place, to which we had to divert resources to meet a tough deadline, and for which several other companies already had more suitable products. I felt that I'd let not only myself down, but also all our employees.

This credit card project was an unforgettable event, but it was dwarfed by our other successes along the way. Within six years, we managed to reach hundreds of clients around the world, a workforce of 200, and annual sales of over $30 million. We were very proud of our product and our results, and in 2021, having already raised

$70 million, we decided to secure another $50 million. Glilot Capital Partners, our first investors, had just started an investment fund for companies in later stages of development, and they jumped at the opportunity. After a short process, they gave us an investment offer.

Meanwhile, another of our investors made a connection between us and the U.S. cybersecurity company Rapid7. We spotted a neat opportunity for cooperation. We saw potential for synergy between our companies' products and believed we could convince them to sell our product together with theirs. Rapid7's product was famous for being able to detect vulnerabilities in companies' computers, alerting security teams to fix them. We believed that our intel, including information scooped up from conversations between hackers online, could help Rapid7's clients prioritize the most problematic vulnerabilities that they needed to fix, knowing which ones were the subject of the most online chatter among hackers.

We decided to meet up. We came to an online meeting with a fairly big team from Rapid7, during which we pitched our product and explained the potential for the products to be sold together as a package, creating major value for clients. The feedback was enthusiastic, and at the end of the conversation, one of Rapid7's team members asked me whether I could stay on the call. I agreed. When only the two of us remained, he asked me whether we would be interested in exploring a "strategic" option. I got the hint: that's code in the industry for an acquisition. I told him on the spot that such an option was not in the cards.

Why did I supposedly reject this offer, which other entrepreneurs might have jumped at? The answer is twofold. First, we really did have an investment offer and were planning on taking it and running ahead. And second, this was a standard maneuver in negotiations, to get a better deal. That said, although we were not looking to sell the company, we did have questions about the future of the market. We were asking ourselves whether there was really any justification for a company that focused exclusively on cyberintelligence, or whether the right place for an intelligence solution was alongside a set of other products that would help to detect and respond to cyberattacks. "In any case," I told him, "if you've got a very good offer and want to move quickly, we'd be willing to look into the option." I told him the honest truth: that was the situation we were in.

We entered a weeklong marathon in which Rapid7 explored the option of an acquisition. Rapid7's team was based in Boston. At the end of each working day—the middle of the night for us in Israel—the team sent us a list of questions and information that it wanted. Every morning, we woke up to a new list in our inbox and sat down to assemble the materials. In the afternoon, morning in Boston, we met online to present the information and answer any questions. As the process moved ahead, both sides felt that the natural place for our intelligence product was alongside the sort of detection and response product that Rapid7 was selling its clients. There was also a great connection between our teams. We felt that we were all on the same wavelength and that joining forces across both organizations was natural. At the end of the week, both sides expressed a desire to complete the process. In time, we also agreed on the price tag for Rapid7 to acquire and incorporate IntSights: $350 million.

The moment of sale was one of satisfaction and pride. Such an exit, at such a price, is an incredible achievement that few startups reach. That's not to say we didn't have plenty of "what if?" questions: what if we had refused to sell and kept growing? Would we have climbed even higher? Thoughts like these can trigger pangs of discomfort, about having to give up your "baby" after working so hard for so many years to raise it. But looking back a year and a half after the acquisition, I'm much more convinced that this was the right move for the company and for me personally, and I feel so much prouder of this achievement—a feeling that will probably stay with me for the rest of my life.

CHAPTER 9

From Crisis to Crisis—Israeli Cyber Grows Up

"What have we done to ourselves?" Assaf Rappaport asked himself as he watched the news in shock in March 2020. A new and mysterious virus had started spreading from China, striking major cities around the world. Governments were imposing strict lockdowns from New York and Italy to Israel. Many businesses were closing their shutters and sending workers home on unpaid leave, and nobody knew for how long. And that was exactly when Rappaport and a couple of friends had walked out of Microsoft, where he had worked as the director of its Israeli development center, with the aim of embarking on a new adventure and building their own startup. "We've just founded a startup with the worst possible timing," Rapaport thought to himself. But his feeling of hopelessness quickly proved misplaced.

Rappaport's cybersecurity and technology journey began during his military service. "Before the army, I'd never written a single line of code. I wasn't interested in computer science at all," he recalls. But the army would soon whip him into shape. Rappaport won a spot in the prestigious Talpiot program, which aims to find the most outstanding youngsters and turn them into the next generation of managers of the military's R&D systems. He chose to study computer science and was assigned to Unit 8200, and then to Unit 81. After nine years in the IDF, he was released back into civilian life. "I dreamed of being the commander of Unit 81, but I felt I wanted to see the world," he says. Rappaport joined the McKinsey management consultancy, introducing him to a world that was, for him, no less exciting than the army, but the experience led him to a clear conclusion: "As a consultant, your influence maxes out with a PowerPoint that nobody's going to implement. As a founder, you do everything, and whatever you don't do, nobody's gonna do it for you."

In 2012, Rappaport joined up with friends from Unit 8200, Ami Luttwak and Roy Reznik, to found Adallom. They started without any sense of direction or a clearly defined idea, but they were determined to think of one that would cause shockwaves in the market. Eventually the three friends developed a cloud security product and received a $1 million investment promise from the hi-tech investor Zohar Zisapel, one of the founders of cybersecurity firm Radware.

Another investor who took an interest in the team was Gili Raanan, who was at the time the sole Israeli partner at the U.S. venture capital fund Sequoia Capital. Raanan heard through Unit 8200's alumni network about this intriguing up-and-coming team, and he started courting them. Rappaport, for his part, tried to avoid him, spooked by stories about American investors who ended up replacing startup founders with more experienced American managers. Sequoia Capital is one of the most successful venture capital funds in the world, and it is not used to getting rejected out of hand, but that was exactly what happened.

Raanan did not give up, and after promising the three entrepreneurs that Sequoia was not planning on taking over their company's management, he managed to drag them along to a meeting. They met Sequoia's managing partner, Doug Leone, and pitched him their product and their plan. That night, Raanan called Rappaport and told him, "Assaf, your presentation was awful. Your product's a bad fit and the market doesn't need what you pitched," and then showered him with more criticism. "But," Raanan added, "despite everything, we still want to invest in you. You're a team with great potential and we believe in you. Let's arrange a meeting to close the details."

Rappaport, stunned, could not wrap his head around the sudden switch. "I thought it was some kind of inside joke at Sequoia," he later recalled.[1] In our conversation, Raanan remembers this incident with a chuckle. "The presentation was nothing special, but the people were incredible, and part of the story was just for negotiation purposes," he admits. On the first day after their meeting, Rappaport and Raanan sat for breakfast at a gas station north of Tel Aviv. After that, Raanan sent Rappaport a term sheet for a $4.5 million investment.

"Raanan's first request was to wait before deciding on a direction," Rappaport recalls. "The message was: you've got a full tank of gas with $5 million. You need to think hard before you step on the gas." Sequoia ran the entrepreneurs through a refinement process: they spent three weeks in Silicon Valley, meeting industry leaders, and they understood on the one hand how unsuitable their idea was, and on the other— exactly what the market needed. It was an eye-opening experience for the young entrepreneurs, which let them focus on their concept: the security solution they needed was a digital agent to monitor cloud services, which were only just rising in popularity. They chose the name Adallom, in a play on the Hebrew phrase *ad halom* ("up to here"), used to refer to the furthest point that Egyptian forces reached in the 1948 war, because their new startup's role was to block access to unwanted intruders.

Success was almost instantaneous. In less than three years, they managed to develop a product, sell it to corporations all around the world, raise $45 million, and sell their company to Microsoft for $320 million. Adallom became the anchor of Microsoft's cloud computing division, which Rappaport headed. Microsoft had developed a strategy of investing in cybersecurity solutions based on the research center that it would open in Israel, a process that began with its acquisition of Aorato in 2014 (for $200 million), continued with Adallom, and was completed with its purchase of Secure Islands ($150 million), Hexadite ($100 million), and CyberX ($170 million).

The contract required Rappaport and his team to remain at Microsoft for just two years, but they ended up staying for five.

After five years, Rappaport felt that he couldn't stay at such a massive corporation and wanted to go back to being an entrepreneur and to start his own company. In December 2019, he and his partners left Microsoft, and together they set out, once more, on the bumpy road of the startup world. Rappaport and his old partners from Adallom founded a startup called Beyond Networks. They started planning a firewall for cloud services, but like at Adallom, they quickly dropped their original idea. They decided to change the company's name to something that suggested nothing in particular, so they could fill it with whatever they stumbled on at the end of the journey. That's how Wiz was born.

It was not an easy decision. Rappaport is open about his concerns: "As an entrepreneur hitting the road for a second time, after one success, people expect a lot from you. Anything less than your first success will be considered a failure. At this point, you also know how hard and stressful the journey of an entrepreneur is, while you could be sitting relatively comfortably with some senior, well-paying job at a major company." They hesitated, but the entrepreneurial bug had bitten them hard. They decided to get going—and they aimed extremely high.

Back when they ran Adallom, the idea of selling the company quickly was always on the table. This time, they made a different decision: they were going to throw themselves into building a major company. The concept behind Wiz was to build a comprehensive security solution for customers' cloud environments. Unlike Adallom, here they were not going to create a security solution that did not exist before, but the opposite: the market had been crowded and extremely noisy for a decade, but nobody had managed to come up with a satisfactory solution. This time, they did not have to learn what clients needed, only how to face off more competitors than they could count. Wiz aimed to introduce something completely different, which would pull the rug out from under everyone's feet and push all the older players aside—including Check Point and Palo Alto, which were already supplying similar solutions.

When the COVID-19 crisis hit Israel in March 2020, Rappaport and his friends were already sitting on $21 million, invested in them simply on the basis of trust in their team. But when businesses were suddenly forced to focus only on survival, who was even thinking about cybersecurity for businesses? Looking back, it turned out to be the best possible time to build a cloud security startup. Workplace projects were shelved, people switched to working from home, and so much business migrated to the cloud, which could be accessed from anywhere. In each of 2020 and 2021, the cloud computing infrastructure market grew by more than 40%, hitting $91 billion in 2021.[2]

The migration of business activity to the cloud unleashed incredible demand for cloud security services and a solution like Wiz's, and the new company grew at breakneck speed. Within just nine months, it was declared a unicorn—a startup worth over $1 billion—and in less than two years, it hit a market value of $6 billion. Wiz also broke the record for fastest revenue growth: in a year and a half, it went from annual revenues of $1 million to an annual recurring revenue of $100 million. Wiz became a symbol of the Israeli "unicorn age," with a new generation of Israeli cybersecurity startups growing at a dizzying pace and attracting interest from investors and clients all around the world.

Wiz's success raised eyebrows in the industry and economic media. Was Wiz's enormous market value, in terms of the investment it secured and sales of its stock, a real reflection of its worth? Some began to see it as a reflection of something else: a cyberbubble that was doomed to burst. Rappaport and his friends insist that the value they have created is real, citing the business's reported revenues as proof. We'll return to the underlying question—whether the Israeli cybersecurity market is overvalued—later in this book.

Safe browsing: Island & Co.

Wiz was not the only company to benefit from the COVID-19 crisis. Another startup that took off rapidly during the pandemic was Island, which developed a secure web browser. Island spotted a major weakness in remote work: in the office, it is relatively easy for organizations to monitor their networks and what their employees are doing on their computers, what websites they are surfing, and what files they are downloading. But with the switch to working from home, this oversight became much harder. At the same time, more and more people were using browsers for basically everything they were doing on their computers, such as sending emails directly from Gmail, not Outlook. Browsers had become the gateway to computers and major targets for potential hackers.

One of the entrepreneurs behind Island is Dan Amiga, another Unit 8200 veteran. In 2013, Amiga founded Fireglass, which provided security solutions against attacks on computers through web browsers. In 2017, the firm was sold to Symantec for $250 million, a whopping 12.5 times the original investment. At Symantec, Amiga met Michael Fay, the company's American president and chief operating officer. They spotted an opportunity in this new situation—the difficulty of monitoring employees at home, and the fact that browsers had become the main gateway for attackers into computers—and they decided to develop a special browser for secure internet activities, giving organization's information security managers tools to detect attacks on their employees. Island was founded in 2020, and in less than two years, it became a unicorn, raising hundreds of millions of dollars based on a market valuation of $1.3 billion.

The growing market for secure browsers is not controlled by Amiga alone. His main competitor is an Israeli start-up called Talon, founded in 2021, which also developed its own secure browser. In August 2022, at the peak of the slowdown in the cybersecurity market, Talon raised $100 million. Besides Amiga and Talon, the market is bustling with other actors, such as LayerX, another Israeli company founded in

2021, which offers a solution that helps organizations secure whatever browsers they are already using. Which company will control the market, and is there room for multiple players? Only time will tell.

The massive switch to networks

When we founded IntSights, it was obvious that the CEO would have to work in the United States. "There's no market in Israel; your market is the United States, and you need a physical presence there," were the lines we kept hearing over and over again from investors and entrepreneurs alike. The coronavirus crisis fractured this widespread understanding. The United States is obviously still the biggest and most advanced market for cybersecurity solutions, but it is now less important to have a physical presence there. The restrictions on face-to-face meetings taught companies to explore security products through Zoom, whose popularity skyrocketed. This shift caused several major changes.

First, closing deals worth hundreds of thousands of dollars without any in-person meetings with a sales rep has gone from unimaginable to commonplace.

Second, the transition to doing business remotely has reduced the inherent advantage of U.S. over Israeli firms. The hardline pandemic restrictions in the United States, which prevented Americans from meeting face-to-face, taken together with the possibility of closing deals on Zoom, has reduced U.S. firms' comparative advantage and pushed Israeli startups ahead.

Third, this new situation has also helped startups compete with major companies. Major companies have big clients, which their salespeople stay in touch with and visit regularly. Some salespeople are in such close contact with their clients that they have their own access passes to their offices, giving them a huge advantage over startups that are just getting going and need to create these contacts from scratch. As of 2022, for example, Palo Alto Networks has over 85,000 clients, and when it launched its latest cloud security product, it could go straight to its clients and sell it to them. Wiz, however, had to put out initial feelers to each new client to grab its attention. During the coronavirus pandemic, Palo Alto's sales reps could no longer visit their clients' offices to catch their executives for a quick chat in the corridor and tell them about the new product they had launched—eroding the company's competitive edge.

The pandemic also highlighted the advantages of hi-tech over other industries. While retail, tourism, transport, and other companies took a serious hit from lockdowns and quarantines, the hi-tech sector flourished, generating unprecedented growth for its firms in 2020–2021. By way of example: the value of U.S. cybersecurity company CrowdStrike jumped by over 300% in this period; Palo Alto's value rose by over 130%; and many other hi-tech and cybersecurity companies posted highly impressive growth figures. These companies' market valuations soared by much more than their sales figures or profits—a sign of the investment communities' solid confidence in the hi-tech sector. The same confidence in public companies also trickled down to younger startups, which found themselves with astronomically high valuations.

In 2020–2021, no fewer than *13* Israeli cybersecurity startups gained unicorn status, more than doubling the number of Israeli cybersecurity firms worth over $1 billion. At the end of 2019, Israel had only three startups and five public companies worth over $1 billion. Six of the new unicorns worked in securing the cloud services that businesses flocked to during the pandemic.

Is the bubble about to burst?

In early 2022, stock markets around the world plunged into bear territory, with share prices dropping, especially in the tech sector. This dramatic drop raised many questions about the valuations given to tech companies, both public and private, over the past few years. Israeli cybersecurity startups were not immune from these doubts. In June 2022, *The Information,* a tech website, published a list of five companies that were overvalued relative to their actual revenues, and three of them were Israeli: Wiz, Axonius, and Snyk. Wiz headed the list, with a valuation 150 times its revenues,[3] while other excellent public companies, such as SentinelOne and CrowdStrike, were valued at 30–35 times their revenues. Israeli cybersecurity firms had posted unusually rapid growth figures, receiving their valuations on the basis of these numbers and potential for future growth. These valuations were obviously based on a very rosy—perhaps too rosy—picture of their growth forecasts.

In mid-2022, the crisis began to bite when many companies started laying off workers. Imperva, Transmit Security, Cybereason, Snyk, Checkmarx, and many others fired hundreds of workers. This wave of dismissals did not necessarily show that the valuations of 2021 were inaccurate, but they did show that these companies had invested too many resources too early on, and that their growth forecasts, on the basis of which they hired so many workers, were overblown. The crisis made investors and company directors sober up and realize that they had to look also at efficiency, not just growth.

Despite the dissipation of the enthusiasm about the meteoric rise of the cybersecurity market, and despite the sector's difficulties, it still seems that 2020 launched a new chapter for the Israeli cybersecurity market. Its companies are growing rapidly and raising huge sums of money based on very high valuations, even in these new conditions. It is a possibility that the latent anxieties about the future are justified, that the share prices will continue falling, and that we will enter a genuine crisis that will shrink the market to more moderate and realistic proportions. But in a market that is based on confidence in individual entrepreneurs, their experience, and their abilities, and in a country that on a daily basis takes threats and challenges and turns them into catalysts for prosperity and growth—there is plenty of room for optimism.

SECTION 3
Offensive Cybersecurity

CHAPTER 10

Reaching Through the Darkness: NSO and Zero-Click Disruption

C hristmas in San Bernardino should have ended differently.

On the morning of December 2, 2015, the community center of one of California's biggest cities was the venue of a Christmas party. Inside, enjoying the celebrations, were some 80 employees of San Bernardino's Department of Public Health. Suddenly, a man and a woman armed with rifles burst onto the scene and started indiscriminately shooting everywhere. The man, Syed Farook, worked as an environment and food safety inspector in the department and was a colleague of everyone there. Fourteen people were murdered in the attack, over 20 were injured, and the shooters escaped the scene.

The police launched a manhunt and tracked down the duo's vehicle around four hours later. The assailants opened fire at the police officers, wounding two of them; after a brief spate of gunfire, the shooters were shot and killed. The police investigation, launched immediately that day, found that the woman, Pakistani-born Tashfeen Malik, holder of a Green Card, had sworn allegiance to the Islamic State of Iraq and Syria (ISIS) before embarking on this murderous rampage. The pair had also managed to do something else before the attack: they destroyed their cell phones.

During the investigation, a federal detective managed to get his hands on Farook's work iPhone, which hopefully would provide priceless information about anyone he had been in contact with, including potential terror cells or other attackers. But then it turned out that the iPhone was locked with a four-digit passcode and a failsafe mechanism that would wipe the phone clean after 10 unsuccessful attempts. Embarrassingly, the FBI was forced to admit that it could not break into the phone and turned for help to the NSA, which also had to admit that it was powerless to act.[1] They both asked Apple for assistance, in the hope of solving the case and nabbing any other potential terrorists.

But Apple refused.

On February 16, Apple CEO Tim Cook wrote an open letter to the company's customers:

> *We were shocked and outraged by the deadly act of terrorism in San Bernardino last December. We mourn the loss of life and want justice for all those whose lives were affected. The FBI asked us for help in the days following the attack, and we have worked hard to support the government's efforts to solve this horrible crime. We have no sympathy for terrorists.*
>
> *When the FBI has requested data that's in our possession, we have provided it. . . . We have also made Apple engineers available to advise the FBI, and we've offered our best ideas on a number of investigative options at their disposal. We have great respect for the professionals at the FBI, and we believe their intentions are good. Up to this point, we have done everything that is both within our power and within the law to help them. But now the U.S. government has asked us for something we simply do not have, and something we consider too dangerous to create. They have asked us to build a backdoor to the iPhone. Specifically, the FBI wants us to make a new version of the iPhone operating system, circumventing several important security features, and install it on an iPhone recovered during the investigation. In the wrong hands, this software—which does not exist today—would have the potential to unlock any iPhone in someone's physical possession.*
>
> *The FBI may use different words to describe this tool, but make no mistake: Building a version of iOS that bypasses security in this way would undeniably create a backdoor. And while the government may argue that its use would be limited to this case, there is no way to guarantee such control.[2]*

In effect, some might say cynically, Cook spotted an opportunity in this terrible event to launch a campaign championing the security features of Apple's products and its commitment to its customers.

The strongest and most sophisticated security agencies in the world were left powerless.

The FBI sued Apple, but even before the trial began, it found an even simpler solution: it turned to Azimuth, an Australian firm, which managed to find a vulnerability in Apple's code and disable the failsafe mechanism that would have erased its memory after 10 unlocking attempts, allowing the FBI to break into the device without harming its memory. The FBI paid Azimuth $900,000 for the service, but it failed to produce any material of value.

The San Bernardino investigation was a key milestone, marking the dramatic propulsion of the worlds of security and intelligence into a new era: small companies, founded by young people in their twenties, had surpassed the technological capabilities of even the FBI. The authorities were left helpless as technology raced ahead, and young companies rewrote the rules of modern espionage.

The real game changer was the invention of the smartphone. It was relatively easy to wiretap old phones, and at least in the case of landlines, there was never any question about the location of the caller. But the offensive cyberindustry's main targets are computers. Apple launched the iPhone in 2008, and within two years, national and international intelligence agencies found themselves at a dead end: suddenly cell phones were encrypted, and it was somewhere between difficult and impossible to track and wiretap them. Government and security agencies were thrust from a position of almost total freedom of maneuver into the "going dark era." The events of San Bernardino made the problem clear beyond all doubt: even if intelligence agencies had known that Farook and Malik were planning an attack, they would have had no effective means of monitoring their communications with hostile actors.

The crime, terror, and pedophilia that started running amok under cover of darkness was the trigger for private companies to start competing with each other to supply the best flashlights. All states, especially militarily weaker ones, started looking for technologies to illuminate their way.

The cyberblacklist

"What's offensive cyber?" asks Shalev Hulio, straightening up in his seat. "It means using cybertools to target real-world infrastructure.

Using a cyberattack to make a centrifuge explode—that's an offensive cyberoperation. Blowing up gas tankers, putting chlorine in water—those are offensive cyberoperations. Collecting intel from a cell phone is cyberintelligence; that's not an offensive cyberoperation."

I met Hulio for a conversation in the living room of his apartment in Tel Aviv's glistening YOO Towers, home to the Israeli industry's newly minted. Hulio is the founder (and was, at the time, also the CEO) of the NSO Group. NSO has developed the world's most advanced offensive cybertechnology—or as Hulio calls it, cyberintelligence technology—and in 2021, the company raked in over $100 million in revenues. Hulio is a large, cheerful man, who considering how much pressure I know he is under, is astonishingly calm. Nothing in his behavior would suggest that he founded and runs one of the most successful, famous, and indeed, infamous cybertechnology firms on the planet.

Until October 2018, NSO was just another offensive cybertechnology firm, no more and no less controversial than others, with contracts with foreign governments and leading spy agencies. But one morning, the world awoke to shocking headlines about the gruesome murder of Jamal Khashoggi, a Saudi journalist. Khashoggi, a member of the Saudi nobility and a fierce critic of Crown Prince Mohammed bin Salman, had entered the Saudi Consulate in Istanbul to process some personal paperwork, only to run into a hit squad, who murdered him and chopped up his body. His murder horrified the Western and Muslim worlds alike, especially because of suspicions that bin Salman had ordered the killing to "dispose" of a popular journalist who had dared to criticize him. Two months after the murder, one of Khashoggi's colleagues, a Saudi journalist who had received political asylum in Canada, sued NSO in an Israeli court. The plaintiff, Omar Abdulaziz, claimed that his cell phone had been infected with NSO technology—which is expanded shortly—allowing the Saudi royals to monitor his text messages with Khashoggi.

Khashoggi's murder focused world attention on research conducted by The Citizen Lab, an academic institute based at the University of Toronto in Canada, about NSO. Since 2016, the Citizen Lab has been publishing papers on NSO, claiming that it knowingly sold its flagship product, Pegasus, to governments that violate human rights. According to the allegations, Pegasus is used to monitor journalists, opposition figures, and dissidents in countries such as Mexico, the United Arab Emirates (UAE), Saudi Arabia, and more.

A few months after Khashoggi's murder, in January 2019, Shalev Hulio gave an interview to the *Yediot Aharonot* journalist

Ronen Bergman, who was also covering the affair and its connection to Israel for the *New York Times*. Hulio used the interview to shake off the allegations:

> We conducted a thorough inspection of all of our clients, not just the one client who could perhaps be a potential suspect for involvement in the affair, but also other customers who may for some reason have had an interest in monitoring him. We also checked whether maybe someone went to a certain other country and asked their intelligence services "to do him a favor." We checked all of our clients, both through conversations with them and through technological testing that cannot be forged. The systems have records and it is impossible to act against a target such as this without us being able to check it. After all these tests, I can tell you, in an attributed quote, that Khashoggi was not targeted by any NSO product or technology, including listening, monitoring, location tracking and intelligence collection. Exclamation mark. The story's just not true.

According to the lawsuit, in June–July 2018, Abdulaziz and Khashoggi were working on a project to help dissidents organize on Twitter and confront the network of Twitter accounts operated by the Saudi regime. Groups of Twitter users "were receiving orders from Saudi regime figures . . . and their objective was to attack Saudi opposition leaders and spread negative rumors about them, while at the same time praising the decisions and actions of Crown Prince Mohammed bin Salman." Khashoggi had sent Abdulaziz $5,000 to support the project, and in Abdulaziz's estimation, "the details of the project were known practically in real time to Saudi government officials, thanks to their surveillance of him using the Pegasus system. This project infuriated Saudi government officials more than anything, and in his assessment, this was the project that cost the deceased [Khashoggi] his life." Two months later, Khashoggi was murdered.

An insider with knowledge of the episode pulls out his cell phone and shows me screenshots of tweets sent by Omar Abdulaziz. They include an oath of allegiance to the leader of the Islamic State terror group, statements of support for Hamas and Al Qaeda, and expressions of fierce anti-Israel hatred. This insider, who prefers to remain anonymous, has no doubt that his lawsuit against NSO is a fundamentally anti-Israel initiative: "The guy doesn't recognize the State of Israel's existence and calls for its destruction. We submitted evidence to the court and we asked to see forensic evidence that he had Pegasus [on his device], but he didn't hand it over. The Citizen Lab said that it had 'seen strange stuff' on his phone, but that doesn't prove anything."

Since there is a gag order on the proceedings, the insider cannot elaborate, saying only that the whole case is a "blatant lie" intended, in his view, to defame Israel on the world stage.

Pegasus is spyware that can be installed on practically any cellular device. What makes it extraordinary is the fact that it uses zero-click technology, meaning that targets do not have to click on anything to unwittingly "authorize" it to run on their devices, making it possible to track them without raising suspicions. It's no use ignoring any suspicious links sent to your smartphone; Pegasus can seize control of it anyway.

Shalev Hulio emphasizes that this technology commits espionage, not sabotage; it does not attack targets, but just provides information about them. He argues that this is an entirely professional distinction, but there is undoubtedly also a PR element at play.

Whereas cyberdefense companies develop software or mechanical solutions to protect information, offensive cyberfirms start developing products the other way around: first they explore existing information storage or transfer technologies, and then they look for ways in. These breaches are called vulnerabilities, and they let offensive cybertechnology firms develop malware that works in three stages: exploiting vulnerabilities to install malware, collecting information and sending it to an attacker, and concealing this all with another layer of software.

Most companies that are considered offensive cyberfirms—most notably NSO—do not, in fact, cause any damage in the physical world. They can obtain valuable information, but their effects cannot spill out of the technological realm. The best metric of this distinction is their success: in the case of offensive malware, success is judged by its ability to cause tangible damage to a target's files. In contrast, when a cyberintelligence firm develops spyware, its success, as in the case of Pegasus, is judged by its ability to remain imperceptible. The reason, nonetheless, that both forms of cybertechnology get labeled as "offensive" is that they operate identically: they spot vulnerabilities and exploit them, against the wishes of a system's owner.

The birth of a revolution

Shalev Hulio is anything but the typical Israeli startup entrepreneur: he did not grow up in the greater Tel Aviv area, nor did he serve in the

Israeli military's Unit 8200. Born in Haifa, Hulio spent most of his high school years at the beach with his childhood friend Omri Lavie. On the rare occasions he actually wanted to go to school, he focused on theater and art. When he and Lavie had to choose where to do their mandatory military service, they didn't try to get into a technological unit, signing up instead for combat duty: Lavie joined the artillery corps, and Hulio went into counterterror and search and rescue.

After his military service, Hulio took the traditional Israeli route of a post-army backpacking trip and working abroad. He cut his trip short to fight in the Second Lebanon War, and when the conflict ended, he signed up for a law and politics degree. While he was studying contract law, Omri Lavie came back from his own trip, and together in 2006, they decided to set up their first company. MediAnd developed a platform for people to buy products they saw in videos: people watching TV, for example, who saw an actor wearing a shirt they liked could thus easily get information about how to buy it. The company took off, and the pair raised funds in Israel and abroad—until the 2008 economic crisis, when after what looked like a successful fundraising effort with an American hedge fund, their new investors pushed them out of the company. "It sucked," Hulio says with a shrug, "but it was a good business school."

But the pair refused to give up and founded their second company, CommuniTake, which provided technical support technology for cell phones. The software allowed customer service representatives to take control of customers' phones remotely, just like computer customer service reps can do with computers. They sold the technology to cell phone providers around the world, so that anyone with a problem could call a hotline and get sent a link. By clicking on the link, they allowed their phones to be mirrored in the customer service center, allowing providers to work on them and fix them remotely.

In 2009, they suddenly started getting requests from European police forces and security agencies. They had been used to working with the old cell phone providers and thought that Lavie and Hulio's new technology could solve their difficulties gathering intelligence in this new "dark era." They used to be able to go through cell phone operators, with a warrant from a judge, to access phone traffic, including mainly phone calls and text messages. But these new smartphones used IP-based technology, with end-to-end encryption. That was when intelligence agencies in non-superpower states understood the need to pivot from signals intelligence (SIGINT) to cybersecurity. SIGINT picks up on electronic signals to collect everything passing through the medium between devices; but since the medium was now encrypted, they had to find one of two things: either a way to crack the encryption or a way to intercept communications between the medium and the end device. And that was how Shalev Hulio and Omri Lavie decided to develop technology that could be implanted in end devices.

They went to CommuniTake's investors and described their new dream product. "And then," Hulio says with a smile, "they told us it was the stupidest idea they'd heard in their lives. Their reason made total sense: you're doing well in the civilian world, but you don't have a clue about the security world, and you don't even have access to anyone there—so who'd buy anything from you? You've already got a product that works. If it ain't broke, don't fix it. It won't catch on."

Let down by their investors, Hulio and Lavie dropped the idea. But they kept getting calls from intelligence agencies, until they decided to give the idea a shot anyway. But their investors remained stubbornly opposed, placing them at a crossroads: they had to decide whether to leave CommuniTake or to give up on their new dream once and for all.

And then, in January 2010, an earthquake struck Haiti.

Hulio was called up, flew to Haiti at the head of an official Israeli rescue team, and came back a different man. It was a "crazy" event, as he recalls it. "There was no government because the roof literally caved in on it. There was no law and order, there were 400,000 people dead, bodies in the streets. My team managed to rescue someone who'd been buried under rubble for 12 days. It made me think, *you only live once*, so I decided to go for NSO. It was a gut feeling. A Eureka moment."

Hulio and Lavie told their investors that they were quitting CommuniTake and founding something totally new.

The pair went to Eddy Shalev, who ran the Israeli venture capital firm Genesis Partners, who had already invested in them when they set up MediAnd, along with another roughly 100 hi-tech startups, taking four of them public on the NASDAQ. Eddy Shalev told them they had a fantastic idea but added with a wink that he wouldn't move ahead with "two morons from Haifa" who didn't have a clue about technology or security. He left them with a promise: "Bring me a security expert and techie who can do what you want, and you've got $1.5 million."

One of Hulio's roommates, in his student apartment in Herzliya, introduced him and Lavie to his friend, Niv Carmi. Niv was not a bigshot in his field, but he had at least served in various intelligence roles, giving him an aura as a "security expert." The company was founded in January 2010, taking its name from the initials of its three founders and first partners: Niv, Shalev, an Omri—NSO.

But the technological leap that they had in mind still looked far from reality. The remote installation of Trojan horse software was essential to their vision, but they kept running into a brick wall.

NSO's founders spoke to hundreds of experts and asked them how they might remotely install an application on a phone without the owner's permission or knowledge, but they all said it was impossible.

Four months into the experiment, in May 2010, Niv Carmi told his partners that he couldn't carry on without a paying job and that he had received an offer he couldn't refuse: to work in shipping security in the Gulf of Aden. The company still called itself NSO, but it was left without its security expert and in-house techie. Hulio decided to ask Eddy Shalev to invest in the company, and they arranged to meet at a Tel Aviv café. In line at the counter, he overheard the two young men behind him talking about hacking into cell phones. He quickly canceled the meeting with Eddy Shalev, turned to the young men, and said, "Sorry, I'm not a stalker, but can I buy you a coffee?" The pair were surprised but agreed. One of them was Omer Ben-Zvi, a Unit 8200 veteran. Hulio asked him, "Is it possible to remotely install an app on a phone, without the user knowing?"

"Yes," replied Ben-Zvi.

"Do you know how to do it?" Hulio pressed him.

"No," said Ben-Zvi, "but my friend does. Let me give you his email."

"Not his email, his phone number," Hulio said at once. "Call him now."

An hour later, Hulio recalls, he was sitting at a café in Petah Tikva, meeting Alexei, a young man, who, wearing a checkered shirt and large spectacles, "looked like a kid, aged 25 or 26." Alexei told Hulio that he did indeed know how to do what NSO wanted, but that he didn't want to move to the company because he couldn't find anything about it on Google—which suggested that it probably wasn't serious. Hulio persuaded him that the company was keeping itself "under the radar," and after brief negotiations, including about Alexei's salary ("I said yes to everything," Hulio laughs, "we didn't have any money anyway") and about bringing two more colleagues from his previous work, Alexei's mind was put at ease. Hulio went straight to Eddy Shalev, armed with their employment contract, and that week, they signed an investment deal for $1.5 million. They appointed Avigdor Ben-Gal, a retired general and hero of the 1973 Yom Kippur War, as their company's chairman and he started making connections with governments and security agencies around the world.

Shalev and Hulio's story would suggest that the advanced hacking abilities that Alexei and his friends developed have nothing to do with their service in Unit 8200. Others in the cybersecurity world suspect things are otherwise. Michael Shaulov served in offensive cybersecurity in Unit 8200 and later founded Lacoon Mobile Security, which was sold to Check Point for $100 million, and Fireblocks, which reached a valuation of $8 billion. He told me about an event at which he bumped into Hulio and Lavie: "When they told me what NSO was doing, I was shocked. My hair stood up on end when we were talking. I told them, 'But you weren't even in the unit!'"

Either way, Eddy Shalev's investment was the only money that NSO ever raised. The company didn't even have a sales department because after its first success everything spread by word of mouth. The NSO Group set up its sales department only years later, in 2014.

The breakthrough

NSO's first success came from "a Latin American country"; Hulio will never reveal his clients' identities, but it was probably Mexico. In October 2011, NSO sold it the first, experimental version of Pegasus, its spyware, named after the winged horse of Greek mythology. NSO's founders reckoned that a flying horse was a good symbol for their new technology because as Hulio explains: "We basically built a Trojan horse that we sent through the air, into end-devices."

Pegasus is not an ordinary piece of spyware; in fact, it's totally extraordinary. It can enter your cell phone without your knowledge and gather up information, whether or not it is already encrypted. Pegasus makes it possible to listen to every conversation on your device, to read every message, to open your phone's microphone and hear everything that is said in the same room, and to take photos with its camera. It also makes it possible to copy passwords, for bank accounts, email, and more—so that whoever is operating the spyware can easily log into these accounts, without needing to try to hack apps protected by extensive defenses. Pegasus' abilities are groundbreaking in their own right, but as we have seen, the tip of the technological spear is its ability to penetrate devices in a zero-click manner.

The usual way of hacking a cell phone is with one-click technology. A link is sent to a device, via SMS or by another means, tempting the victim to click it. Clicking on this link makes the phone download spyware, but savvy targets of espionage should know not to click on unfamiliar links.

Zero-click hacking technologies create threats and opportunities on a totally different scale. They make it possible to introduce spyware directly to someone's phone, no matter how carefully they behave. It is likely that NSO designed its first zero-click capabilities for Black-Berry devices, but eventually Pegasus also found vulnerabilities in other operating systems. In time, NSO became the world's biggest company researching software vulnerabilities; it employed 75 vulnerability researchers, who turned Pegasus into software capable of penetrating any cellular device. In December 2021, Google's Project Zero team blew the lid on Pegasus' sophisticated strategies for penetrating devices using iPhone operating systems.[3] NSO's programmers managed to target iPhones with PDF files disguised as GIFs, which as soon as they arrived, started running a virtual processor that could run lines of code on the hacked devices, acting like a kind of minicomputer hidden in a file disguised as a different file. It was a powerful display of the Israeli firm's advanced abilities, but in those early days in 2010, Pegasus was still, to quote Hulio, "half-baked."

The Mexican government was grappling at the time with rampant crime by drug cartels, and it hoped that Pegasus would help it find and nab the drug lords. NSO hesitated; the Mexican police force was known for being problematic, and the firm was wary of selling it this valuable weapon. Only after Mexico established a separate military agency to take on the cartels did a pathway open up for a massive deal, and NSO started helping Mexico wage war on the cartels.

One day in 2011, Hulio was woken up by a phone call. It was 3 a.m., and the person on the line muttered something in English in a heavy Spanish accent. Hulio had no doubt that it was Omri Lavie pulling his leg. "Drop it, Omri, you jerk, go to sleep," he said and hung up. The phone rang again, but it wasn't Omri; it was someone in the Mexican president's office. It turned out that NSO had managed to do in a month what Mexico's police had failed to do in a decade. NSO's technological breakthrough opened the door to massive deals, even by the standards of the industry at the time.

Pegasus helped to bring down the Mexican drug lord Joaquín Guzmán, better known as "El Chapo," by monitoring the phone calls of the actor who was cast to play him in a biopic. El Chapo was arrested in January 2016 and eventually brought to trial in the United States, where he was sentenced to life in prison plus 30 years. Naturally, as with all reports about the involvement of offensive cyberfirms, it is hard to know what details are true, but NSO can take credit for many other events, including the capture of pedophile rings, the thwarting of mass terror attacks in Europe, and even the targeted killings of high-ranking terrorists. NSO is often attacked over human rights violations, but it takes most pride in cases like these, which usually remain hidden from public view.

Since that phone call from a president somewhere in Latin America, Shalev Hulio's phone has rung many times again in the middle of the night, and on many of those occasions, he was just as surprised by who was on the line.

CHAPTER 11

In the Right Hands— The Israeli Companies That Stretched the Boundaries of Possibility

One day, the offices of Hacking Team, an Italian company, received an intriguing phone call. On the line was a senior official in the Milan police, who wanted to gain access to the company's technological tools in order to record the Skype conversations of a police suspect.

Hacking Team was founded in 2003 as a cyberdefense company.[1] One of the services it offered was penetration testing: running simulated cyberattacks to expose organizations' security flaws. Hacking Team decided to take this service a few steps forward, and its teams developed a tool that would prove exceptionally effective for offensive purposes. After the phone call from the Milanese gendarmerie, Hacking Team went from being just another cyberfirm to one of the first companies in the field of offensive cyber, laying the foundations for an entire industry.

Another major player is Gamma Group, an Anglo-German company. Like Hacking Team, Gamma Group also offered the market malware that could be installed on the computers of espionage targets in order to extract documents, keyboard strokes, passwords, records, and more from them. And like Hacking Team, Gamma Group did not start off as an offensive cyberfirm, but when it understood the commercial potential of selling offensive cybertechnology for state espionage purposes, it decided to pivot.

Gamma Group had gotten its hands on a goose that laid golden eggs: its subsidiary, FinFisher, sold malware called FinSpy, which was capable of dodging all the most common antivirus programs. FinSpy was able to hijack computers and its operators' Skype calls, emails, chats, webcam footage, and microphone audio.[2] A document leaked to WikiLeaks in 2014 revealed that, as of that year, the company had raked in €50 million by a conservative estimate. Another document that reached WikiLeaks exposed FinFisher's client list, including Qatar, Pakistan, and Bosnia, alongside the Netherlands, Belgium, and Australia.[3]

When the Israeli offensive cyberindustry got going, it already had to compete with such international giants as Gamma Group and Hacking Team, and to prove that it had something new to offer. The fierce competition only benefited Israeli entrepreneurs: although it is difficult to give precise numbers, we can cautiously say that in 2022, there were over 10 offensive cyberfirms in Israel—and around the same number of recognizable firms in the rest of the world combined.

In time, Israeli companies and their technologies built up a global reputation, and many states are now knocking at their doors to use their products. Israel has become the world's biggest exporter of offensive cybertools, and according to Israeli industry estimates, it controls some 60%–70% of the global market. Industry officials say that practically their only competition is from other Israeli companies. As these companies developed, Western attitudes to offensive cybertools also evolved: a mixture of admiration and concern, a desire to control the best tools in the market, and shock at what they can do. The companies, for their part, have tried to address both ends of this pendulum—the incredible demand and the ferocious criticism.

Candiru: The covert company

Candiru sits in an office block in central Tel Aviv, but you will never find its name anywhere in the lobby. When you step out of the elevator on its floor, you will see only a big black door, a security camera, and a small sign with the company's fake name. The walls of its office are covered murals of silhouetted faces, symbolizing the anonymity expected of its employees. Candiru has no website; its employees do not mention the company on their LinkedIn profiles, saying only that they work at a "cybercompany"; and everyone has to sign a strict secrecy agreement. The company also changes its real name from time to time, at its clients' request: when it was founded in 2014, it was called Candiru; in 2017, it was called D.F. Associates; in 2018, it became Greenwick Solutions; in 2019, it rebranded as Taveta; and in 2020, it morphed into Saito Tech. In any case, it is still most commonly known as Candiru, named after the tiny fish that wriggles into the respiratory systems of bigger fish and sucks their blood.

Candiru was founded in 2014 by two NSO and Unit 8200 veterans, Eran Shorer and Kobi Weizmann. They were soon joined by investor Itzik Zack, a former NSO board member, who had also invested in other companies with Shalev Hulio.[4] Candiru was one of the few companies that developed capabilities to hack not only smartphones but also personal computers.[5] Its technology is exceptionally sophisticated because computers are equipped with many more defense technologies than smartphones, such as antivirus software, firewalls, and more. A document leaked to WikiLeaks in 2020 reveals that Candiru offered clients a range of options to infect other devices, from sending hyperlinks or contaminated files to support in physically installing its malware on target computers. Another option is to use technology called "Sherlock," which works with Windows, iOS on iPhones, and Android devices.[6]

But in 2017, Candiru's sales were close to zero; its founders understood that something had to change, and they decided to bring in a professional CEO. Their new boss, Eitan Achlow, decided to deviate from the company's strategy of not competing with NSO in the phone-hacking market. Industry sources indicate that the decision was made after one of Candiru's clients—a NATO member state—was so pleased with its computer-oriented product that it asked Candiru to work on a complementary product for telephones and bankrolled its development. According to one of the company's executives, the client was disappointed with NSO's product, which was not good enough for its purposes. The competition between the companies caused tensions, which reached a peak in 2021, when Candiru accused NSO of recklessly leading to both companies being blacklisted by the United States, in light of growing public criticism about their activities—a step that seriously hurt them both. It is unclear whether NSO is really responsible for Candiru being blacklisted, but its activities undoubtedly attracted heightened global attention to the entire offensive cyberindustry.

Unlike most of Candiru's management, Achlow came from the business world and had not served in Unit 8200. When he started out, he happened to meet a former head of Mossad, Israel's legendary spy agency, and after their conversation, he understood that in this field, it was extremely important to pick his clients wisely. In addition to building up the company, Achlow decided to set up an external ethics committee to oversee the firm's operations.

Picking clients is a tricky business, requiring an intimate understanding of the background of each potential buyer. One of the requests that reached Candiru in recent years came from an African government, which wanted to get its hands on technology that would help it nab a citizen who was using WhatsApp to share embarrassing images of the country's leader with young women, but as Candiru says, "that's not the reason we founded this company."

The first step that Candiru takes when a potential client makes contact is to collect information from various reports about the threats that the state in question is grappling with, along with more data from the Israeli Ministry of Foreign Affairs. As a rule, Candiru will not sell its technology to any state to which Israel or the United States do not sell weapons. The second stage involves investigating the specific body that wants to buy its offensive cyber capabilities: is it police or military? Is it the whole organization or a special unit? In the case of certain states, Israeli companies will avoid selling their technology to specifically problematic organizations, but will sell it to others. In certain undemocratic states, for example, the military defends the state, while other organizations are in charge of protecting the regime. If the ethics committee approves the sale, therefore, Candiru will sell only to the military, and not the organization shielding the regime. In order to illustrate how strictly separate these organizations are, a Candiru executive tells me about the time it sold technology to the police force in a certain Gulf state, and the system got stuck at customs. Candiru asked its client to speak with customs officials to get the technology released, but officers in this foreign police force told Candiru that the customs authority was a separate body, and they could not intervene.

In 2020, Candiru had an almost-signed deal with a democratic African country, a supposedly legitimate client. The problem was that Candiru could not understand what threat it supposedly faced, to justify the use of its technology. When the president of this country asked to bring forward the signing of the contract and purchase the technology "before the elections," which took place in October that year, Candiru's representative asked whether the reason was that there would not be a budget after the elections. The president explained that there would be a budget, but that he needed Candiru's capabilities "for the elections themselves." Candiru's team got the hint and refused to complete the deal. Ironically enough, it was another Israeli cybersecurity company that sold its technology to this president for some $8 million. Soon afterward, his country's main news site published a photo of this Israeli company's team under the headline "PRESIDENT HIRES ISRAELI SECURITY OFFICIALS TO SWAY ELECTIONS."

In case potential clients nevertheless manage to conceal their illicit intentions, Candiru's system contains all sorts of technical restrictions on unethical uses. It does not work at all in certain geographical areas, such as Israel and the United States, nor does it work on Israeli, U.S., Chinese, or Russian phone numbers; Candiru simply has no interest in getting involved with the latter two. Moreover, the system has to be used with precision and does not allow for mass monitoring. If any user nevertheless tries to attack a forbidden target, the system sends a warning, and Candiru is able to pull the plug.

According to foreign reports, Candiru's technology has been used to spy on people in Lebanon, Gaza, Iran, Yemen, Armenia, Turkey, and other countries. Candiru claims that this list does not suggest a lack of caution, but rather shows that it sells its technology only to states that really are grappling with tangible terror threats. The company's chief marketing officer, who was fired in 2018, waged a high-profile lawsuit against it, which revealed another interesting fact: the litigator claimed that "in early 2016, the company was in the advanced stages of sales to clients in Europe, the former USSR, the Persian Gulf, Asia, and Latin America."[7] When these are your clients, accusations that your tools have been used to monitor civilians are practically unavoidable.

In November 2021, the British newspaper *The Guardian* reported that the Czech security company Eset had detected a sophisticated attack on a U.K. website, leading to Candiru's spyware infecting the personal computers of people who surfed this site. Candiru, like industry counterparts, never publicly responds to accusations and prefers its anonymity to fighting to clear its name.

This extreme secrecy is not, as some might suspect, the result of shame. In no way does the offensive cyberindustry see itself as problematic or illegitimate. On the contrary: its people are proud of their contributions to the war on crime and terror. The main reason for the secrecy is that clients demand it: spy agencies, police forces, and foreign government ministries do not want their targets to know their capabilities. Nor do they want any negative reports about their suppliers to rub off on them because this would only undermine the legitimacy of their operations. Moreover, if any media reports revealed technical information about the security flaws that these companies were exploiting, smartphone and computer manufacturers would simply fix their devices to block espionage using these cyberweapons, denying the clients these abilities until new vulnerabilities could be detected and new methods found.

But this was not the only consideration, it seems. Despite pride in its work, the whole industry found itself in the media's crosshairs, and public attitudes soured because of how these tools were used to violate and harm privacy. NSO and Candiru executives depict their companies, on the one hand, as cautious, and on the other, as powerful enough to stamp out rampant crime and terrorism, but outside critics see things differently. Amitai Ziv, formerly a reporter at *The Marker*, argued in a conversation with me that offensive cybercompanies should be seen as weapons manufacturers and that "for years, this abuse was happening with the approval of the State of Israel." In such a state of affairs, it is only logical to keep a low profile and avoid attracting attention to firms whose products are sometimes used illegitimately. To this, we must add that for workers at these companies, their employment histories at these firms might damage their prospects with employers who see offensive cybertechnology as illegitimate. Some of my industry colleagues, although undoubtedly a minority, are already openly saying that they will not hire people coming from offensive cyberfirms because they were necessarily involved in grave violations of human rights.

"We have made a sweeping decision not to employ people from offensive cyberfirms," declared a founder of an Israeli cybersecurity firm in an interview with *The Marker*. "We don't want to put anyone in our clients' homes or offices who we know is highly motivated by dollars and not the product itself. Anyone who has worked for these companies is used to thinking that you should solve problems without giving any thought to the importance of privacy and data protection. I don't want anyone like that touching my clients' personal data. I don't want to have people whose moral boundaries are up for sale."[8]

Surveillance van hacking: The story of Intellexa

In 2019, *Forbes* published an extraordinary video interview revealing the capabilities of Intellexa, a company founded in Cyprus by an Israeli reserves brigadier-general, Tal Dilian. The report showed how a surveillance vehicle could be used to hack an intelligence target's phone. "We are not the policemen of the world, and we are not the judges of the world," said Dilian in response to a question about the ethics of offensive cybertechnology. "We work with the good guys. And sometimes the good guys don't behave."[9]

Dilian is an unconventional character in the Israeli cybersecurity world. In 1998–2002, he commanded Unit 81, the Intelligence Corps' technological unit, after a long career as an officer in Sayeret Matkal, the IDF's elite commando force. He was a widely respected commander and ran a project for which he won the Israel Defense Prize, but his career took a hit when military police opened an investigation against him in 2002 over financial irregularities in the unit. His promotion was delayed and he retired from military service feeling that he was the victim of an injustice. He was eventually acquitted.

Dilian entered the offensive cyberworld in 2011, partnering with Boaz Goldman to found Circles. Their company sold surveillance technology that monitored cell phones' locations and could intercept their communications, exploiting telecoms companies' vulnerabilities. Circles was sold in 2014 and was eventually incorporated into NSO, but Dilian did not wash his hands of offensive cybertechnology. In 2019, he founded Intellexa, which demonstrated in that unusual *Forbes* report how surveillance vehicles could be used to hack the phones of people standing 1,640 feet away and extract private SMS and WhatsApp messages from them.

Intellexa started life as an analytics company. Originally, it offered ways of connecting databases held by national authorities—including footage, photographs, recordings of conversations, and police materials—and crosschecking them, in order to provide clients as broad information as possible about their targets. The problem with Intellexa, as the company soon discovered, was that its clients were not content with tools that processed specific information for them; they needed the raw material on their targets' devices. In every meeting with a client, Intellexa's team was asked, "Have you got any horses?" (meaning Trojan horse malware), so the team decided to add "horses" as complementary products. The team wanted to position Intellexa as the world's best analytics company and to distinguish it by having its own offensive cyber capabilities. Without this feature, the company's business model would not have stood up because it would have needed to rely on other companies' Trojan horses, but one of the company's employees emphasizes that "the core of the company is still analytics." One of Intellexa's abilities, for example, is to connect materials gleaned through lawful interception (LI) and bodycam footage with other intelligence gathered through cybertechnology. Another service that the company offers is to process information in a way that converts it into a searchable database. Police and security agencies might have plenty of relevant images from security cameras, but without tools that let them analyze these images efficiently, they will not necessarily know that they already hold the winning cards.

What is Intellexa's edge over other offensive cybercompanies? When I posed this question to an industry official, he said that companies such as NSO, Candiru, Quadream, and Paragon have developed trailblazing zero-click technologies, but these abilities are being eroded with time because manufacturers are increasingly discovering and closing these vulnerabilities. Nowadays, he claims, if NSO's technology supports an operation for 90 days straight, it is doing relatively well. These companies take the approach that they provide a service and their customers have to take into account that there may be periods when this service is inactive: the breaches that allow their products to work get closed, and in the meanwhile, they can offer less advanced technologies, which require some involvement by targets to infect their devices.

Intellexa takes a different approach: it offers a whole basket of products that allows access to intelligence on targets, without necessarily aiming to do so with zero-click technologies. In order to get its targets to click on links, it needs a different raft of tools, including social engineering tools. One popular method is to create fake Facebook profiles, which then trick targets into installing certain software on their devices, but there is also another complementary tool that works through targets' SIM cards and cell phone providers—a tool that works best in physical proximity to the target. Intellexa does not offer a single flagship product, but an integrated solution that attacks targets from several angles.

In its three years of operation, Intellexa has managed to insert itself into several international scandals. On August 6, 2022, the chief of Greek intelligence, Panagiotis Kontoleon, announced his resignation.

The Greek government secretary also resigned after it was revealed that Greek intelligence, with government authorization, had used Intellexa's Predator software to monitor an opposition leader and a journalist investigating massive corruption.[10] A few months later, in November 2022, *Lighthouse Reports* published a bombshell investigation with two media partners: Israel's *Haaretz* newspaper and *Inside Story* in Greece. It revealed that surveillance of Dilian's private jet (made possible thanks to an unwise selfie by an Intellexa employee, exposing the plane's registration number) showed that he was apparently doing business with RSF, a Sudanese militia helping the army maintain its military regime, following the toppling of Omar al-Bashir in 2019.[11] It is no coincidence that Intellexa and its subsidiaries are registered outside of Israel, letting them operate without the oversight of the Israeli Defense Ministry.

It is possible that Dilian had other reasons for moving to Cyprus, but the weaker regulatory oversight is undoubtedly helping Intellexa grow. In any case, in that interview to *Forbes*, Dilian expresses skepticism about the effectiveness of regulation to begin with. "Most of the products that are sold in this industry you cannot monitor," he concludes. "And more than that, customers don't want you to know who their suspects are."[12]

Dilian's observation points directly at the tension at the heart of the offensive cyberindustry: is secrecy, despite its cost, necessary to make the world a safer place or do even darker things happen in the shadows?

CHAPTER 12

Criticism of Offensive Cybertechnology

On April 6, 2014, a new account appeared on Twitter, called Phineas Fisher. Its Twitter handle was @GammaGroupPR, which misleadingly suggested that it was the official press office of Gamma Group. It tweeted, "Get your free trial of FinSpy Mobile!" with a link to a website hosting a treasure trove of 40 GB of information, including client lists, a price list, source code, details about the effectiveness of its malware, and information used for training and customer support.[1] Years later, it was reported that Gamma Group had sold its holdings in FinFisher back in 2013, but the parent company was still identified with the spyware at the time.

"Phineas Fisher" claimed he had proof that Gamma Group's technology had been sold to the Bahraini government to spy on Bahraini activists during the Arab Spring of 2011, and that this was what made him decide to hack the company's servers and leak its information.[2] Gamma Group, the cyberexpert that had just become the victims of a cyberattack, suffered a major blow to its reputation. The company was forced to rewrite the sections of code that had been leaked, to deal with a lawsuit from Bahraini activists claiming that its program had been used to spy on them, and on top of all that, to grapple with a British government report claiming that the company had violated Organisation for Economic Co-operation and Development (OECD) guidelines on "responsible business conduct."[3] Despite all this, FinFisher did not disappear from the market in the immediate run; business continued to boom, thanks to the growing demand for offensive cyberweapons. In 2015, it was revealed that there were no fewer than 32 states on the company's client list, and cybersecurity company Kaspersky revealed in 2019 that FinFisher has even expanded its basket of products in the meanwhile to include cyberweapons targeting smartphones.[4] But in the long run, the damage was too serious. In 2017, it was revealed that a Turkish website popular with opposition activists had been exploited to infect visitors with spyware. In 2019, an investigation was launched against FinFisher, on suspicion that it had exported its software without a license in violation of German law, and in 2022, the company went bankrupt.[5]

Around a year after the FinFisher hack, Phineas Fisher struck again.[6] On this occasion, the target was the other cybersecurity giant, Hacking Team, and the leaked information was posted to Twitter again—this time, through the company's own Twitter account, which was also hacked. The data leak contained evidence of negotiations with Nigeria and Ethiopia, as well as malware sales to Gulf states and Sudanese intelligence—all countries with problematic records on human and civil rights. The leaked materials also contained code sequences and commercial information, as well as internal emails, exposing the company's day-to-day conduct. Here, too, the reputational and commercial damage was significant, but it did not bring the company down. Hacking Team merged with another company and changed its name, and it is still active in the market.

These attacks are only the tip of the iceberg of ideological opposition to offensive cyberfirms, opposition that highlights the major battles taking place behind closed doors within governments and intelligence agencies all around the world in an attempt to find a gentle balance between two important values: privacy and security.

The enemy of offensive cybertechnology

"Mercenary spyware firms are causing widespread harm globally. Left unchecked, they have become a major crisis for global civil society, and ultimately, liberal democracy itself." So says Professor Ronald J. Deibert, founder and director of the Citizen Lab, in a message to the prime minister of Israel in an interview with *Haaretz*.[7]

The Citizen Lab was founded in 2001 with the self-proclaimed mission of investigating the intersection of information technology, national security, and human rights.[8] The lab, based at the University of Toronto, quickly proved the bane of the offensive cyberindustry, becoming the flagbearer of the battle against it. Citizen Lab is a center of world-leading technological knowledge and research, allowing it access to malware, its creators, the states using it, and the targets of their attacks.

The Citizen Lab can claim credit for some of the biggest exposés in the field, raising public awareness about the use of tools developed by NSO and similar actors to spy on journalists and human rights activists. It exposed the use of Pegasus against *Al Jazeera* journalists and attributed it to Saudi Arabia and the United Arab Emirates, along with an espionage campaign against social activists who criticized the Bahraini regime.[9] In the course of its research, the Citizen Lab was even able to get its hands on a version of Pegasus and to expose the iPhone vulnerabilities that it was exploiting to install itself on people's devices, an exposé that pushed Apple to release software patches to block such attacks.[10]

In 2020–2021, the lab published 12 reports about offensive cyber-technologies, 11 of which investigated Israeli companies, and nine about NSO. The Citizen Lab's researchers have built a list of activists, journalists, and dissidents in over 40 countries, all of whom had devices infected with Pegasus. Its report was one of the reasons why the United States ultimately placed NSO on a government blacklist.

The Citizen Lab's focus on Israeli companies and NSO, in particular, can be understood as evidence of these companies' dominance, but some see things completely differently. "The Citizen Lab writes about NSO 85% of the time, and Candiru another 5%," an industry official told me. "Where's Russia? Where's China?" Others point out that the lab's biggest donors are individuals and foundations known for funding anti-Israel activities, including the Ford Foundation, the Sigrid Rausing Trust, and George Soros's Open Society Foundation.[11] They argue that the Citizen Lab's disproportionate criticism of Israeli companies is just another form of Israel-bashing under the guise of human rights activism.

Bad publicity

The criticism of offensive cybersecurity, in general, and NSO Group, in particular, reached a boiling point with reports about Pegasus Project in July 2021. A few months earlier, a list of 50,000 people around the world had leaked—individuals whom NSO's clients had marked out for potential attacks using Pegasus. The list was sent to two nonprofits: human rights organization Amnesty International and the Forbidden Stories website that specializes in stories about journalists under all sorts of threats. Instead of publishing the leak, these two organizations decided to keep it a secret and investigate its veracity. For their investigation, they brought on board 80 journalists from 17 media channels and newspapers, across 10 different countries, including reporters from the Israeli newspapers *Haaretz* and *The Marker*. They also mobilized Amnesty International's own security research lab and the Citizen Lab to investigate the technical details.

This consortium of journalists found over 180 journalists' names on this list, alongside human rights activists, academics, lawyers, and politicians. Everyone in Saudi journalist Jamal Khashoggi's inner circle was also there: his wife, son, friends, and even the Turkish prosecutor in charge of investigating his murder. The highest-profile name on the list was French President Emmanuel Macron, who had been marked down for potential surveillance by Moroccan intelligence.[12] Afterward, the investigative journalists tried to track down the people on the list and check their smartphones. Of the 67 smartphones that they checked, they found evidence of Pegasus attacks on several of them. The researchers did not share exactly which phones were found to have been infected, raising suspicions that the number was, in fact, quite low, but the fact that they managed to find traces of this malware is hugely impressive because Pegasus is programmed in a way that is supposed to make it hard to detect.

The investigation showed that Pegasus had been used not only to fight crime and terror, but also to advance all sorts of political goals at the expense of ordinary citizens' freedom of expression and human rights. Pegasus had been exploited by authoritarian regimes, such as Azerbaijan, but also by democratic countries, such as India. The investigation also reveals that while NSO has clients from some 50 states, around 10,000 of all the phone numbers on the hit list were targets of the Moroccan government, revealing that it had been using the spyware in a sweeping fashion with very little oversight.

The Pegasus Project makes harsh allegations against NSO, but questions remain. For starters, it is unclear where the target list even came from. Each NSO client is supposed to receive a separate system, completely disconnected from other customers' systems, and since this information is highly sensitive, it was obviously heavily guarded by NSO. If the journalists indeed got their hands on real information, they could have revealed its source, even if the information itself could not be published for privacy reasons. The sheer number of targets on the list is indeed disturbing, especially in relation to Morocco, and seems to suggest that Pegasus was used indiscriminately. But on the other hand, out of 50,000 phone numbers, the journalists were able to find only 180 illegitimate targets—relatively few political as opposed to security targets, which would suggest that the damage to freedom of expression and human rights was not as sweeping as it might seem. Moreover, as for the 67 phones that they checked, the journalists claimed to have "exposed successful infections," but we are not told how many; the number of infected devices might, in fact, be very low, which would strengthen the claim that any damage was limited. Either way, the Pegasus Project achieved its desired effect: it created a lot of noise and raised awareness of how states could violate human rights using Pegasus.

The Pegasus Project inflicted serious reputational and commercial damage on NSO Group and the Israeli offensive cyberindustry in general. iPhone vulnerabilities that were presumably discovered as a result of the investigation were closed by Apple soon afterward, making them unusable.[13]

In November 2021, the U.S. government imposed the harshest sanction that it can slap on commercial entities when it added NSO Group and Candiru to its blacklist, a list of entities that American companies are forbidden from doing business with (even their subsidiaries) without explicit approval. The U.S. Department of Commerce claimed in a statement that these two Israeli companies had acted "contrary to the foreign policy and national security interests of the U.S." It was the first time that any corporate entity had been blacklisted for selling offensive cyberweapons.[14] This move was especially unusual considering that these were Israeli companies, such that the U.S. government was ready to handicap the offensive cyberindustry even if the companies affected came from friendly states. The blanket criticism also caused domestic problems for these firms: the Israeli regulator imposed a de facto freeze on approval for many deals, and Israeli industry officials expressed serious concerns that this would halt the growth of Israel's offensive cyberindustry and would send business to places with much less regulation and oversight.[15]

Reputational damage has another effect on offensive cybercompanies. The blow to the image of the industry seen as the tip of the spear of the fight against crime and terrorism is also affecting its workers.

After the United States announced that NSO and Candiru would be blacklisted, Israeli lawmaker Mossi Raz tweeted that NSO was "shaming us around the world" with its "dangerous and harmful business" and that he was writing to the minister of defense "to demand that he take action against NSO as soon as possible."[16] This criticism came on top of even earlier allegations against the Israeli offensive cyberindustry, such as when the Israeli media watchdog *The Seventh Eye* blasted the *Calcalist* newspaper for inviting NSO representatives to its conference.[17]

The industry's dubious reputation has also affected its ability to recruit and maintain manpower, or as one industry official says, "nobody wants to be bombarded with these questions at the dinner table." Hulio also says that the negative coverage pushed him to give more media interviews, an unusual step in such a secretive industry, to defend his employees. In order to compensate for the reputational damage, these companies offer higher salaries, better conditions, and more impressive corporate events. Salaries in the offensive cyberindustry can range from 80,000–90,000 NIS ($22,500–$25,500) a month, and in some cases, even 120,000 ($34,000) and higher. NSO is also known in the industry for throwing some of the most lavish corporate events in the industry at the most exotic locations. These companies are doing their best to suffuse their employees with a sense of mission and pride, telling them that above all else, they are helping to protect the world from terrorism and crime.

Between privacy and security

The attack on the Twin Towers on September 11, 2001, shocked the Western world for several reasons. One was the intelligence failure that meant that such a massive operation by a terrorist organization to strike the heart of the United States and commit mass murder on such a horrific scale managed to get past U.S. intelligence agencies. This rude awakening led to sweeping change in the structure of the U.S. intelligence community and an understanding that, in order to thwart terrorist threats, citizens' privacy would have to take a hit.

The idea of giving the state more power to protect its people already appears in the writings of some of the greatest philosophers of the modern state, such as Thomas Hobbes and John Locke. Both men argued, each in his own way, that state authorities would have to be entrusted with some aspects of personal liberty, based on the understanding that it is better for citizens to sacrifice a small amount of their liberty than to risk losing it all.[18]

These terror attacks showed that overzealous protections of privacy could cost human lives on a massive scale, and there were good reasons to fear more attacks by Al Qaeda on American soil. About a month after the attack on the World Trade Center, President George W. Bush signed the Patriot Act, or to use its full name, the Uniting and Strengthening America by Providing Appropriate Tools Required to Intercept and Obstruct Terrorism (USA PATRIOT) Act of 2001. The law relaxed restrictions on gathering intelligence on U.S. citizens and gave federal authorities broader powers to exercise their own judgment in acting to thwart terrorism. From that moment, the United States started beefing up its ties with offensive cybercompanies.

But the shock of 9/11 soon faded. Zealous support for privacy came back in fashion, and with it, suspicions that the government might abuse the information it was gathering. When former NSA employee Edward Snowden leaked masses of documents about government surveillance of U.S. citizens, the revelation sparked outrage in the media and American public, leading President Barack Obama to promise to rein in surveillance. In an interview to *The Guardian* from his place of asylum in Russia, Snowden framed the core issue:

It may be that by watching everywhere we go, by watching everything we do, by analysing every word we say, by waiting and passing judgment over every association we make and every person we love, that we could uncover a terrorist plot, or we could discover more criminals. But is that the kind of society we want to live in?[19]

Snowden described a situation that he claimed was routine: one of the NSA's young employees found an image of someone they were monitoring in an intimate situation and thought the image was "extremely attractive":

So what do they do? They turn around in their chair and they show a co-worker. And their co-worker says, "Oh, hey, that's great. Send that to Bill down the way," and then Bill sends it to George, George sends it to Tom, and sooner or later this person's whole life has been seen by all of these other people . . . the fact that records of your intimate moments have been taken from your private communication stream, from the intended recipient, and given to the government, without any specific authorisation, without any specific need, is itself a violation of your rights. Why is that in the government database?

It was in this context that offensive cybercompanies came under intensified criticism, as the security benefits of their technologies were overshadowed by a growing appetite for privacy. This shift was seen clearly in the events of San Bernardino, as is mentioned in the previous chapter, when Apple refused to help the FBI hack a terrorist's iPhone. The fact that Apple CEO Tim Cook wrote an open letter defending his decision to "protect our customers' personal data" even at the cost of obstructing a counterterror investigation shows that he assumed that this was exactly what the public wanted to hear.

Something similar happened with the abduction of three Israeli teenagers on June 12, 2014, by Palestinian terrorists. Naftali Fraenkel, Gilad Shaer, and Eyal Yifrach were kidnapped from a bus stop in Gush Etzion near Jerusalem and disappeared without a trace. Israel launched a massive intelligence and military operation to find the boys, and it had asked Apple to assist with the manhunt because Eyal Yifrach had an iPhone. An Israeli intelligence official tells me that Israel asked the U.S. government to give Apple approval to try to find Yifrach's iPhone: a capability that the company definitely has, and to which it often grants access to the Chinese and Russian governments.[20] When Apple locates one of its devices, it can mark its location on a map with incredible precision—a circle with a diameter of a couple of feet. The U.S. government quickly gave its approval because one of the other kidnapped boys, Naftali Fraenkel, was a U.S. citizen, but Apple dragged its feet. Only 10 days later did it return a reply. It sent back a circle encompassing the whole State of Israel, including parts of Iraq and Cyprus. In other words, Apple granted the request, but had no interest in helping find the boys' exact location, supplying totally useless information instead.

The sales dilemma

The Khashoggi murder was an extreme example of a regime that used cybertechnologies to fight not enemies threatening national security, but "domestic enemies" threatening the regime. Snowden raised the issue of the cost of privacy violations in the United States, but the cost in nondemocratic states is much higher. Besides authoritarian regimes' use of spyware to track dissidents, it is not rare to see attempts to spy on Western states, such as Morocco's espionage against France. In this sense, offensive cybertechnology is a fully fledged weapon, and that is how any Israeli company weighing up whether to sell malware to foreign governments should think of it.

That said, offensive cyberindustry professionals argue that it will be harmful to have too many restrictions. Nondemocratic states also suffer from terror attacks and rampant crime, even more so than democracies. Restricting sales to such clients would hamstring their ability to maintain law and order, and protect their people from terrorists. Should the desire to protect a country's citizens from regime surveillance trump the desire to protect them from violent attacks? This is undoubtedly a genuine dilemma. Shalev Hulio claims that tools like Pegasus that require surgical precision, in fact, *solve* the problem of privacy violations caused by the mass surveillance of U.S. citizens. Espionage against innocent citizens might be undesirable, but it is definitely preferable to indiscriminate mass surveillance.

That said, after the publication of NSO's clients' target list, when it turned out that Morocco was tracking some 10,000 phone numbers, it also turned out that even surgical instruments can be used for spying on a massive scale. In order to deal with this problem, some offensive cybercompanies have built technological restrictions into their products, preventing large numbers of targets from being attacked and requiring their clients to select targets with more precision.

Another issue with restricting this export market is that crippling the offensive cybersecurity market would prevent companies from helping advanced, democratic countries. Just as the State of Israel sells weapons to various countries to make the production of weapons for its own military economically feasible, the same is true of offensive cybertechnology: Israel needs these capabilities in order to confront its enemies, but in order to remain at the forefront of the global industry, it's got to be profitable. Moreover, since the demand exists—and it's massive—whatever does not come from regulated companies will come from actors under less oversight, or under no oversight at all, and will therefore do more damage. If African countries use Intellexa's services, which are under looser regulations than Israeli standards, or those of foreign companies offering even more dubious espionage services, privacy protections for their citizens are unlikely to get any tighter. It is much better, all in all, for these services to be bought from companies that, for all their complications, are still regulated and meet high ethical standards, and can therefore pull the plug on their customers' illicit activities when needed.

Offensive cyberindustry insiders claim, correctly, that companies like Apple that wave the banner of privacy rights are nevertheless willing to let China and Russia dictate the terms to enter their markets, effectively letting these governments collect massive amounts of data about their citizens. In my dozens of interviews with leaders of the Israeli offensive cyberindustry, despite the professional and ideological differences among them, they all repeated the point that this criticism from outside is hypocritical, and at least partly, contaminated by anti-Israel politics. Moreover, criticism of the Israeli industry and steps to restrict it have undoubtedly benefited the rival U.S. industrial complex, which raises suspicions that special interest groups have been fanning the flames and profiting from the free-for-all against Israeli companies.

Offensive cyberfirms were conscious of these intense dilemmas, resulting from the interaction among technology and democracy and human rights, long before regulators entered the frame. While writing this book, I was often asked whether all these industry insiders I was interviewing "would basically do anything for money." The answer is unambiguously *no*. There are definitely fundamental disagreements about how much responsibility these companies bear, or about how far they should go to make sure their technology is not abused, but all the industry executives I interviewed fully understand the significance of the tools they have engineered, and they are committed to using them to make the world a safer place. Each company has developed its own mechanism to supervise its deals.

Back when NSO was founded and the industry was still in its infancy, long before people started debating its legitimacy, the company set itself four rules: 1) sell only to governments, not private actors; 2) sell only to governments that will probably not abuse them; 3) do not operate the technology for clients, but rather only sell technology that end users can run independently; and 4) request Ministry of Defense oversight—a decision that was made, according to Shalev Hulio, long before such supervision was mandatory. Every offensive cyberfirm has the same basic mechanism of filtering end users. Without exception, all Israeli companies in the industry sell only to states (not private actors) and refrain from selling to Israel's enemies or to countries that might abuse their tools.

Earlier, I mentioned the distinction that companies draw between different state agencies, such that an Israeli company might sell software to an authoritarian country's armed forces but not to its monarch's private guards. This approach rests on the assumption that all security forces want operational independence in order to complete their missions, and they have zero interest in sharing their capabilities with other, potentially rival, agencies in their own country.

Competition between branches of the security forces is also a factor in democratic states. Thus, for example, one might imagine both Mossad and the IDF operating in Iran, both gathering intelligence there and sending it to the same decision-making echelon in the government. In this case, both organizations would be competing over which could bring the most high-quality intelligence, creating a negative incentive for each organization to help its counterpart with intelligence tools

Moreover, in the offensive cyberworld, every organization has an inherent interest in restricting other entities' access to the same technologies, in case this ends up exposing their operating methods, causing the vulnerabilities to be closed, and rendering their technologies worthless.

But it is not always possible to draw watertight distinctions between organizations in the same country, especially if that country is not a democracy. These technologies might still find their way to different agencies, and critics claim that when companies say they are only selling to "legitimate" bodies, they are simply playing the fool or trying to pull the wool over people's eyes. It is important to note that offensive cyberfirms limit the use of their technologies to the specific organizations that paid for them, and different bodies within the same countries sign separate contracts for similar capabilities.

But all this said, the problem with self-regulation is that it is a classic case of letting the fox guard the hen house. Multimillion dollar deals are almost impossible to resist, and fears of losing potential clients can push companies to come up with all sorts of excuses to justify sales. The fact that democracies also abuse these tools shows that even cautious sales to nondemocratic states can have unwanted effects. In order to grapple with the complex task of sifting clients, and to deal with inherent conflicts of interest and to maintain a degree of objectivity, some companies, most notably NSO and Candiru, have established their own external ethics committees to set criteria for any deals they sign.

These Israeli companies firmly insist that they do not sell espionage services, but only a finished product that their customers can use by themselves. They see private spy services, like those offered by companies active in places like India, as illegitimate. In order to understand the difference, let's compare the situation to weapons sales: if a manufacturer sells weapons to a country, anything that country does with those weapons, good or bad, is its own responsibility. But if a company acts as a mercenary force wielding those weapons, it subordinates itself and its activities to the discretion of its clients—and bears responsibility for the results. Offensive cybercompanies have no direct access to targets or the operations conducted using their technologies, but they can preprogram their systems to restrict certain activities. Industry insiders say that a technician from a certain company was sent to help a customer set up its system—and took the opportunity to spy on his girlfriend. He was caught and sent to jail in that country, and his boss was forced to negotiate his release. In order to avoid such situations, some companies require at least two operators to identify themselves and give approval in order to attack a target.

Moreover, all these systems are programed to store their operational history, so if there is any suspicion of improper use, the manufacturer can look into it. In the case of the Khashoggi assassination, NSO used this capability to investigate allegations that Pegasus was involved (which it was not, according to NSO). Likewise, when the Israel Police was accused of using Saifan, a weaker version of Pegasus, to monitor a whole range of people, these claims could be checked, and the results of the commission of inquiry acquitted the police.[21] NSO even sued the *Calcalist* newspaper after it reported that the Pegasus system came with the option of not keeping tabs on its operations.[22]

Besides ethical concerns, one criticism that has received less media attention but Israel intelligence veterans often mention is about the employees that these companies recruit. Many of the researchers busy discovering vulnerabilities on smartphones or computers come straight from the Israeli security forces' technological units. It is possible that after years of investigating and uncovering vulnerabilities for the military or spy agencies, they are simply taking their knowledge with them to the offensive cybersector. This raises concerns that they are effectively developing technologies based on classified military knowledge and hawking it to customers around the world. All this raises the likelihood that the vulnerabilities they exploit will be discovered and patched up, harming not only these private vendors, but also the Israeli security forces that relied on them. Each company is grappling with the essential challenge of separating military insider knowledge from professional know-how in its own way, and I will elaborate on this later on.

In conclusion, evolution of the Israeli offensive cyberindustry can be divided into three waves, or generations, of companies: the first wave was the pioneering wave of NSO, with self-regulation and no state oversight. Then came second-wave companies like Candiru, subject to both self-regulation and official oversight by Israeli authorities. The third wave came in response to the growing awareness and criticism of the offensive cyberindustry, with the establishment of companies like Intellexa on the one hand, which moved operations to countries with weaker oversight, and companies like Paragon and Toka (which are discussed soon) on the other, which aim to be even tougher than the regulators.

Whether in the case of trailblazing companies or more cautious ones, the offensive cyberindustry will undoubtedly continue to debate and be challenged by dilemmas about the boundaries of the use of these technologies.

CHAPTER 13

Selling to the Good Guys—Regulation, Self-Criticism, and "Clean" Offensive Cybertechnology

A few years ago, Ehud Schneerson, a former commander of Unit 8200 and the founder of its cybersecurity branch, received an offer that was practically irresistible: a foreign state had earmarked a $500-million, two-year budget and asked Schneerson's company, Paragon, to build its offensive cybercapabilities. It was an extremely generous offer: "Invest all the money you need to build such a company, and keep the change." Soon after that, Schneerson's company received another request to buy the operating license for Paragon's technology. The state in question was offering $40 million, and when Paragon declined, it kept raising its offer, up to the totally fantastical figure of $600 million.

In both cases, despite the immense temptation—Schneerson said no. It was a country with a dodgy human rights record, and Paragon had a different vision of offensive cybersecurity: *clean* offensive cybersecurity.

Paragon was founded in 2019 and designed its policy largely in light of the growing criticism of NSO and similar firms. The problem with NSO was not only ethical but commercial: operating in this gray zone risked turning off customers who did not want to be implicated with their negative reputation, or even to be dragged under sanctions, such as being placed on the U.S blacklist. But Schneerson is under no illusions: he knows that there is no chance of persuading the most extreme voices who believe that all forms of offensive cybertechnology are necessarily evil. "You've got to have a conversation from a place of consensus," he says. "The people generating the headlines in this world are the most extreme privacy zealots, they're not the consensus."

Schneerson came to realize that cell phones were an invaluable resource of high-quality intelligence when he headed Unit 8200. In 2018, he and Idan Nurick, another Unit 8200 veteran, joined the U.S. venture capital fund Blumberg Capital. Ten months later, they received an offer from Igor Bogudlov and Liad Avraham, who had worked in offensive cybertechnology in the IDF, to set up a company that would search for vulnerabilities in technological systems. It was a good idea, but it was a proposal to develop a service, not a sellable product. After they spent a long time thinking about how they could turn this service into a product, one morning they had a brain breakthrough: they built the concept for their product and understood that "this was exactly what the world needed during the ISIS era." Schneerson doesn't elaborate, but he seems to be hinting that ISIS jihadists had used old and unfamiliar devices, and that offensive cybercompanies had struggled to develop technologies to hack them. Bogudlov and Avraham set out to run a technological feasibility study for their new product, and Schneerson and Nurick tried to come up with a suitable ethical charter.

Paragon's founders adopted this formula: they would sell only to democracies, and of these, they would not sell to states with a history of abusing surveillance technologies for nefarious ends, such as spying on political rivals. Paragon drew up a list of fewer than 40 countries, but the brevity of this list was compensated for by the fact that it contained only stable Western states, which would sign sufficiently large deals. Paragon also decided not to hire people who had done the same work in the army that they would be doing there.

This insistence on ethics proved its worth. Paragon now has 150 employees "of the highest possible caliber," according to Schneerson. Other industry officials also admit that "nowadays, Schneerson's got the best talent you'll find." This combination of genuine interest and an ethical work environment did the trick.

Paragon is not the only company that sticks to a fixed list of legitimate customers. Alon Kantor, who founded the offensive cyber-firm Toka in 2018, told me when we met about how he decided to draw up a list that later served not only other companies, but also regulators: "Some guy who had been in the army's advance intelligence course, ARAM, came to me for an interview, and we really wanted to hire him. He was in two minds about whether to join us, and I was asked to try and persuade him. He said he had moral reservations about the offensive cyberindustry. He asked us, 'How can I know that none of our clients will abuse whatever I develop here?'" Kantor promised him that none of their technologies would be abused and that they would only go to the safest hands.

After that interview, Kantor left the room and started thinking about how he could honor his promise, and then the penny dropped: Paragon simply had to sell only to the "good guys." Toka started investigating and found various metrics for assessing countries' corruption levels and human rights records. "In the end, it's kind of intuitive," Kantor explains, "But there are very few countries where you've got doubts. We work with 25 countries, out of a list of 30-something," and he admits: "I don't know whether selling only to these countries is a big enough market for the whole industry."

"Offensive cybersecurity is a market with all sorts of fixers," he continues. "You show up in some African country, for example, and there's an Israeli there who knows the chief of the police. You pitch the technology, they ask you a couple of questions, and then the police officer goes. The Israeli comes up to you and says, 'No problem, let's close for $1 million.' You're left with no idea whether the police have even understood how to use your product.

"Or you might have another country, where some other fixer has connections with the commander of the local version of Unit 8200. You meet all sorts of military figures, and finally, the Israeli guy says, 'Listen, no problem, we'll do a deal for $4 million, and you'll get $1 million from it.' Where's the other $3 million disappeared to? 'It changes lots of different hands, just make sure you've got the money in cash, because that's how things are done here.' Try claiming later that you didn't know the deal was corrupt, or that there'd be abuse. It's not even clear if they understand why they need it."

Kantor started his career at Check Point and climbed up its management ranks until he was promoted to chief business development officer. As part of his job, he interviewed programmers applying to

Check Point, and thus, got to know what he called "cybersecurity's Generation Zero": the first waves of employees who had gained their cybersecurity knowledge in the army and had developed the civilian cybersecurity industry. In 2018, he and a friend from reserve duty, Kfir Waldman, who happened to know Nadav Zafrir, a former Unit 8200 commander, had an idea. They decided to develop a product to sell to states, but they wanted to be able to be selective about their customers without having to grab every deal for their company to survive. When they applied for investments, all the Israeli funds turned them away, claiming their field was "sensitive," "problematic," and "unsuitable for funds," and that it has a "bad reputation." They tried private investors in the United States and fairly quickly managed to raise $10 million.

Their idea was based on the assumption that the offensive cyberindustry was already saturated with companies hacking computers and telephones, and that they would have to move on to the next challenge. They decided to develop a product that would connect to other devices connected to the IoT, such as loudspeakers, cameras, cars, or anything else with internet connectivity that could be hacked to obtain intelligence. Kantor does not elaborate, of course, but we can assume that unlike companies that hack devices through computers' or phones' operating systems, Toka would break into them directly through the internet. The whole IoT world is much less aware of the threat of cyberattacks and has far fewer protections than technologies that have already been online for ages, such as computers and phones, as it stands.

The founders managed to get an interesting and surprising partner on board: former Israeli Prime Minister Ehud Barak, who was not only a former IDF chief of staff, but also a former commander of military intelligence. "The story begins with Pavel Gurvich, from cybersecurity's 'Generation Zero,'" Kantor recalls. Gurevich had founded Guardicore in 2013, and Ehud Barak sat on its board of directors. Guardicore was already a success story, and in September 2021, it was sold for $600 million to Akamai, a U.S. company. "We asked Pavel to make an introduction. We sat at his home and told him our whole story. Barak was enthusiastic and asked to be a founding partner." The entrepreneurs were excited by the fact that a former prime minister wanted to team up with them, but they wanted to get to know him a little better first. "We met a few times and found that he was simply incredible: friendly, gentle, responsive, modest, clever, full of good advice," Kantor says. Their partnership proved a dizzying success: Barak must have fallen in love with the offensive cyberworld because a year later he also roped Ehud Schneerson into Paragon as an investor and board member. "We've been working together for five years," says Kantor, "and whenever he needs to be flexible, he's flexible."

But still, even though Toka has armed itself with a hardline ethical code and a former prime minister, dilemmas around the delicate interplay between ethics and realism, top-secret security agencies and a civilian industry, still crop up. In the beginning, they thought of setting up an ethics committee like NSO did, but they realized its power would be limited anyway. "What could it tell you about a specific organization in Morocco?" Kantor wonders. "And how can you control what it gets up to?" Thanks to this policy, at least according to him, there has never been a case of any customer abusing Toka's technology.

Besides the basic ethical problems, there is, as we have seen, a serious problem of information leaking from the Israeli military's technological units to industry. One of Toka's flagship causes is "being fair" with these top-secret units and making sure that sensitive information does not cross over from Israel's intelligence agencies to the private sector. "Let me give you an example of how careful our workers are, separating what they learned in the army from what they're doing here," Kantor stresses. "We once had a situation where someone well-connected in the industry gave us a tip-off that a certain vulnerability was about to be closed. Suddenly one of my guys said, 'Yeah, I knew that.' In other words, he knew about a certain piece of intel but didn't use it till we had it officially." Toka's employees even do reserve duty, but they help the army using the tools they learn in the private sector, not vice versa.

The Israeli regulator

NSO's decision to subordinate itself to Israeli regulation turned out to be a major step in terms of Israel's ability to supervise the industry on the one hand—and its ability to use it as a geopolitical tool, on the other. Since 2006, the Israeli Ministry of Defense has kept an eye on the cyber-industry through its Defense Export Control Agency (DECA). Under Israel's Defense Export Control Law, companies must obtain a license from DECA in order to export defense-related equipment, technology, knowledge, and services. The purpose of the law is to protect Israel's security interests and its foreign relations to stop its enemies from getting their hands on these sensitive technologies and to stop these capabilities from being sold to enemies of Israel's closest allies. The passage of the law was motivated by Israel's desire to align with the Wassenaar Arrangement, the international export control regime governing conventional weapons and dual-purpose goods and technologies, which serves to protect global stability by preventing weapons from reaching regimes that threaten it.

When DECA was founded in 2006, Israel had no offensive cyber-industry to speak of, and the agency focused on restricting and supervising the export of conventional weapons and any other goods or technologies that might have a military use. After NSO was founded, Israel began to realize that the company was also selling sensitive technologies and that it was important to ensure that they not fall into the wrong hands. In time, the world came to understand that some regimes might use them to violate human rights, such that exports to these countries would also have to be curtailed, and in 2013, the Wassenaar Arrangement's list of export-restricted technologies was expanded to include "internet-based surveillance systems" in order to restrict exports of offensive cybertechnology. DECA is now seen as a natural part of the industry landscape, and when my partners and I founded IntSights in 2015, we also knew that one of the first things we had to do was to check if we needed a license.

DECA issues two kinds of licenses: a security marketing license that stipulates which countries or entities a company is allowed to sell to, and a security export license that approves the sale of specific technologies to those approved customers. Israeli defense exporters must also get their foreign customers to sign end-user license agreements with the head of DECA in the Defense Ministry, representing the State of Israel, in which the customers must commit to meet certain standards, even though DECA has no real abilities to monitor whether the customers are actually honoring their agreements.

Naturally, DECA is not immune to criticism. "DECA wants to have its cake and eat it," claims one industry official. "It doesn't categorically ban countries that aren't on its approved list. If you want to do business with a certain African country, for example, they don't say 'that's not allowed,' they say, 'apply for a marketing license and we'll see.' So if you work with these countries, and that's basically the whole industry, you're stuck in limbo and can't go anywhere."

What's the reason for this halfway house? In recent years, there have been several cases of Israeli technology being approved for export to controversial countries. There have been several proposals for legislative amendments, submitted mostly by the Knesset opposition, to require DECA to take human rights considerations into account when granting export licenses, but none of these changes have passed. Why does Israel not adopt the strict criteria of companies such as Paragon and Toka and categorically ban the sale of offensive cybertechnologies to non-Western countries?

One easy answer is economic interests because offensive cyber-technology is undeniably a booming business that employs several thousand workers, many on extremely high salaries. These companies' headquarters are all in Israel, and they employ not only software engineers there, but also accountants, managers, salespeople, and others. If offensive cybersales were dramatically restricted, the industry would wither.

But this easy answer is too easy in Israel's case: according to Israeli Defense Ministry figures for 2021, only 4% of security exports count as "intelligence, information, and cybersecurity," bringing in little more than $450 million. Meanwhile, Israel is home to over 200 defensive cybersecurity firms, alongside dozens of global companies with defensive cybersecurity R&D centers there. These companies are all thirsty for skilled employees, and at any given moment, they have thousands of vacancies. If the offensive cyberindustry were to shut down, everyone it employs would probably find work very quickly in the defensive cybersecurity sector, giving it a boost, sending its exports soaring, and bringing in enough money for the Israeli treasury to compensate.

Israel's main interest lies in the special knowledge that this industry cultivates. Already discussed is how cybersecurity researchers at Google's Project Zero describe NSO's ability to hack iPhone devices as creating one of the most technologically sophisticated vulnerabilities they have ever seen. Google's researchers are some of the best in the world, making their assessment of NSO's abilities especially important. Offensive cybercompanies in Israel are developing and cultivating this knowledge in order to give their customers the world's most advanced capabilities in cyberspace. This knowledge strengthens not only Israel's offensive cyberindustry but also its defensive cybersecurity industry: its most advanced defensive inventions are based on an understanding of cyberattackers, their capabilities, and their technologies. The free flow of employees between offensive and defensive cybersecurity firms enriches their knowledge and helps them improve their defensive products. There are many cases of experienced offensive cyber professionals who become defensive cybersecurity entrepreneurs; one good example is Noname Security, founded by two NSO veterans, which became a unicorn in two years flat.

But the biggest reason why the offensive cyberindustry is important to Israel has to do with security: in January 2021, an investigative report in *Calcalist* revealed that the Israel Police was using Pegasus to spy on civilians. The exposé created massive public shockwaves and sparked outrage at the conduct of the police and NSO. An official commission concluded that the police had only used the spyware subject to judicial warrants, but in doing so, it confirmed that Pegasus and other companies' cyberweapons were being used by the police to fight terror and crime. The incident raised public awareness about Israeli security agencies' use of offensive cybertechnologies, but not only for purposes that might be controversial. In interviews I conducted with industry insiders, some of them said explicitly that certain terror attacks were stopped by the Israeli security forces thanks to their use of their companies' tools.

Offensive cyber as a geopolitical tool

The offensive cyberindustry offers Israel another special, geopolitical advantage. When Russia invaded Ukraine in February 2021, Ukraine understood that it was in a position of military inferiority. Ukrainian President Volodymyr Zelensky launched a campaign to mobilize international support in the form of funds, arms, military aid, and economic sanctions on Moscow. As part of this drive, Zelensky addressed the Knesset on Zoom and concluded his speech by praising Israel's missile defense and weapons systems, forcefully calling on Israel to help Ukraine by sending it weapons and imposing sanctions on Russia. Three days later, *The Guardian* in the United Kingdom revealed that in the three years before the invasion, Ukraine had tried to get permission from Israel to buy Pegasus—and was rebuffed. *The Guardian* connected the dots between Zelensky's speech and Ukraine's demand for access to Pegasus, and suggested that Zelensky's demand for Israeli weapons included this spyware. The next day, Zelensky's chief of staff and right-hand man, Andriy Yermak, said in an interview with Israeli media that Ukraine was indeed expecting to get approval for this purchase.

The story of Ukraine and Pegasus shines a spotlight on the enormous political power promised by offensive cybertechnology on the world stage. The spying technologies needed to hack smartphones are incredibly sophisticated, and so few countries have sufficient capabilities to meet their own needs. Since such capabilities are critical for any state to safeguard its security interests, there exists immense demand for these technologies all around the world. The fact that Israel is home to offensive cybercompanies that are supervised by the State of Israel, which dictates to whom and how they can export their products, gives Israel political power to maintain its own security interests.

A far-reaching investigation by the *New York Times* showed that Israel's ability to control the export of NSO's tools helped it achieve tangible diplomatic and security gains. Certain states swung their votes in Israel's favor on important resolutions at the United Nations, and Pegasus exports were also key in paving the way to the Abraham Accords in 2020: the groundbreaking treaties normalizing relations between Israel and the United Arab Emirates and Bahrain.

"As part of the Abraham Accords, they decided that what would bring the sides closer together was Israeli technology," an industry insider tells me. "And that's what interests these countries. It was the first time Israel agreed to supply technology to Saudi Arabia, and it happened with the support of the United States. It opened the door to lots of things, including the opening of Saudi skies to Israeli air traffic."

According to reports, Saudi Arabia's operating license for Pegasus expired in 2019, and the Israeli Ministry of Defense refused to renew it because of reports of human rights violations. Saudi Crown Prince Mohammed bin Salman phoned Israeli Prime Minister Benjamin Netanyahu and demanded that the license be renewed, using the leverage the Saudis had at their disposal: the kingdom did not sign a peace treaty with Israel, but it did not oppose the United Arab Emirates and Bahrain normalizing relations with it, and it allowed direct flight between Israel and the Gulf to use its airspace. Without the Saudis' consent, the accords would have been in danger. Netanyahu ordered the renewal of Saudi Arabia's operating license for Pegasus, and it was renewed on the spot.

Final reflections

What is the right way to navigate the ethical and economic minefield of the offensive cyberindustry? Technological and procedural mechanisms have their place, but in the end, the most important thing is to build an organizational culture of ethics and healthy priorities. From my conversations with industry leaders, it is clear that many of the differences between companies revolve around this issue. They all have their own checks and balances, in addition to regulatory oversight, but the fear is that a company that places its short-term profits at the top of its priority list will end up finding its technologies abused.

In contrast, companies where ethics and privacy protections are an integral part of the discourse, and where senior managers can turn down quick and easy money when needed, will be able to drastically minimize any abuse of their technologies. Culture is an elusive concept, which is hard to evaluate and even harder to enforce. Industry leaders argue that criticism of their industry is making it harder to hire and retain talent, and that one of the most effective ways of dealing with the problem is to maintain a moral backbone, giving employees confidence that their company is working for a good cause. Companies that adopt such organizational cultures will be able to turn their ethics into a competitive advantage in hiring workers and selling their products to customers.

Taking a comprehensive view of the situation, criticism of the offensive cyberindustry's mere existence is clearly unjustified. The public really does need to be protected from a range of threats, and offensive cyberfirms play a significant role in this effort. Moreover, extreme criticism and overly strict restrictions may end up diverting business from regulated to unregulated companies, which would only hurt the general public.

That said, proportionate criticism and sensible oversight on the part of regulators, civil society, and the media can work to effectively minimize the exploitation of offensive cybertechnology for the purposes of oppression and other nasty abuses. The right way to treat the offensive cyberindustry is, to some extent, like the weapons industry: a vital and important industry that requires moderate regulation, but not too tight, to avoid creating a black market. The cyberindustry must stick to this golden mean in the years to come.

SECTION 4

Building a Cyberstate

CHAPTER 14

The Israeli Silicon Valley—Small State, Big Data

"Israel's cybersecurity industry is worth as much as Silicon Valley's," says Dino Boukouris, co-founder of U.S. consulting firm Momentum Cyber—and he's not alone.

There was a time when any comparison between this tiny and diverse Middle Eastern state, encircled by existential threats, and the world's richest and most prosperous superpower would have sounded ridiculous. But over the years, and especially the past decade, the State of Israel has managed to create a whole raft of capabilities, products, and services that have transformed it into one of the central and dominant players in the global cybersecurity market. A Tel Aviv University study in January 2021 mapped out the major hubs of the global cybersecurity industry and found three: Silicon Valley, Washington D.C.—and Israel.[1] "There's not much difference between Israel and Silicon Valley," agrees Shlomo Kramer, adding that "it's a world-class industry." Kobi Samboursky, co-founder of Glilot Capital Partners, which specializes in cybersecurity firms, goes even further and says, "In the past, Israel was second only to California, and today its industry is probably even better than California's." Assaf Rappaport takes a similar view: "Israel's ecosystem is very strong, globally. Silicon Valley might be its only serious competitor."

In June 2021, the International Institute for Strategic Studies, a British think tank, sorted the world's leading cybersecurity powers into three tiers. The top tier includes only the United States.

The second tier contains seven countries: Australia, Britain, China, France, Canada, Russia, and Israel. The tiny State of Israel, with a population of less than 10 million, thus joined an exclusive club of major states with populations running in the tens or hundreds of millions.

I got a personal sense of Israel's cybersecurity reputation when my partners and I hit the road with IntSights in 2015. In the world of cybersecurity managers and investors, Israel was already a global brand, known for its expertise and quality, and we decided to start conversations with clients or new investors by dropping that we had served in the IDF's technological units. We were not alone: all Israeli cybersecurity entrepreneurs brandish their "Israeliness" as a way of seducing new clients and investors. It is relatively easy for big international corporations to access Israeli companies because, unlike elsewhere, the Israeli market is already geared toward a global, not local, clientele.[2]

Israel's territory is only 0.2% that of the United States, and it accounts for only 0.12% of the world's population. But despite its tiny size, Israel's cyberdefense firms alone account for 10%–15% of the world's cybersecurity firms, a factor of 58 times greater than Israel's share of the global population.[3] Measured by cybersecurity firms per million people, Israel leads the world with a ratio of 25 companies per million, followed by Singapore with 4.8. The United States, with over half of all companies in the industry, comes only fourth—with 4.7 cybersecurity firms per million people.[4]

Israel stands out not only in terms of how many cybersecurity companies it has produced, but also their market share and turnover. As of June 2022, 15 of the world's 57 private cybersecurity "unicorns" (companies with a market valuation of over $1 billion) are Israeli or Israeli-American—a staggering 25%.[5] The list is indisputably dominated by U.S. firms, but it also contains representation from only four other countries besides Israel: Canada (three companies), Switzerland (one), Lithuania (one), and China (one).[6] The cybersecurity company at the top of the list—Tanium, with a market valuation of $9 billion—is an American company, founded by David Hindawi, an Israeli expat who served in the Israeli Air Force, and his son Orion.

It's a similar picture with public companies, those traded on global stock markets. As of June 2022, 5 of the world's 26 public cybersecurity companies worth over $1 billion are Israeli or Israeli-American or were otherwise founded by Israelis: Palo Alto Networks ($50 billion), Check Point ($15 billion), SentinelOne ($7 billion), CyberArk ($5.6 billion), and Varonis ($3.6 billion). Much like the previous list, this one contains only five non-American companies: Avast from the

Czech Republic, Trend Micro from Japan, Mimecast and Darktrace from Britain, and Secunet from Germany.

Likewise, when measured by profits and revenues, Israel has produced two of the nine cybersecurity firms in the world with annual revenues of over $1 billion: Israeli company Check Point, and Israeli-founded company Palo Alto Networks (founded by Nir Zuk). Even if one argues that most Israeli companies are headquartered in the United States and that many of their executives are Americans, it is still hard to dispute the dominance of companies based on entrepreneurs, products, and technologies that have come out of Israel.

The investment community keeps expressing its confidence in Israeli cybersecurity. In Part 2, we saw that when the Israeli company SentinelOne went public in June 2021, its IPO was based on a valuation of $9 billion, and on the first day of trading its value hit $12 billion, more than any previous cybersecurity company. SentinelOne received such a gigantic valuation despite posting annual revenues of "only" $160 million, attesting to investors' ironclad confidence in its future. This might have been the result of hype around the global cybersecurity market, which was at its peak at the time, but broader international investment figures also point to Israel's leading position in this market: in 2021, Israeli cybersecurity firms raised between $6.6 and $8.8 billion in their funding rounds,[7] attracting over 20% of all global cybersecurity investment.[8] Most of this investment came from foreign (mainly American) investors, who saw these Israeli firms' potential and believed that they would balloon extremely quickly. Their confidence was also reflected in the especially high valuations given to companies with relatively low turnovers, and thus in 2021 alone, 11 Israeli companies reached unicorn status, despite reporting revenues of no more than a few tens of millions of dollars each.

Israel also stands out in terms of startup exits. Of the 195 cybersecurity firms acquired in 2021, 32 (16%) were Israeli. Acquisitions are usually a sign that international cybersecurity companies value not only these startups' products and technologies but also their talent, and want to incorporate them into their workforces. On the one hand, this "exit rate" can be a misleading metric because it might point to a failure to build big, sustainable businesses. But in Israel's case, the combination of lots of exits with so many companies going public or reaching unicorn status is undoubtedly a sign of success.

Israeli exits can also be measured by the sums that these startups are acquired for: in 2021, acquisitions of Israeli cybersecurity firms totaled over $3.2 billion—some 4.5% of all money invested in cyber-security firms *around the world* that year.[9] This figure is also striking relative to Israel's population size—bigger by a factor of 37 than Israel's share of the global population—although it is not as staggering as earlier metrics. Given how many Israeli startups are making exits, we can assume that they are being sold relatively cheaply, or at earlier stages of their life cycles, explaining the low price tags. In other words, Israel is quickly churning out major companies, but also ones that stop being independent at relatively early stages. This picture reflects the ethos of the Israeli entrepreneur, who aims for a rapid exit—an ethos that is beginning to evolve, as we shall soon see.

The success of Israel's cybersecurity industry can be seen not only in the creation and sale of companies; the fact that so many international companies have built major centers in Israel also points to its status as a global cyberhub. Of the 10 biggest non-Israeli cybersecurity firms in the world, 6 have R&D centers in Israel, including the 4 leading companies: Palo Alto, Fortinet, CrowdStrike, and Zscaler.

Israel is even more dominant in the offensive cybersecurity industry than its defensive equivalent, although it is hard to find precise data for the offensive cyberfield because there are few investments or acquisitions, and of course, because offensive cybercompanies are so secretive.

"Most of this world [of offensive cybersecurity] speaks Hebrew," says an industry leader, speaking also of companies such as Intellexa, which are based outside of Israel but were founded by Israelis. Shalev Hulio from NSO agrees, adding that most of the competition with other cybersecurity firms is with fellow Israeli companies. The CEO of another major company estimates that "at least 60%–70% of the market is Israeli, and if we're talking about those with the most advanced capabilities—90%." Israel's dominance can also be sensed from public criticism of the industry. In reports by the Citizen Lab and similar organizations, almost all the companies discussed by their security researchers are Israeli ones. One might argue that Israeli companies are the world's biggest human rights violators, or that these watchdogs have an anti-Israel agenda, but either way—it's hard to deny that this attention has something to do with Israeli companies' absolute dominance in this industry.

All these figures raise an important question: what are the factors that have made Israel such a key player that it can be seen as the Middle East's answer to Silicon Valley? The next chapters are devoted to answering this question.

CHAPTER 15

Unit 8200—Secrets of the IDF's Success

In December 2019, the commander of Unit 8200 was shocked to discover a giant SentinelOne billboard opposite the entrance of the IDF's intelligence base in Glilot, north of Tel Aviv. "WE NORMALLY HUNT ATTACKERS. NOW WE'RE HUNTING TALENTS. JOIN US," read the English-language sign.[1] The Israeli military was furious. "Placing a commercially funded recruitment billboard at the entrance of Unit 8200's base is a cynical and reckless act that I am not sure will succeed," wrote the unit's commander in a letter to his soldiers that week, signing off with the words: "For us, our defensive mission and choice to keep contributing to the State of Israel and its future are a way of life. Big signs can't stand in the way of big values."[2]

SentinelOne's shameless advertising campaign was no mere annoyance for Unit 8200's commander. Its campaign might have been especially explicit, but it illustrated what had been an open secret for over 20 years: the IDF's technological units, and especially Unit 8200, are the Israeli cyberindustry's main sources of talent. Ironically, however, SentinelOne's founders are not Unit 8200 veterans—a distinction of which they are proud.[3]

If you have read this far, including all the history of the Israeli cybersecurity industry, you can't have missed the fact that almost all the entrepreneurs in this field come from the IDF's elite technological units. The majority come from Unit 8200, followed by Unit 81, and even units in the C4I Corps, such as Matzov and Mamram, have a place on this list. It is hard to avoid the conclusion that the IDF's technological units are some of the most important forces behind the success of the Israeli cyberindustry. I could even hear echoes of IDF military jargon in the language of the industry insiders I interviewed, who used phrases such as *chamal* ("war room") to refer to their operations centers. Unit 8200 has such a reputation as Israel's cybersecurity incubator that CEOs of international corporations make pilgrimages to its HQ to try to crack its secrets.

When I was in high school, the army called us up for tryouts, including for units in the Intelligence Directorate. My parents, who usually took a liberal approach to my education, suddenly changed tack and urged me to invest in acing these trials. My dad, who worked in hi-tech, saw how intelligence veterans were going straight into the booming hi-tech industry as entrepreneurs and executives and understood that serving in intelligence was a potential springboard for serious positions in the private sector. He drove me early in the morning to all my tests, even when rushing to work, and told me many stories about Unit 8200 veterans' achievements. With his encouragement, I invested in my exams and got accepted to a prestigious track in the Intelligence Directorate, but in the end, I decided to give it a miss. I felt that if I was already going into the military, then I might as well do combat, so I signed up for Egoz, an elite infantry unit. Only after my hearing was damaged and I was transferred to Unit 8200 did I begin to realize what my dad had been talking about.

My dad was not alone in taking this view. Everyone knows that the IDF's technological units, especially in the Intelligence Directorate, produce huge numbers of tech entrepreneurs and serve as a gateway to the hi-tech world. But Unit 8200 does not teach its soldiers how to be entrepreneurs, build companies, or sell products. The military world is completely different from the business world, and none of the IDF's intelligence units give their recruits any special preparation or guidance for careers in hi-tech, innovation, or marketing. So how have these units nevertheless become incubators for innovators and industry leaders?

"We've got to go up a notch"

To try to answer this question, I asked Professor Isaac Ben-Israel, a major-general in the reserves, whose life story is interwoven into the story of the Israeli technology and especially cybersecurity establishment.

Ben-Israel served in the Israeli Air Force in a host of technological and intelligence roles. In 1992, he became the head of R&D at the Israeli Ministry of Defense Directorate of Defense Research and Development, known by its Hebrew initials as "MAFAT." In 1998, he became the director of MAFAT itself, where he served until he left the Ministry of Defense in 2002. He won the Israel Defense Prize twice, once in 1972 for the development of the Phantom fighter jet's bombing mechanism, and again in 2001 for a project cryptically described as "giving expression to an innovative conception of the battlefield of the future." In his public remarks, Ben-Israel also addresses computer warfare, a field that he was already speaking openly about in the late 1990s.

I know Ben-Israel from my studies at Tel Aviv University, where he heads its Blavatnik Interdisciplinary Cyber Research Center—the first and biggest cybersecurity research center in Israel, which now has 280 researchers, including 60 faculty members from a range of disciplines. Before writing this book, I wanted to hear from Ben-Israel more about his experience, so I made my way to his office on campus.

When we sat down, I laid out my overview of the factors behind the Israeli cybersecurity industry's success, including the IDF's technological units. He agreed with my analysis but insisted: "The reasons you mentioned are the trees in the wood, but you're missing the wood for the trees." Ben-Israel points to a fateful decision made even before Israel was established, to address Israel's strategic inferiority in the face of its surrounding enemies through technology and science. Israel's pre-state leaders understood that to confront brutal enemies who didn't want their country even to exist, they had only one choice: to be strong enough to exhaust them and force them to give up their efforts to annihilate the Jewish state. The way to do this was to leverage the comparative advantage of the Israeli population. David Ben-Gurion, Israel's first prime minister, expressed this most clearly in 1953 when he said, "Since we fall behind them in numbers, we must surpass them in quality."

"That quality," says Ben-Israel, "is the human factor, or as they called it back then, 'the Jewish genius': science and technology." That is why Israel placed special importance on its technological units from day one, even setting up an IDF Science Corps to provide science and technology for warfare. (These army scientists proved a poor fit for the military lifestyle, so the corps became a department of the Defense Ministry.) Based on the same strategic doctrine, Israel placed a similarly heavy emphasis on technology in military intelligence.

The story of Unit 8200

Unit 8200 of the IDF Intelligence Directorate is now one of the biggest units, if not *the* biggest, in the Israeli military. Commanding thousands of soldiers, Unit 8200 alone is believed to be around the same size as the entire Israeli Navy.

Before Israel's independence, in the early twentieth century, the intelligence services of Haganah, the pre-state paramilitary, were based mainly on human intelligence: agents or collaborators, who supplied information about the Jews' enemies in the Land of Israel. In the British Mandate period, the Jewish community started developing technological abilities to intercept enemy communications for reconnaissance purposes.[4] In 1940, the Haganah set up its own special intelligence body, called Shai.[5] This agency comprised several informal units that eavesdropped on enemy communications and deciphered their encrypted messages.[6] During the War of Independence, Shai became the official Intelligence Directorate of the IDF,[7] and soon after that, all the units involved in intercepting and deciphering communications were merged into a single unit called "S.M. 2." This unit was headquartered in a two-story building in Jaffa, and brought together the best minds in the country to intercept and decrypt enemy communications. They built a radar on the roof to pick up Morse code signals, transcribed the encrypted messages, and cracked them using paper and pencils. S.M. 2 went through several incarnations, each time with a new name, morphing into Unit 515, and then Unit 848, and then after the Yom Kippur War it received the name it has had ever since: Unit 8200.

Over time, with advances in communications technology, Unit 8200 had to keep running after changes in enemy communication strategies to detect and decipher them. At first, it had to pick up on Morse code signals over radio waves. Then it had to intercept landline telephone calls and later conversations between cell phones and through internet-based communications. With each change, the unit had to make a technological leap to pick up on and decrypt these new forms of communications. This reality, and Israel's existential need for real-time intelligence about the enemy, pushed Unit 8200 to be on the constant search for the latest technologies, while also developing its own technologies to pick up on and decipher enemy communications.

To complete its mission, Unit 8200 hunted and recruited the Israeli military's most brilliant young conscripts. It put some of them through academic studies first and then gave them an enormous responsibility: to develop the most innovative technologies and devise the most creative solutions needed to grapple with technological changes on the enemy's side. This responsibility, in such a technological environment, produced a class of elite technologists, who then finished their military service and started working in the same field. Many of them found work as engineers in the private sector, but many others leveraged their distinctive knowledge to build companies in the same fields in which they had gained experience and understanding.

One good example is NICE Systems, founded in 1986 by a team that had met in Unit 8200. NICE developed a system to record phone calls based on technologies its employees had learned about in their military service. "I had no doubt the company would succeed. It's something you can feel in your bones," said Didi Arazi, one of NICE's founders, in an interview. "I knew that if I had these guys with me, we could go anywhere."[8]

By the 1990s, Unit 8200 was known as Israel's leading incubator for hi-tech entrepreneurs and executives, as the unit's veterans founded one hi-tech company after the other. The most striking example was, of course, Check Point, the first hint of the Israeli cybersecurity industry. Check Point founder Shlomo Kramer confirms: "Check Point was a direct continuation of Unit 8200."

Unit 81: Making the impossible, possible

Unit 8200's little sister is Unit 81. Its soldiers and veterans swear by its motto, "Knowledge, Will, and Dedication Make the Impossible, Possible," even in civilian life. The unit's core purpose is to supply the Intelligence Directorate's special operations units, such as the elite Sayeret Matkal commando force, with advanced technological means, reaching capabilities that are scarcely imaginable. Imagine a Sayeret Matkal operation deep inside Syria, with Israeli commandos planting some technological device at a strategic site. That device, which must not be allowed to fail or be discovered, is planned and built by the men and women of Unit 81. But the unit does so much more than that, and its operations are shrouded in strict secrecy. Its tasks are extremely challenging, demanding almost impossible deadlines and uncompromising excellence.

Unit 81's intense secrecy, and the huge budgets pumped into it for unknown technological purposes, have led in the past to financial irregularities.[9] But these scandals—however colorful and headline-grabbing, are ultimately minor details in the truly outstanding role and performance of Unit 81.

Cyberintelligence: Challenges and opportunities

The major changes introduced by the computer and internet revolution of the 1990s rocked the intelligence world. Until then, communications had been based on analog broadcasts (represented by various wavelengths), but now intelligence agencies had to develop technologies capable of intercepting and deciphering digital communications (represented by just two values: 0 or 1). Until then, communications had largely been based on radio and cellular devices, and spies could set up antennae to catch them midair, but now communications were traveling through underground cables. Until then, communications traffic had moved openly, or encrypted in a way that could often be deciphered, but in 2000, the world saw a leap in encryption methods using mathematical models that were difficult, if not impossible, to crack. It was obvious that the enemy's communications methods were changing, and this required IDF Military Intelligence to adapt itself to this new reality to continue supplying high-quality, real-time information.

The Intelligence Directorate soon realized that this challenge was also an opportunity. If it could reach the enemy's computers, it could get its hands on emails and any other information the enemy was sending and receiving over the internet. Unlike encrypted information transferred between computers, when information is still *on* a computer, it is hardly ever encrypted because the end user needs to access it. The IDF Intelligence Directorate also understood that cybersecurity operations held even more promise than just intercepting enemy communications. Microsoft Office started taking off in the 1990s, as people used it to create and save files on their computers. Until then, most documents had been stored as hard copies, and the only way to access them was to send agents to physically go and nab them. But Israeli military intelligence understood that cyberspace now offered a new way of reaching files on enemy computers, using technology to poach data that would have otherwise been almost unobtainable. Pinhas Buchris, who headed both Unit 81 and Unit 8200 in the 1990s and played a leading role in the development of Israel's cybersecurity sector, told me: "When everyone started falling in love with the same programs, those programs could be used to sabotage an organization's operations. I realized that cyber was a revolutionary tool to penetrate organizations and nab information without them even knowing you were there."

"That was the point when everyone, including intelligence agencies worldwide, understood that the internet was transforming the nature of the espionage game and reconnaissance," says Lior Div, an officer in Unit 8200 at the time. And thus, approaching the new millennium, Unit 8200 decided to throw itself into the field of cybersecurity with all its might.

Building the Israeli military's cybersecurity apparatus

How did the IDF's cybersecurity apparatus begin? Isaac Ben-Israel, one of its founders, as we know, sits down to tell me the story. The IDF had already penetrated enemy computer systems to obtain intelligence snapshots back in the 1980s. As soon as radar systems were computerized, for example, it was only logical to try to hack the computers that controlled enemy radars. But in the 1990s, it began to dawn on the Israeli military that a whole new domain of warfare had been born.

"One day in 1992," Ben-Israel recalls, "I'm sitting in my office, and technicians walked in and started drilling a hole in the wall. 'We're hooking you up to the internet,' they said. 'What's the internet?' I asked them. I was the head of R&D at the Ministry of Defense, and I'd never heard of it. So they gave me an explanation. I sat and thought, and in the end, I went to talk to the chief of staff. I told him, until now, wars were always waged using kinetic energy: a sword through a soldier's body, a bullet or a shell that whizzes through the air and hits troops.

In the 1970s, a new form of warfare entered the picture—electronic warfare: the ability to use electronic signals to strike the enemy and seriously sabotage its fighting abilities. The internet, which is starting to spread around the world, is proving that really soon there'll be a computer in every important system, and all these computers will be interconnected, giving us a third option for warfare. We'll be able to get into the enemy's computers and scramble their systems—planes, tanks, cannons, or anything else controlled by a computer." Ben-Israel suggested leveraging this new interconnectivity for a new form of warfare: attacking infrastructure through computers.

Sometime in the mid-1990s, the chief of the Israeli military let Isaac Ben-Israel hire 75 people for a new offensive cybersecurity unit. "The question was where to set up this unit. The organization I headed, the R&D section of MAFAT, was inherently unsuitable: it's a management body. It can allocate budgets, and it's got officers who can supervise things, but it's not a unit that recruits and trains new soldiers. I told the chief of staff, if you want to use this mode of warfare to neutralize enemy surface-to-air missile batteries, for example, then it'd make sense to set up the unit in the Air Force."

But the commander of the Israeli Air Force couldn't understand what anyone wanted from him. "Itzik, how long's it been since you left us?" he asked Ben-Israel. "Half a year," Ben-Israel replied. "Something messed you up quickly," the air force commander said. "You've just crossed over to the 'greens' [ground forces—ed.] and already you're playing around with science fiction." So Ben-Israel went to the Israeli Navy, where he got a similarly chilly response; only then did he ask the Intelligence Directorate. The number one purpose of offensive cyber-operations was not necessarily reconnaissance, but Ben-Israel assumed that at least the Israeli military's intelligence chief wouldn't tell him this was all science fiction. After all, he already had 10 years of experience hacking computers for intelligence purposes. But the intelligence chief rebuffed him for another reason: "We do intelligence," he told him. "Since when should intelligence officers be attacking targets?" Salvation finally came from somewhere unexpected: Pinhas Buchris, the commander of Unit 81.

When I discuss this with Buchris, he says that he remembers Ben-Israel as a dominant and highly creative character. "We did some amazing things together," he says. "One day Isaac Ben-Israel came up to me and said, 'I want you to read a book, then let's talk about it.' He gave me a copy of *War and Anti-War* by Alvin and Heidi Toffler.

It's a tedious and repetitive book, but I liked the ideas it developed about cybersecurity. I told him, 'I'll take cybersecurity, it's on me.'" A few years later, Buchris became the commander of Unit 8200 and set up his own offensive cyberunit.

"I understood that Unit 8200 was the right place for such an out-fit," Buchris says, "and I started things off as a dialogue. I started creating a conversation within Unit 8200 about cybersecurity, and I kind of imposed the solutions that I wanted them to think about onto them. They learned to develop capabilities, understood the potential for these tools for getting to sources of information that nobody had thought of trying to reach before, and then they became extremely creative with this whole subject."

Unit 8200's offensive cybersection was established in the late 1990s with high expectations, and it pushed technology to the limit. "We did some pretty wild stuff," recalls Michael Shaulov in an interview with me. Shaulov, who would go on to found Fireblocks, was awarded a presidential citation for one of his projects at the unit. He still remembers his service vividly. "I remember that once, there was an opportunity for some operational scenario, and we didn't have a system that was ready for it," he recalls. "For 72 intense hours, I sat down and worked to write the whole system. I didn't sleep, but the system was ready in the end. I installed it on a cell phone, and our forces took it with them. It's the kind of thing you never forget."

The ARAM Course

Once the whole world was online and the public became aware that cyberspace could be used to wage attacks, teenagers across Israel started studying and experimenting with cybertechnology. When these curious teenagers enlisted in the army at the age of 18 for their mandatory service, the IDF had a golden opportunity to recruit them for its intelligence drive. Having found the most talented young men and women, it sent them on a course to prepare them for the cybersecurity world and plug gaps in their knowledge. The IDF Intelligence Directorate thus became one of the world's first hacking schools.

This course was known as ARAM, the initials of its Hebrew codename: the Special Welding Studio. "I set up the ARAM Course," Buchris tells me. "I understood that we had to run a different kind of cybersecurity training from ordinary programs. We had to make our guys think differently. There was a lot of resistance from inside the system. People said, there are so many courses, what's the point of another one? But we launched it anyway and it was a huge success. Everyone who came to the ARAM Course understood that it brought something to the table that nobody else was delivering."

The ARAM Course provided a constant flow of cybersecurity experts into Unit 8200 until by around 2010, its graduates formed the core pillar of the unit's offensive and defensive cybersecurity research. "Once ARAM started dealing with hacking—the cyberindustry was born," concludes Toka founder Alon Kantor. This was neither the IDF's first nor last program for training talent. One of its oldest schemes is the Talpiot Program, an academic track for new recruits carefully selected for excellence, operating alongside its intelligence-specific counterpart, Havatzalot. Like Unit 8200, these and similar programs not only trained the IDF's best tech experts; they also pumped outstanding engineers and entrepreneurs into the industry. What distinguished the ARAM Course was that it trained people who already had a special interest in cybersecurity and were blessed with a rare capacity for out-of-the-box thinking.

Until 2015, the IDF maintained a simple distinction: offensive cyberoperations were run from the Intelligence Directorate; cyberdefense was run from the C4I Corps. But that year, IDF Chief of Staff Gadi Eizenkot pushed for the military's offensive and defensive cyberoperations to be merged into a single cybercommand, but this plan has yet to be implemented.[10]

From offense to defense

With thousands of IDF soldiers finishing their military service and founding their own cybersecurity companies, we might expect to see C4I Corps veterans setting up cyberdefense firms and Intelligence Directorate veterans working on offensive cybertechnology. Reality is quite different: most of Israel's cyberdefense entrepreneurs have come from its intelligence units, and I was able to see the reason why up close. Anyone who's been on the offensive side realizes how vulnerable computer systems are to cyberattacks, understands the need for solid defenses, and knows various ways to protect systems. It is precisely because cyberattacks often require so much more sophistication than cyberdefense that the skills that seasoned attackers gain are no less useful than those of soldiers who have "only" been responsible for defense. Lior Div is a classic example of an entrepreneur who gained in-depth knowledge of cyberattacks while in Unit 8200 and learned to adopt the attacker's perspective. When he decided to become an entrepreneur, he understood that existing defensive solutions were not based on an understanding of how attackers actually operated—which was exactly what they were missing to be effective. It was this insight that pushed him to found Cybereason.

Some military intelligence veterans who entertained the idea of setting up offensive cybersecurity startups ended up backing out for various reasons. Aviv Gafni, co-founder of Hyperwise, told me that he and his partner Ben Omelchenko originally thought of the offensive cyberroute, which looked like a good fit given their service in Unit 8200, but "we found out, the offensive cybersecurity world isn't for us." The problem wasn't the ethical challenge: the offensive cyberindustry market is small and most of its customers are governments, while the cyberdefense industry spans billions of potential clients—in fact, anyone with a business or a computer, phone, or any other internet compatible device. When Gafni and Omelchenko consulted with Amos Malka, a retired major-general who headed the Intelligence Directorate in the early 2000s, he replied bluntly: "Go into defense, there's more money there." And that's what they did.

The key to success

Interestingly, the interplay between military intelligence and the cyber-industry in Israel does not seem to exist in other countries with the same intensity.[11] The Kirya, the nerve center of the IDF and Defense Ministry in Tel Aviv, is encircled by dozens of cybersecurity firms, and the whole Israeli industry is concentrated in the greater Tel Aviv area. If we look across the sea, however, the NSA is headquartered in Maryland, for example, while most of the industry is in California. In 2021, 60 cybersecurity firms based in Maryland or neighboring Virginia raised investments, while companies based in California completed 195 investment rounds.[12]

What explains the difference? There is no ignoring the fact that the IDF, almost uniquely, is based largely on mandatory conscription.

This system lets its technological units scout the most talented young people in the country, picking the absolute best from an enormous reservoir of options. Foreign intelligence organizations, in contrast, must actively attract the best people to work for them, and they cannot be too picky about the supply.

The disadvantage of the Israeli model, from the army's perspective, is the length of time that these recruits stay in its intelligence units. Whereas foreign spy agencies—just like Israel's civilian spy agencies, such as the Shin Bet and Mossad—hire agents who want to build long-term careers, IDF intelligence conscripts leave after just a few years. But these units have recently found a way to compensate for this drawback: they are so attractive and enjoy such a reputation for preparing soldiers for successful civilian careers that they are able to make admission conditional on recruits agreeing to sign on for longer. In order to get into most of Unit 8200's cybersecurity and AI tracks, new recruits must sign on for an extra four years of service: seven years in uniform in total.

Of course, even seven years is not long compared to the standard decades-long careers in equivalent intelligence organizations. But in time, this drawback proved incredibly valuable for the cybersecurity industry: the Israeli army finds the most talented young people in the country, puts them through intense and advanced training, gives them lots of experience—and then pumps them into the private sector.

This process is not without its costs. Israeli taxpayers currently invest huge sums in manpower that stops serving the public after a few years. This is a windfall for the cybersecurity industry, but not necessarily for the rest of the economy. Second, there is also an invisible cost to channeling talent into cybersecurity because the people taking this cybersecurity experience from the army into the private sector could have gone into other hi-tech sectors, such as fintech or health tech, or even unrelated fields. This entails a hidden cost for other sectors, which are deprived of talented manpower, and thus, develop less than they could have if so many people had not been steered into cybersecurity.

But still, the Israeli model's advantages seem to trump its downsides. In such a small country, the concentration of resources in specific fields is vital for building a supportive ecosystem for an industry, including specialist funds, global partners, a national reputation, and accumulated experience. It is possible that if this talent were spread across many sectors, none would have developed the critical mass to justify such an ecosystem, and they would have all been worse off.

Overcoming any obstacle

What truly makes Unit 8200 and the IDF's other technological units and programs so special is their internal culture, which fosters innovation and problem-solving. As Gil Shwed says about his service in Unit 8200: "I learned that every problem can be solved." Despite being a military framework, Unit 8200 encourages its soldiers to think creatively and solve problems by any means possible. "That's impossible" is simply an unacceptable answer. Ofer Schreiber, the CEO of venture capital fund YL Ventures, who served in Unit 8200 and has met with hundreds of other technological unit veterans, has a similar sense of things: "The unit gives you incredible drive to succeed. You get the feeling that you'll succeed in anything you do, and there's no technological challenge you can't rise to because that's just who we are. The message that Unit 8200's best technologists keep hearing is that there's nothing they can't do."

Unlike other branches of the military, Unit 8200 expects all its soldiers to speak their minds to much higher-ranking officers, so that even the most junior soldiers can have a critical impact on intelligence missions. When I was moved from combat service into Unit 8200, I had a major culture shock. I'd come from a world in which discipline and obedience were the most important things in the world, and where your commander's commander was about as important as God himself, and suddenly, I landed somewhere that had much less room for hierarchy and much more for creativity and challenging authority. I'll never forget how, at the start of my service there, I was in a meeting where I had a chance to deliver a presentation to the unit's commander, Brigadier General Nadav Zafrir. It's a culture that creates an incredible sense of aptitude, which gets translated into entrepreneurs who aren't afraid of sticking their necks out and founding their own startups, or finding work at innovative and groundbreaking companies.

Unit 81, many of whose veterans still swear by its motto, "Make the Impossible, Possible," has a similar culture. Its soldiers are told to find technological solutions for problems that at a first glance look impossible. "What we did was to keep building whole new startups inside the army," says Yevgeny Dibrov, a Unit 81 veteran and co-founder of Armis. "Solving problems at all sorts of crazy hours with limited budgets—that's just like a startup. After that, you've got to raise money, but you're no Cisco or Microsoft, and you've got to beat them with your product." The Unit 81 experience is not like managing a commercial company, with marketing and sales, but it definitely fosters a culture that encourages creative solutions in an environment of limited resources. Everyone has to operate under the same demands, from the most junior soldier to the most decorated general.[13]

That is not only the case in military intelligence. Alon Cohen, co-founder of CyberArk, used to run the information security department at Mamram, in the army's C4I Corps. He was effectively responsible for securing the biggest computer center in the whole of Israel at the time. "It's the kind of education you don't get anywhere else in the world," he says. "Only in the army can you reach such a senior management position at the age of 25."

In the last week of my military service at Unit 8200, I told my friend Gal Ben-David, "Mark my words, one day we're gonna do something together." He thought I was crazy, but that's what ended up happening. In the years after I was out of the military, we stayed in touch, met up occasionally for a coffee or a burger, and brainstormed all sorts of ideas for startups. By the time we got to our idea for IntSights, our connection already felt totally natural. My promise to Gal at the end of my service might have been unusual, but it did not come out of nowhere. The atmosphere in Unit 8200 is one that empowers and strengthens people with entrepreneurial ambitions. It's completely natural and unremarkable for soldiers to have lunchtime or watercooler conversations about start-up ideas.

Nadav Zafrir is well acquainted with this mindset. "If I'm a soldier and I see my team commander or someone else from my desk going out and founding a company, that's not a story I'm reading in the newspaper about Larry Page or Sergey Brin. They're people I know, and what I'm thinking is: I'm no less talented than these guys, I can do that too. It's really personal."

This entrepreneurial spirit is amplified even more by reserves duty, which brings soldiers into contact with veterans who have already become successful entrepreneurs or hi-tech executives. When Amichai Shulman, co-founder of Imperva, was a young officer in an IDF tech unit, Nissim Bar-El used to come back to his unit for reserves duty. Bar-El had already founded ComSec, one of the first and biggest cyberdefense consulting and service companies in Israel. "He was Israel's king of information security," says Shulman. Bar-El was joined by other reservists who had led their own companies to successful exits. These interactions with reservists who have hit the jackpot in the private sector are inspirational for soldiers nurturing their own entrepreneurial dreams. It was obvious to Shulman that he would end up working for Bar-El, but his comrade Mickey Boodaei convinced him to join him on their own entrepreneurial journey together—and that's how Imperva was born.

The old boys' club

Thanks to the network effect, entrepreneurs can find partners and talent on the basis of personal acquaintance. When we founded IntSights, two of the four engineers we hired in our first few months were friends who'd served with us in Unit 8200. Soon after that, we hired our development manager, who had also served with us in Unit 8200. There was nothing unusual about that. When veterans of Israeli technological units launch startups, they often hire their old army buddies as their first engineering teams. "The army not only creates really in-depth knowledge about the cybersecurity world; it's also a huge reservoir of brainpower from which you can hire your first people as a company," explains Cohen. One of the biggest challenges in starting a business in Israel is the shortage of quality manpower, especially engineers. Being able to rapidly assemble an initial team of engineers gives entrepreneurs an incredible advantage and an excellent starting position. It lets them start developing their products immediately, throw themselves into the market quickly, and create a high-quality core of engineers who can set their technological standards for years to come.

Veterans of Israel's technological units find themselves getting along not only if they served together, but even if they never met during their service. It is not rare for Unit 8200 veterans who served at different times to meet up and start throwing around concepts and figures that nobody else would understand. They click naturally, like any other group of people with similar roots or backgrounds. This familiarity makes all sorts of connections possible: job opportunities, partnerships for joint projects, and connections between investors and entrepreneurs.

Adallom is another good example of a company built on the basis of an acquaintance from Unit 8200. "I met my partners in the army," says Assaf Rappaport, one of the company's founders. "In 2012 the three of us decided to quit our jobs and set up our own operation. We all agreed that we were starting a process of at least a year, in which we'd look for a startup idea."

The fact that they knew each other from the army helped them make the decision to drop everything and throw themselves into founding a joint venture for a whole year. Their background also helped them reach their first investor. "I heard about Adallom's team through the Unit 8200 alumni network," says Gili Raanan, founder of the Cyberstarts venture capital fund. "I was told they were a very talented team and that I had to meet them."[14] Some of Adallom's first employees were also people they had known from Unit 8200 and Unit 81. Back in Unit 81, Rappaport headed a team that included Yevgeny Dibrov, who would later co-found Armis Security. "One day I get a call from Assaf," says Dibrov, "and he tells me that he and two other entrepreneurs are raising money for a startup and he's offering me to be their company's first employee." Dibrov was working at Mellanox at the time, a large and respectable company, but he decided to quit his job for a startup that was only just getting going, headed by his former army commander.[15]

Closed club?

The criticism of the close connection between the cybersecurity industry and the Israeli military's technological units practically writes itself. These units' alumni networks are often seen as "old boys' clubs" that are hard to break into, and where people who do not come from the "right" backgrounds will find it even harder to blend in. This criticism is even more intense when you compare soldiers in technological units, who serve in air-conditioned offices in the greater Tel Aviv area, to their comrades in combat, exerting immense physical and emotional efforts out in the field, often risking their own lives. While the former gain professional experience and an entry pass straight into the lucrative world of hi-tech, combat soldiers performing grueling and exhausting service are thrown back into civilian life to build their own careers from scratch.

Some try to blunt this criticism by arguing that the Israeli hi-tech industry suffers from a serious and chronic shortage of manpower, so anyone who wants to study and gain experience in software development, even without having served in a technological unit, can crack the industry with relative ease. The argument is that the network effect is not a zero-sum game, nor does it come at the expense of anyone outside it: this network has built a technological center in Israel, which in turn, consumes more manpower, so nobody gets left out at all. Or as

I heard Gil Shwed say in 2022 at a conference on the subject: "Even if you bring me a cat that knows how to code—it's hired."

But the criticism is still valid, especially in the case of nontechnological roles, where there is no manpower shortage and the right connections definitely help to get ahead. The same is true for entrepreneurs asking investors for funds, where a background in a technological unit is definitely a good starting point.

It's hard to fight this kind of universal phenomenon. Push comes to shove, people end up connecting with others like them. If they've experienced success with others from a certain background, they will naturally tend to minimize risks and prefer people with a similar background. Nevertheless, major efforts are being made to bridge this gap, which has created widespread unease. The IDF has started running a program for combat soldiers to spend some time in Unit 8200 or other technological units near the end of their service, to give them some experience and add to their networks of connections.[16] There are also civil society organizations that help discharged soldiers get into hi-tech,[17] and investors are making an effort to open up to candidates from diverse backgrounds.

In any case, nobody disputes that Israel's technological units have had a critical impact on the success of its hi-tech industry, as almost every industry leader says. They have trained and cultivated entrepreneurs (including me) who have gone on to found companies, shaping them professionally and ethically, and giving the industry a constant stream of cybersecurity professionals, catalyzing its growth. Despite the criticism and challenges, nobody can ignore this mechanism's contributions to the cyber and especially hi-tech industry.

CHAPTER 16

A Professor and a Hacker—Academia and Cybersecurity

"When Yuri, a Ben-Gurion University student, started working with us, he realized the language he and his classmates were studying in their computer science classes was irrelevant," Liron Tancman, who founded CyActive with Shlomi Boutnaru, tells me. "He asked the university to teach them Python because that's what's relevant in the industry, and they switched to Python. At one point, Shlomi was teaching at the university, his classes were 600% oversubscribed, and every year, we could fish all the most suitable candidates. Later on, our partnership expanded to internships and joint research projects."

Israel's major academic centers are not, for the most part, private institutions, but state-funded bodies under the Council for Higher Education. Despite taking a few cybersecurity courses as part of my law degree, I don't personally feel that my academic education has made much of a difference to my path as an entrepreneur; what pushed me and my friends into this field was our shared background in Unit 8200. But many other leading cybersecurity entrepreneurs *did* acquire their education and skills at Israeli universities: Check Point's Gil Shwed studied computer science at the Hebrew University, and his partner Shlomo Kramer studied math and computer science there too. Mickey Boodaei, Kramer's partner at Imperva, studied computer engineering at the Technion; Island's Dan Amiga studied math and computer science at the Open University; Marius Nacht, the third co-founder of Check Point, studied physics, math, and computer science at the Hebrew University as part of his service in the IDF's Talpiot program, later completing a master's in electrical engineering at Tel Aviv; Adallom's Assaf Rappaport and Wiz's Ami Luttwak met each other on the Talpiot program; Aramis Security founders Yevgeny Dibrov and Nadir Izrael met at the Technion; Nir Zuk studied math at the Hebrew University; and despite not sensing much of a connection between my academic education and entrepreneurial career, even I met my future partner Guy Nizan through my studies and received support from my university as I took my first steps into the world of entrepreneurialism. In fact, our first office as entrepreneurs was the basement of Tel Aviv University's social sciences library.

Nevertheless, most of the people interviewed for this book did not even mention their academic studies as a significant influence on their life stories or the Israeli cybersecurity industry in general. Others mentioned it in passing. Rappaport told me that "all in all, Israeli academia is solid on cybersecurity, but the innovation in the field isn't coming from there. Unlike other fields in the tech world, where academia's at the forefront, like in biotech, there's another set of factors with cyber—like Unit 8220 or existing startups."

One former high-ranking Unit 81 officer takes a similar view, in light of his personal acquaintance with ARAM Course graduates. "We decided not to wait for these talented guys to spend three years at college and only then loop back to us. ARAM Course graduates no longer need to go to university," he explains because of sending talented young recruits to college, the army uses this course to train them in-house. "Twenty percent of them go onto academic studies, but that's not because it'll help them in their careers." He believes that universities are still not the best places for training manpower for cybersecurity. "The things you learn nowadays in computer science and the three-year model don't produce suitable people for the cyberworld, and definitely not for offensive cyber, but probably not for cyberdefense, either. That kind of training is enriching, it's educational, but how relevant is it to the industry? That's an open question." He doesn't mean to say that universities do not produce talented engineers, only that they do not actively cultivate researchers who will dive deep into the technology, think extremely creatively, and deliver the next breakthroughs.

It is hard to say, given all this, what the secret is behind Israel's outsized presence in the cybersecurity industry, but reservations aside—it would be wrong to downplay the role of the universities. Michal Braverman-Blumenstyk, the general manager of Microsoft's R&D center in Israel, attributes the success of the Israeli cybersecurity industry to the unique ecosystem that exists in Israel, which includes not only the military's technological units and the hi-tech sector, but also the universities. In fact, Braverman-Blumenstyk was originally planning an academic career, but during a sabbatical in the middle of her PhD program at Columbia University in New York, she discovered that she enjoyed working in industry much more. "The industry is the engine, but the academy is the brain that makes it possible for that engine to climb up to new heights," she says. "The military also benefits from academia and sends soldiers there; you can't separate them." Braverman-Blumenstyk believes that the state must keep strengthening academia, to train the next generation's human capital.

"Academia has been the main tool for the advancement of knowledge for the last few hundred years," says Professor Isaac Ben-Israel, "and technology is built on top of that: when you know what the rules are, you can build something functional for the benefit of humanity on top of it. Without academia and science, none of this would happen." Ben-Israel points out that Israel was the first country in the world to have cybersecurity programs at every university, and even some high schools—a system without parallel anywhere in the world.

In November 2010, Prime Minister Benjamin Netanyahu tapped Ben-Israel as the head of a new cybersecurity taskforce, which would formulate Israeli policy about the new domain of cyberspace. "In 1999, as the head of MAFAT, I wrote a letter to Prime Minister and Defense Minister Ehud Barak, arguing that Israel was the most vulnerable country in the world in this new cyberspace environment because its infrastructure was so much more computerized than its enemies, and we had to prepare accordingly," Ben-Israel recalls. "In 2010, when the whole world starts talking about cybersecurity, Prime Minister Benjamin Netanyahu is worried. I get invited to his office, and he sits there and puts down in front of me the letter I'd written 11 years earlier." It turns out that Netanyahu's military secretary, Yochanan Locker, a former deputy chief of the Israeli Air Force, knew Ben-Israel from their service together there—and the warnings he was already making, back then.

Ben-Israel says that he understood that in such a rapidly developing field, it would be difficult to plan a defensive strategy against threats that Israel didn't even know existed. "Take ransomware, for example—viruses that get into your computer and lock you out until you pay a ransom. The field has really taken off recently thanks to the rise of cryptocurrencies, posing a grave threat to civilian systems, but in 2011, when the cybersecurity taskforce published its report, with a list of potential threats—ransomware attacks weren't on the list. Out of a hundred experts, not a single one imagined the possibility that hackers might break into computers in order to lock them.

"It was clear to us that with technology evolving at such a pace, we couldn't predict the future. I told the prime minister, I can't tell you today what capabilities the country will need to build against future threats. 'So we're just going to sit and wait for threats to arise, and then get to work?' the prime minister wondered, and here's what I told him: we'll have to prepare sufficiently flexible capabilities to be used against any possible threat. That means first and foremost the human factor: lots of people who understand cybersecurity and know how to adapt to rapidly changing threats."

And one of the top institutions for training such talent is academia.

"In 2011, there wasn't a single university that taught cybersecurity because the whole field was top-secret, and in academia, professional progress is measured by how many papers you publish. The first country in the world to decide that every university in the world should teach cybersecurity and that every research university should establish its own cybersecurity research center—that was Israel," says Ben-Israel, who now laments the Finance Ministry's decision to withdraw its special support for these academic cybersecurity centers on the pretext that academia can support itself alone.

Despite Ben-Israel's analysis, the gulf between the importance of academia for cybersecurity in principle and its real-world impact on Israeli companies is striking. Cybersecurity firms draw mainly on their own internal research, not academic papers, and only in few companies has innovation been driven by academic discoveries. Moreover, even though all Israeli universities offer cybersecurity studies, the bulk of the growth of the Israeli cybersecurity industry, with the emergence of the biggest companies, happened before these programs even started.

But still, the three main partners in the Israeli cybersecurity industry—military, industry, and academia—undoubtedly have a symbiotic relationship: Israel's army sends soldiers to study at the universities, and talented engineers acquire tools not only in the army, but also in academia; the industry itself, which desperately needs quality manpower, invests in academia. Check Point, for example, has had a longstanding partnership with Tel Aviv University as part of which, in 2008, it founded the Check Point Institute for Information Security. In 2019, the university inaugurated a whole Check Point Building, which houses the university's School of Computer Science.

That said, relations among these three actors are not only symbiotic, but also cannibalistic: the industry is able to attract the best manpower and promise significantly higher pay to the most talented candidates. In a country like Israel with a relatively small population, this tug-of-war between the army, academia, and industry can prove especially significant. Israeli academia might not have produced Israel's cybersecurity industry or significantly fostered innovation, but through its critical role in the IDF's elite programs, serving also as a springboard for people who have not climbed up through military intelligence, it has played a key role in turning Israel into a cybersecurity superpower.

CHAPTER 17

Free Hand or Bear Hug—The State's Role in the World of Innovation

"The state's job is first and foremost not to get in the way," says Gil Shwed when I ask him about the State of Israel's role in fostering the cybersecurity industry. "The hi-tech world is quite disconnected from states and governments, and that's a good thing. It's one of the best things about it—there are few laws, and there's little regulation. That suits me as an entrepreneur, and that's also why software is the fastest-developing field in the world."

Shwed's answer is a faithful reflection of the thinking among Israeli entrepreneurs in the hi-tech industry, in general, and in cybersecurity, in particular. In their view, it was only thanks to the spirit of entrepreneurialism, human capital, and the specific nature of software as an industry where services and products can be supplied to anywhere in the world at the click of a button that a tiny country in the Middle East could produce such successful international companies. And since that is the case, their top expectation from the government is that it not interfere with too much regulation or taxation.

But there is also another side. Nobody can deny that massive state investment was responsible for fostering the IDF's technological units, which have been so critical for the industry's success—and the State of Israel is now also trying to invest even more widely to help the business world.

One of the markets that we, at IntSights, found hardest to crack was Germany. It is the fourth-largest economy in the world and home to many major corporations, such as Volkswagen and Siemens, so we had no doubt that we had enormous potential for sales there. Nevertheless, Germans love doing business in German, so international companies have to find German representatives. For years, we retained three German salespeople, but they were unable to shift large volumes. We decided to change tack and instead of waiting to find the right salesperson, we recruited local partners to distribute our product.

Exactly then, we heard that official Israeli economic attachés around the world were helping Israeli startups enter foreign markets. We called up the Israeli trade office in Munich and asked for help making connections with potential partners. After a few days, its officials got back to us with information about Performio, a company that worked with one of our competitors in Israel, which wanted to switch to working with another company. We met with Performio's people and clicked almost immediately. Within a couple of months, they were able to find our first major customer in Germany, one of the country's largest pharmaceutical distributors. Meetings with economic attachés do not always bear fruit—in the United States, for example, they were unable to reach any potential clients—but here and there, they can give pinpoint assistance. That said, the most significant connections usually come from investors or straight from local partners who already know the Israeli scene and like working with it.

Given all this, let's now examine the various attempts the State of Israel has made to develop and foster its cybersecurity industry, trying to come up with some rules of thumb to measure how effective they have been.

The Yozma Program: Government-funded venture capital

Until 1990, Israel did not have a venture capital industry to invest and pump money into early-stage startups. Nor did foreign investors see Israel as an attractive target for investments. Israel was widely seen as plagued by wars, with a couple of religious tourist sites—not a country capable of producing successful tech companies. "It was very clear that something was missing in Israel at the time," says Yigal Ehrlich, Israel's chief scientist starting in the 1980s. "While Israel was very good at developing technologies, Israelis didn't know how to manage companies or market products."[1] The venture capital industry is critical for a hi-tech industry's development, not just for funding, but also for the knowledge and connections needed to build global companies.

Ehrlich concluded that the only way to solve the problem was to create a governmental venture capital industry. In 1993, together with Finance Minister Avraham Shochat, he established the Yozma (literally, "initiative") program, in which the state would invest $100 million in 10 venture capital funds. These funds would be allowed to keep the State of Israel as a partner or return the money with interest after five years, letting them access cash without the risk of not being able to pay it back. This investment in Israeli funds was a positive signal to foreign investors and pushed them to invest their own money too.

When the results of the Yozma program were assessed in 2004, every single fund that had received public money had returned it with interest.[2] Yozma-backed funds had invested in 168 companies, of which 103 survived, 26 went public on the stock markets, and 30 were acquired. That year, companies supported by Yozma employed 6,000 people in Israel. All in all, the program was a roaring success and laid the foundations of the Israeli venture capital industry, which in turn, contributed to the growth of the hi-tech sector, in general, and the cybersecurity industry, in particular.

The program invested another $20 million directly in startups. Israel stuck to its model of direct investment even afterward, to encourage startups that were struggling to raise funds from the venture capital industry. In 2016, it upgraded the chief scientist's office into a separate government authority called the Israel Innovation Authority, to encourage innovation in Israeli industry, and especially in hi-tech. Through the Israel Innovation Authority, Israel's chief scientist continues to distribute grants to early-stage tech companies, making the Israel Innovation Authority "the biggest early-stage investor in Israel," according to Sagi Dagan, its Vice President for growth and strategy.

The Yozma program also inspired other countries. In 2008, Ireland launched its own innovation fund, earmarking €500 million to attract the venture capital industry. "The Irish state—ironically for a country that didn't have diplomatic relations with Israel for the first 40 years of its existence—has copied the Jewish state," explains the Irish economist and journalist David McWilliams. "Israel is the most successful high-tech country in the world."[3]

Few similar government programs in other countries in the 1980s and 1990s were as successful. Researchers who investigated this subject concluded that part of the reason why Israel's programs were successful is that they were targeted: decision-makers did not just throw money at the challenge. They emphasized that Israel already had the basic conditions in place: the Yozma program lit the spark, but it unleashed possibilities that already existed.[4]

The innovation and bureaucracy authority

Having secured our first round of funding from Glilot, we rented our first offices from the company and started working feverishly to develop our product and sell it to customers around the world. Soon after that, we heard about the grants offered by the chief scientist in the Economy Ministry. After raising money for our company from a venture capital fund in exchange for a substantial proportion of our stock—this sounded like a dream, practically free money. The chief scientist's program let us secure investment without having to dilute our ownership of the company, under conditions that kept the R&D inside Israel and let the country enjoy some of the fruits of an eventual exit—a success-based model that involved no risk on our part, while letting us retain our share of the company's ownership. Like all Israeli cybersecurity companies, we were planning on keeping our R&D in Israel anyway, so we didn't mind this demand. What could possibly be better?

We started working like crazy to submit all the forms. Guy Nizan led the project and took responsibility for all the commercial questions, while Gal Ben-David worked on the technological specifications of the product we were developing. We worked on these forms intensively for several weeks, but eventually, we decided to give up. In the middle of all this work, we realized it would take up too much time and investment and that there would still be lots of bureaucracy ahead. In any case, these grants came with all sorts of conditions about intellectual property that we didn't want to hold us back. We already had money from Glilot, so we didn't need the money from the chief scientist, but above all, we understood that we were better off investing our time in developing our product and attracting new customers rather than raising funds. There were so many investors who were happy to invest in successful cybersecurity firms, and we understood that if only we could get our product ready and bring it to market, we were sorted.

Although we started applying for investment from the Israel Investment Authority, it turned out that it rarely invested in cybersecurity companies like ours, for the same reason we stopped in the middle. "We don't invest in cybersecurity," Dagan told me, "because the private sector's meeting the demand for funding. The state's contribution to the cyber world is mainly through vision, raising awareness, and helping synchronize different actors."

The venture capital industry believes deeply in the Israeli cybersecurity industry and is happy to invest in young companies without much bureaucracy or conditionality. Moreover, venture capital funds have much more flexibility and are willing to make massive investments when needed, while the Israel Innovation Authority has a cap on how much it can give each company. Venture capitalists can also advise entrepreneurs on how to build their companies, connect them to customers and potential buyers, and help them raise more money down the line—support that the state simply cannot provide. One industry leader shared with me his conclusion from his attempt to secure funding from the chief scientist: "They're offering grants of 100,000 NIS [around $30,000], which is nice, but obviously in cyber terms, that's peanuts. Trust me, when I raised $2 million for my startup I didn't go through one-tenth of what the chief scientist put me through for a 100,000 NIS grant." We agreed that it's an admirable initiative to give a leg up to early-stage startups with grants, but in the end, the sums are too small and the bureaucracy's too heavy.

It turns out that Israel's efforts to nurture the cybersecurity industry directly—unlike the Yozma program, which invested directly in companies—have been quite ineffective.

Capital of the Negev, capital of cybersecurity

"Beersheba will be the cybersecurity capital of the eastern hemisphere," declared Prime Minister Benjamin Netanyahu at a conference ahead of International Science Day in 2014.[5] This was great news for the city of Beersheba and Israel's southern periphery. The main hub of the Israeli hi-tech and cybersecurity industry is, famously, in and around Tel Aviv. There are few companies in the north, and at the time, there were hardly any in the south. By attracting cybersecurity companies to Beersheba, Israel would create jobs, generate business for these companies' suppliers, bring in money for the municipal government, and attract educated, middle-class families to the area. This was also excellent news for the cybersecurity industry. The prime minister's statement promised to boost the industry's reputation in the public's eyes and send even more manpower its way, while also signaling the government's willingness to support the cybersecurity industry in the long run. Moreover, opening another hub could attract an influx of talent from southern Israel—as opposed to the Greater Tel Aviv area—and thus, strengthen the industry even more, despite the difficulties attracting quality manpower.

Beersheba has several anchors that should have helped it become a hi-tech center. The city has an established university with engineering and computer science faculties, and a train station connecting it to the greater Tel Aviv area. In order to support the vision of turning Beersheba into a cybersecurity capital, the Israeli government decided around a year after Netanyahu's declaration to give cybersecurity companies that relocated to Beersheba grants equivalent to up to 30% of their R&D employees' pay.

Netanyahu's announcement of Beersheba's transformation into the "capital of cybersecurity" made headlines, but it was not necessarily his most important statement at that conference. He added: "We are moving Unit 8200 and our cyber directorate [to Beersheba]; for the first time, we are seeing positive migration to the Negev Desert." Indeed, the Israeli government had made an official decision six years earlier to relocate the IDF Intelligence Corps, including its technological units, to the Negev.[6] When I joined the unit in 2009, people were already talking about the move to Beersheba, but everyone realized this would take a long time. It was already clear that one of the most influential factors, if not *the* most influential factor, behind the cybersecurity industry's success was the IDF's technological units. Moving these units to southern Israel would also make soldiers and officers relocate there and motivate them to launch their own projects or find work in cybersecurity companies in Beersheba.

About a year later, Beersheba witnessed the first acquisition of a local startup, CyActive, by PayPal—the first exit from Israel's new cyber capital. PayPal also announced that it would open a Beersheba office, in addition to its Tel Aviv branch. In my conversation with Liran

Tancman, co-founder of CyActive and Shlomi Boutnaru (veterans of Unit 81 and Unit 8200, respectively), he told me how their company had become a local success story: "We started out in Beersheba out of necessity. We didn't want to be there at first. We got an investment from JVP, and the company conditioned it on us moving to the hi-tech incubator in Beersheba. Then we discovered a few interesting things: we found out we could work with Ben-Gurion University. My first employee was a guy who'd grown up in Beersheba, a genius, a Unit 8200 vet who was in college there, and so were all our first employees—students who'd come through Unit 8200 and Unit 81."

The two entrepreneurs decided to take advantage of the government's investment in Magshimim, an excellent computer science and cybersecurity program for high schoolers (more on this soon), and they started doing *pro bono* training for around 20 high school students. After that, Tancman describes, "We decided to pick five or six to work for us between high school and the army, for low pay. Then they enlisted, and we opened a WhatsApp group, where we kept in touch with them through their service till today. We met them when they were 16–17; they went into the army, and now—they've come back to us. My team leaders—all from Magshimim. Seniors—from Magshimim. After a year in Beersheba, we went from being opportunists to believers. We saw that it was interesting, that it worked; we saw that they were doing well. I've never had any trouble hiring and I don't think you'll hear that from anyone else."

Such cases, together with government announcements and state support, have made many Israelis feel that David Ben-Gurion's dream of making the desert bloom is coming true with a modern twist—with cybersecurity companies instead of agriculture.

In January 2022, the Knesset Finance Committee approved a support package for the hi-tech sector in Beersheba worth 25 million NIS (around $7 million).[7] The plan had been submitted for the Knesset's approval by the Israel Innovation Authority, which wanted to help attract more hi-tech firms and startups to this desert town. This was great news for Beersheba and it was widely praised, but there was also some bitterness around the fact that despite the efforts invested in the city, it had not yet grown as predicted. In its request to the Knesset Finance Committee, the Israel Innovation Authority explained the need for this program: "Over the years, the Israel Innovation Authority has invested resources to try to build and lay down serious anchors in Beersheba, based on the understanding that the city is the metropolis

of southern Israel, with potential to advance the Israeli hi-tech industry. Despite these investments, Beersheba remains far from fulfilling its
potential for innovation."

While Beersheba has managed to attract several international
hi-tech companies, such as Wix, Dell, and IBM, few of them have been
able to grow much in the city. When the Israeli government announced
its grant program to offset employment costs in Beersheba, the support
was capped at 2,500 cybersecurity employees. Israel clearly had high
expectations, but in practice, in 2019, there were only 330 recognized
employees under the program. "It's really hard to find suitable people
and to grow. The state's got to invest in infrastructure," explained Nir
Zohar, the president of Wix.[8] PayPal, which festively announced the
opening of a Beersheba office, has already quit the town. It said that it
was doing so for cost-cutting reasons, on the orders of the company's
global management, but there's no doubt that a better supply of talent
would have kept PayPal running operations in Beersheba.

For startups, the situation is even tougher. Startups have limited
resources, and they can't afford to train people without the right quali-
fications. Moreover, in order to justify their existence, startups are
engaged in a constant war for survival, so they can't afford to delay
their growth or promote unrelated ideologies. The difficulty hiring
suitable talent has pushed many startups founded in Beersheba to
relocate to the greater Tel Aviv area as soon as they started taking off.
"What's clearly missing here is exits," says Daniel Einhorn, CEO of
Tech7, an organization trying to promote the industry in the city. "You
can count on two hands the total exits the Negev has produced. That
tells you that startups are finding it tough staying here after they reach
a certain size. We need new success stories."[9]

As of 2022, Beersheba is home to around 8 cybersecurity startups,
out of nearly 250 around the country, most of which are based in and
around Tel Aviv. Even the JVP venture capital fund, which set up an
incubator to support new startups in Beersheba, especially in the cybersecurity sector, is no longer sure that it will maintain its operations in
the city. Around half of the companies it invests in end up moving to
Tel Aviv.[10] "We'll be there for the next few years," said Yoav Tzruya, a
partner at JVP, in July 2019. "We've got companies there and we'll keep
supporting them. That said, I can't ignore the fact that companies are
deciding to relocate elsewhere in Israel. We're looking to invest in new
companies, but it's becoming difficult."[11]

The numbers are backed up by a general sense of lost momentum. "In recent years, Beersheba has been visited by dozens of groups, coming to see this wonder of a cybersecurity desert oasis," says Tzruya, but notes that fewer delegates at Israel's cyberconferences are now visiting the desert city.

Some believe that moving the IDF Intelligence Corps' technological units to southern Israel could turn the tide. Streaming the units' quality manpower into the region could make them feel connected to the south and give a critical boost of oxygen to the whole industry in Beersheba. Israel's original target was to move the Intelligence Corps to the south by the end of 2015,[12] but as of 2022, that relocation is nowhere on the horizon. The IDF's technological units explain the delay in their relocation to the south by saying that it will make it difficult to retain quality manpower. They find themselves in a constant battle with the private sector for talent, and this is even more of an uphill climb in the south, which is much less attractive, as the difference in house prices between Beersheba and Tel Aviv shows. The units' soldiers have also put up stiff resistance to the planned relocation. A former high-ranking officer in Unit 8200 told me he sees no problem with the move south, and "there are challenges, although they're surmountable"; but the units' commanders fear a brain drain, which they call an "existential threat."[13]

Morphisec is the biggest cybersecurity startup in Beersheba. Its technology was developed at Ben-Gurion University before it moved to JVP's incubator, and from there became an independent company. Ron Reinfeld, its CFO, is a colorful and humorous guy—not the typical profile of a financial manager—and he's also an ideologue. "The reason we stayed in Beersheba," he says, "is 100% ideological. There are good people there, but the promises aren't happening yet." Beersheba's impact on the Israeli cybersecurity industry so far has undoubtedly been minimal. The great promise for the Israeli south and the industry has yet to be realized, as it stands, in reality.

The implosion of Israel's "cyber capital" dream illustrates the weakness of the state in artificially creating a business environment that suits its leaders' political ambitions. As we shall soon see, the structural concentration of the cybersecurity industry in a single place, Tel Aviv, has played a major role in pushing the Israeli industry forward, and other locations in Israel are expected to remain its less important satellites. Despite the government's efforts and differential tax incentives, it is highly doubtful whether we will ever see Beersheba becoming a cybersecurity capital, and Tel Aviv will probably remain the cybersecurity capital of Israel—if not the whole eastern hemisphere.

Just keep out of the way

Nadav Zafrir served for 25 years in the IDF in a range of high-ranking roles as an officer in the Infantry and Intelligence Corps, culminating with his command of Unit 8200. After he left the army, he joined the private sector and founded the company-building platform Team8, a kind of venture capital fund and syndicate hybrid, which invests in startups, but also generates its own ideas and founds its own companies. His work gives him a unique vantage point because he gets to see the cybersecurity world from both a military and a civilian perspective. When I ask him what explains the Israeli cybersecurity industry's success, he mentions the government's policy of supporting the industry, especially through tax breaks.

First, the corporate tax rate in Israel stands at 23%. Under the 1959 Encouragement of Capital Investments Law, exporters pay only 12% corporate tax, and if they are based in the country's periphery— just 7.5%. Moreover, these companies enjoy a reduced 20% tax rate on dividend withdrawals, instead of 25%–30%. Hi-tech companies are almost all classified as exporters and so benefit directly from this benefit. This tax perk is not relevant to startups because they rarely generate profits, but it is hugely significant for big and profitable hi-tech firms like Check Point. According to Gil Shwed, this benefit has a direct impact on companies' decisions about where to register their operations, attracting major firms to base themselves in Israel.

Another aspect is the tax policy for international corporations, like Microsoft and Palo Alto Networks, with R&D centers in Israel. Israel does not tax R&D centers on their profits because it is very hard to attribute parent companies' profits to specific research and development projects. Let's say Microsoft makes $1 billion: how could anyone say how much should be chalked up to its R&D center in Israel? These R&D centers are taxed, therefore, on a "cost plus" basis, which calculates their total costs— salaries, office rentals, payments to suppliers, and so on—and assumes that their profits are 10% of that, and this is what is taxed. For example, if a company's total expenditures were $10 million a year, its profits would be presumed at $1 million, which would then be liable for corporation tax. This is a relatively low tax rate considering the profits that such R&D centers produce for their parent companies, making Israel highly attractive to global companies. This tax benefit encourages firms to acquire Israeli startups and keep them as R&D centers, thus continuing to invest in the local industry. Israeli tax authorities understand that this is a low tax rate and are trying to find ways to tax the real profits attributable to these R&D centers, but no such reform has occurred to date.[14]

Israel also encourages its hi-tech industry through its "Angel Law," passed in 2011 as a temporary law. Israel recognized the importance of angel investors in the local venture capital ecosystem. Angel investors have more appetite for risk and are often more willing to deviate from normal investment patterns and go with a team or idea they believe in. They are especially important for fields and teams that do not fit the standard mold. The law treated investments in hi-tech firms as tax-deductible expenses, but it expired at the end of 2019. There was an attempt to revive it in 2022, and it even passed its first reading in the Knesset, but the change of government stopped it in its tracks.

Israel's tax policy on the stock options of hi-tech employees who work in the country is similarly restrained. Hi-tech startups offer their employees stock options, giving them a share of the company. When these startups make an exit and get acquired, their employees receive a windfall in proportion to their share of the ownership. Since this counts as money paid for labor, you might expect employees to pay income tax on it, like on their salaries—with a top band of 50%. In practice, Israeli tax law lets them pay only 25% tax for their options. The combination of intense competition among hi-tech companies for scarce talent and this tax benefit creates an incentive for Israelis to work for startups instead of major companies, despite the risk that startups can always collapse. Startups are the main engine of innovation in hi-tech, especially in cybersecurity, making this perk very important for fostering innovation.

When you look at other tech industries, such as life sciences or medicine, or even more traditional industries, and see how much regulation they face, it is possible to appreciate the cybersecurity industry's relative freedom. It is important to remember that politicians are under constant pressure to finance national projects, and the hi-tech industry is a convenient cash cow. Nevertheless, over the years, the industry, and especially the cybersecurity sector, has not been drowning under their tax burden. The politicians have let it flourish. Given all their competing pressures—that can't be taken for granted.

The prime minister's agenda

Nadav Zafrir points out another major contribution the Israeli state has made to the cybersecurity industry: "I don't know many other leaders at the national level who keep saying at every opportunity: we're going to lead the cyberworld." Zafrir is referring to Benjamin Netanyahu, Israel's longest-serving prime minister, who has given the industry a moral and practical tailwind.

Netanyahu has appeared at every international cybersecurity conference in Israel, speaking about the importance and success of the Israeli cybersecurity industry. At the 2019 Cybertech Conference in Tel Aviv, which attracted thousands of cybersecurity professionals from all over the world, Netanyahu explained in flawless English: "Every country needs the combination of a national cyberdefense effort and a robust cybersecurity industry and I think Israel has that and has that in ways that are in many ways unmatched. . . . Every single country here in Israel's expanding diplomatic horizons is talking to us about cyber. They all want to share in our knowledge of cyberdefense."

Such a presentation by the Israeli prime minister in front of an audience from all over the world sends a clear message: the cybersecurity industry is a matter of strategic importance for the State of Israel, which will therefore continue supporting it in order to guarantee its continued prosperity. It is a message that instills confidence in Israeli companies' partners and customers, boosting the Israeli cybersecurity industry's global reputation.

"There aren't many countries," Zafrir says, spelling out Israel's support for the industry, "with an economic attaché in every relevant city in the world to help Israeli startups and make connections for them. There's an Israeli pavilion at RSA." The RSA Conference is one of the biggest annual cybersecurity industry's mass gathering in the world. It draws industry leaders from all over the world, who meet in San Francisco to do business with and pitch their wares to other participants. The main event is an expo at which almost every cybercompany in the world sets up shop, from CrowdStrike and Microsoft's massive complexes to the stands of early-stage startups. It's a real extravaganza. One of the only stalls that does not represent a cybercompany belongs to the Israeli Economy Ministry, a familiar sight at the conference, which lets Israeli startups present their products without having to spend tens of thousands of dollars on their own stalls. This won't change the rules of the game, but it's another powerful statement that the State of

Israel considers the cyberindustry strategically important and intends to invest in it.

In sum, it would be hard to overstate the value of the State of Israel's efforts to create a comfortable environment for the cyberindustry, but it is important to be specific and see which efforts are really turbocharging the industry and which have had only a minimal or symbolic impact. What cybercompanies mainly need is the freedom for the private enterprise, talent, and capital in the country to work together in the best way possible. The impact of tax relief and minimal regulation is so much greater than any attempt to create a whole new cyberhub in Beersheba, any expo stall, or symbolic support from the Israel Innovation Authority. The unwavering support of Israel's leaders and government authorities for the Israeli cyberindustry is a statement of confidence in its abilities— but its growth will depend not on what the state does, but mainly on what it does *not* do. Successful industries need space to flourish.

CHAPTER 18

Small and Nimble— Being a Small Island- Nation in the Middle East Is Not Such a Bad Start

The State of Israel's starting conditions make it hard to build major companies. A nation of nine million Hebrew speakers is a tiny market for any product. Israel is also a kind of island nation, without open trading relations with its neighbors: it has no relations at all with Syria and Lebanon, and despite peace treaties with Egypt and Jordan, Israel's relationship with them looks more like a cease-fire than genuine peace, and free trade is not in the cards. In all the Middle East, Israel has open long-term commercial relations only with Turkey, and more recently also with the UAE and Bahrain. So with such a small local market, how can Israelis build major companies? On the face of it, this situation should have condemned the Israeli economy to producing only small, domestic companies. In practice, the cyberindustry tells a completely different story.

"Obviously you can't build a major business in Israel alone," says Assaf Rappaport, explaining the basic assumption of Israeli entrepreneurs. Developing cybersecurity products demands a huge investment of resources, both in in-depth technological research about attackers and their methods, and also in developing the technology for a product that global companies with high standards will want to buy. In order to justify this investment and make it pay off, entrepreneurs need huge markets. In order to justify their companies' existence and make them profitable, entrepreneurs need lots of big customers to pay them massive receipts. Given all this, you might expect Israel not to produce any cybercompanies at all, only businesses that require low enough R&D costs to be profitable domestically. In reality, it was the clear realization that it is impossible to launch a cybercompany relying only on the Israeli market that generated Israeli entrepreneurs' significant competitive edge.

The key is, therefore, to think globally from the beginning, and this is where the cyberindustry has an advantage. In any sector involving global marketing, entrepreneurs belonging to the most similar culture to their largest markets have a comparative advantage over their competitors because it is easier for them to communicate with potential customers and build the most suitable products for them. But in the cyberindustry, the situation is different. When customers look at cyberproducts, they put a bigger emphasis on technology and less on marketing messages. "The advantage Israelis have in the cyberworld is that it's completely technical," says Gil Shwed. "It's a market where, bottom line, you're judging capabilities against other capabilities, and that blunts the comparative advantage of local companies in major markets."

Hackathons lead to global thinking

Jay Leek is one of the standout figures in the American cyberindustry. For over 20 years, he worked as the information security manager of such major corporations as Nokia and Blackstone, one of the world's biggest financial institutions. At Blackstone, Leek was one of IntSights' first American customers, and he was so pleased that he became the main engine behind Blackstone's investment in our company. After several years as a customer, in which he got to know the industry inside out and saw hundreds of security products, he decided to become an investor who could bring value, using his connections and knowledge, to the companies he was investing in. Leek joined the Clear Sky venture capital group as a partner, later founding SYN Ventures, which invested in companies around the world, including several in Israel.

I ask him what differences he sees between companies from different places. "European companies start their operations on their home turf and then slowly, slowly expand," he says. "In contrast, U.S. and Israeli companies have this crazy motivation to take the whole world by storm as quickly as possible." That sums up the Israeli entrepreneurial mindset in the cyberworld and shows how Israel has transformed a disadvantage into an advantage: it is precisely because the market is so small and *should* have pushed Israeli entrepreneurs to found small companies that they developed an ambition to conquer the world.

When Israeli entrepreneurs build companies, they already start off planning to take them global and serve customers across the planet. They use English as their official language from day one. Their Israeli employees speak Hebrew among themselves, but their software only ever contains English text, which gets proofread by native speakers. Their documents are all in English and so is all their internal correspondence, even if all the parties speak Hebrew.

Beyond the question of language, this global mindset means that products are developed from the outset with an eye on international customers' needs. Israeli entrepreneurs will always aim to meet their customers outside of Israel in order to target their products at these foreign markets, and their first interactions with customers largely dictate what their products will look like. Every market has its own needs and characteristics, such as local regulation affecting cyberdefense needs, and even if their needs are similar, priorities usually differ across markets. For example, if there are far more phishing attacks in Israel than in other countries, then protections against phishing will be much more important to Israelis. When Israeli companies receive feedback from domestic customers, they will always think about whether the demands they are getting are only relevant for Israel or also for other countries before they act on them.

One of the main things I pushed for in this context at IntSights was a customer advisory board. Precisely because of the physical distance from our customers, it was important for us to invest in a customer forum that would meet face to face every year, where customers could give us feedback about our plans for the direction of our product. It was a hugely expensive and logistically complicated operation, bringing together people from across Europe and the United States, but there was no way we could compromise on this. It was clear to us that we had to make sure our product fit the needs and priorities of the market, and that the best way to get such feedback was directly, face-to-face.

Israelis aiming for the global market quickly learn to walk a tightrope act and adapt themselves to different markets. "What we learned right at the start was that you have to go for a glocal strategy—a combination of global and local—and adapt yourself locally even if you're a global company," says Lior Div, who co-founded Cybereason. "If you don't understand the culture, you won't manage to generate the trust that's essential in the field of cybersecurity. We learned very quickly to listen more: to use our ears more than our mouths."

The "American Dream"

Despite the cultural differences, which definitely exist, Israelis and Americans have more in common with each other than other cultures, such as in China, Japan, or even Europe. The typical Israeli absorbs a lot of American culture, and in both cultures, people are usually willing to say what they think and feel.

"From day one of our company, we knew our HQ would be in the United States," Div tells me. "We understood that to have a big company that's close to the market, we'd have to be there, and we'd have to talk the language and inhabit the U.S. ecosystem." For the typical Israeli entrepreneur, Div's insight is practically trivial. The United States is the world's biggest economy, represents an enormous potential market, and above all, leads the global cyberindustry. Making it big in the United States is the key to success in the global market. As a result, it is normal for at least one Israeli founder to move to the United States right after setting up their company. That was the case with Alon Cohen from CyberArk and Shlomo Kramer from Imperva, who both moved to the United States in 2000 soon after founding their companies, and startups such as IntSights and Cybereason kept up the tradition. In IntSights' case, it was clear to us that as the CEO, Nizan would have to move to America as quickly as possible, and he even brought up his wedding date to move earlier. Relocating to the United States not only brings you closer to customers; it also lets you build your first marketing and sales team to focus on the U.S. market. Israelis might be good at technology and innovation, but when it comes to managing massive markets, Israelis with enough expertise are a rare commodity.

Backs against the wall

The Israeli satellite industry, a world leader in miniaturizing satellites and their components, is outstanding precisely because of Israel's geopolitical constraints: around the world, space rockets are launched toward the east, in the same direction as the earth's rotation, to make it easier to leave earth's atmosphere. But in Israel, this is impossible because there are enemy states in the east, so Israel has to launch rockets to the *west*, against the earth's rotation. This meant that Israel had to launch lighter payloads, so what could it do? It made them smaller. Israel, therefore, invested huge efforts in miniaturizing satellite components, and a constraint became a competitive advantage.[1]

Likewise, Israel's small market has led to the building of better products. Gil Shwed traces Check Point's success to precisely this point: "When I started Check Point, I told myself, I'm in Israel and I'm far away from my customers. My competitors, meanwhile, are in Boston and New York. I need a super-simple solution that can be installed in 10 minutes because I won't be there with the customer during the installation. That gave Check Point power. When the market grew, our competitors could reach dozens of customers a month, while we could reach hundreds in the same timeframe." The fact that Check Point's product required little work to install meant that it could shift it in much bigger quantities than its competitors. This feature also made it possible for Check Point's partners, which naturally understood the product less well, to sell its product to customers and install it for them. Paradoxically, sometimes it is physical distance that creates the best products for U.S. and global markets.

Shwed says that only when he acquired an American company from San Francisco did he understand another advantage of Israel's distance from customers: it builds a better organizational structure. "We bought a company in San Francisco that had a very big customer that was also in San Francisco," he says. "This customer had massive support problems and couldn't understand why they weren't getting solved." After Shwed dug into the weeds, he understood that the company maintained a strict separation between technical support people and engineers, in order not to bother the engineers with customer problems. "I told them to cross the street and have the development team talk to the company," he says with a smile. "It's precisely because we're so far away that we make an effort to understand our customers. As an Israeli, I said that since I'm so far away from the customer, I'll let my engineers talk to them. In America, they didn't even cross the street; in Israel, you'd put your engineer on a plane to solve the problem." Israelis have to make efforts to compensate for physical distance and cultural differences, to bridge the gaps with their customers, leading to quicker solutions and better service.

All this said, Israel's distance from the world's biggest markets undoubtedly puts Israeli companies at a disadvantage, definitely compared to U.S. companies, which are right next to their customers and know the local culture well. "With Israeli companies, marketing, and sales are always in the United States and product development's in Israel," says Assaf Rappaport. For Israeli entrepreneurs, this means starting companies that are split between the United States and Israel, with a workforce split between the two countries and separated by at least a seven-hour time difference, often creating communication and coordination problems and slowing down their growth. I experienced this myself: one of our major challenges at IntSights was consolidating a global team. Even after countless workshops and team bonding exercises, we still had occasional miscommunications and coordination glitches.

Two degrees of separation

Israel is a small country not only in population but also in territory: just 8,494 square miles, even smaller than Massachusetts, one of the smallest U.S. states. Around 40% of Israel's population is crammed into the greater Tel Aviv area, a region of just 1,158 square miles, or 14% of the country's territory. For historical and geopolitical reasons, Israelis are never more than a few degrees of separation from each other, a hop of just one, two, or at most, three friends from anyone else in the country. "In Israel you'll find lots of people from similar backgrounds, making it easier to create partnerships and set up companies," says Nir Falevich, who led the cybersecurity sector at Start-Up Nation Central. And as Yossi Vardi, one of the leading figures in Israeli hi-tech, says, "the social graph is very simple here: everybody knows everybody."[2]

Military service, of course, has a huge impact on this culture. Besides the high levels of familiarity among the IDF technological units' veterans, the army is a framework that concentrates lots of people, often against their own will, in a single place. Soldiers' limited choice about where to serve, combined with the fact that they are then often posted far from home, creates connections between diverse sections of the population. This has the effect of bringing together citizens from across the country and making it easier for them to meet in the first place. Personally, having grown up in the religious school system, my only chance of meeting partners like Ben-David or Nizan was in the army or college.

Israel's cyberindustry is based not only on connections forged in the army, but also on geographic proximity. Most Israeli cyberfirms are based in and around Tel Aviv, making it easy for them to collaborate. Nir Zuk, the founder and CEO of Palo Alto, also notes that the Israeli startups that his company acquires are not "from Israel," but specifically from Tel Aviv. "They're not from Haifa, not from Jerusalem, and not from Beersheba. The furthest away is Herzliya," he says. For hi-tech companies, it is very important to be close to other companies and their engineers' homes, and this might be the main reason why the idea of transforming Beersheba into a cyber capital, as we saw in the previous chapter, has no chance of success.

Alon Cohen from CyberArk highlights another aspect of Israel's dense social graph: the communal sense of family, which maintains long-term ties. "In Israel, there are two powerful hubs where friendships are made: high school and the army. In most Israeli companies, the partners met in the army, but there are also partnerships that date back to high school." Like many other entrepreneurs, Cohen recruited for his company people he had met in the army, but his partnership with Udi Mokady goes back to their high school days. NSO's founders, Shalev Hulio and Omri Lavie, also know each other from back when they used to ditch school and go to the beach. "Partnerships that go back to high school are very rare in the United States," says Cohen. "Every time we told American reporters that Udi and I met in high school, their jaws dropped."

When I was at Rapid7, I had a parallel team in Boston that worked on developing a different product. They wanted to create connectivity between their project and one of Microsoft's products, and one member of the Boston team sent me a message asking whether I knew someone at Microsoft called Yael Ganot. When I saw her name on my screen, I chuckled. Yael's brother was Gal, one of my best friends, who also worked with me at the company. I called him straightaway and made an introduction. Only in the cybersecurity sector can two American companies create a partnership through an Israeli branch office, and only in Israel can someone ask you whether you know someone random, and you answer she's actually your close friend's sister.

This intense interconnectivity is constantly creating introductions between entrepreneurs and investors, and companies and customers. This is incredibly valuable for early-stage entrepreneurs, for whom these connections are a genuine lifeline. Kobi Samboursky of Glilot Capital Partners sums it up well: "Everyone here knows everyone, so a young entrepreneur who invests in connections will very quickly find himself connected to the right people."

"You can see it in the United States, in Seattle, for example," explains Dan Amiga from Island. "If Microsoft or Amazon move employees to Seattle, those employees will find it harder to quit for other companies." The United States is an enormous country, with companies scattered across the continent. Amazon employees in Seattle will find it hard to move to Google, all the way in California. Changing jobs would mean packing up and relocating far away, whereas in Israel, it might mean at most an extra half hour's drive. Check Point, Palo Alto Networks, Cato Networks, Wiz, and Transmit Security's offices are no more than a half hour's walk away from each other.

This creates intense competition for talent and makes it hard for companies to retain workers in the long run, but there are lots of advantages. "People can move inside the ecosystem from one company to another. Their knowledge moves with them and gets constantly enriched," explains Esti Peshin, the manager of the Cyber Division at the Israel Aerospace Industries, a state-owned defense body that also provides cyberdefense solutions. "It's a huge advantage. Sometimes it's frustrating when one of my employees goes to work for another company, but there are lots of companies in the field, and I can take employees from other companies." The knowledge that moves between cyberdefense companies creates a positive feedback loop, cross-pollinating the whole industry. This is especially valuable for early-stage startups, which can hire workers from established firms, and since there are so many startups in Israel, there is competition in basically every sector.

Competition not only benefits strong and established companies; it also provides fertile ground for new entrepreneurs. In 2013, Ofer Bin-Nun founded Argus, a company that provides automotive cybersecurity solutions, and sold it in 2017 for $430 million. In 2021, he founded Talon Cyber Security, which provides browser security, and in the company's first investment round, it raised $100 million. "The only way to build a new field in the cyberindustry is if you've got around 10 companies working on the same category," says Bin-Nun. "It's a big deal to educate the market and find funding. You want to be one of several companies knocking on a client's door and explaining why there's something good here. If we look at Argus's journey, maybe the main reason why customers agreed to listen to us was that they'd seen Arilou, TowerSec, and other automotive cybersecurity companies that week already. So they understood there was a need they had to take seriously. When you're the only company that shows up, people don't think it's going anywhere or it's going to stick, and they don't want to have to explain why they chose to do something crazy." When multiple companies compete in the same field, customers realize that they are selling a hot commodity, and that pushes demand up, not down.

There are also other advantages. "It makes you move much more quickly," Bin-Nun continues. "When you come with a new feature, your rivals copy you, and vice versa. It's dramatic if you've got strong competitors, especially if they're Israeli. At Argus, 70% of our competitors were Israeli. That's also the trend at Talon, and it pushes you even more. All your employees are much more exposed to things. At Argus, there was a day I lost a candidate to a rival, and it was really painful. But the value it creates is so much greater than the potential frustration."

As an entrepreneur, I got firsthand experience of the advantages of competition, especially from Israeli companies. Whenever we had to recruit for a position at IntSights, we started by targeting employees of our Israeli rivals, so that they would arrive with as much relevant knowledge as possible. Indeed, we often hired people who came from rival companies developing similar products. This was a huge advantage because it didn't take long to ease them into their jobs, and the knowledge they brought was an asset for our company. They could not transfer commercial secrets, of course, but technological knowledge, work methodologies, an understanding of cyberattacks, and building products for enterprise customers—all these were hugely valuable. One industry leader told me about the impact these job changes were having on the strong connection between offensive cyber and cyberdefense companies: "There's a symbiosis between offense and defense. There's an ecosystem here that takes everyone up a notch. People switch between companies and it enriches their knowledge because they understand how attackers work and then switch to playing defense."

CHAPTER 19

"Bro"—What Makes Israel's Culture an Incubator of Cybersecurity Innovation?

"If you compare experienced talent in the cyberindustry to uranium," says Ehud Schneerson from Paragon, "then Israel's got reserves of human uranium in concentrations you won't find anywhere else in the world."

When we founded IntSights, we didn't have a product yet. At first, we developed only the interface and Nizan went around pitching it to companies. I did the work that the not-yet-existent software was supposed to do, manually: I browsed hacker forums and looked for information that might threaten our potential clients, like a human cybersearch engine. Gal Ben-David, meanwhile, developed the software itself, which would eventually take over from me.

We followed the golden rule of the startup world—"fake it till you make it"—and our Israeli personalities gave us a big boost as we took the cheeky route. Our first big break came when a contact put us in touch with Yonatan Gad. "You've got to meet him," he said. "He's got a magic touch and he'll help you sell abroad." Ben-David met him and showed him the interface. Gad took a keen interest in it and said that he was in touch with Volkswagen and that he would like us to show them our system. Volkswagen was a huge potential client, so instead of gently telling Gad that it might be best to wait with our pitch until we had a ready product, Nizan picked up the phone to me and said, "Listen, I'm just here doing a demo for Volkswagen, switch the system on," and hung up.

The phone call came out of nowhere. I was just at the garage, getting my car fixed, but I understood the enormity of the moment. I leapt into my car, opened my laptop, turned on a hotspot on my cell phone, and started combing the dark web for information on Volkswagen. I picked up on lots of warnings and sent them on, and the system— that's me—went into overdrive, until I realized they'd turned off the lights in the garage while I was sitting there in my car with my laptop. When I felt I had exhausted all the alerts I could find, I shut my laptop and prayed for the best. On my drive home from the garage, Nizan called again. "Listen, he loves it, it was a success." It was, thanks to that moment sitting in a garage and manually doing the work of a system that was in development, that we also reached our first investor, Glilot, and five new customers.

This kind of anecdote keeps coming up in stories about new startups: these companies have to find customers and investors pronto, and often it's impossible to wait for the product to be ready because investors need to be shown results and because rubbing along with customers at an early stage creates a better understanding of the product that you need to develop. The hi-tech startup world requires daring, improvisation, and good old chutzpah, which are essential elements of Israeli culture.

Tony Velleca, the founder and CEO of CyberProof, an Israel-based consultancy, recalls such a story that made clear to him the advantages of the Israeli character. His company was competing for a contract with a major insurance firm against massive corporations, including IBM. The Israeli team managed to sell a solution that was not ready yet. It was based on a connection to a Microsoft product, Azure Sentinel. The Israelis leveraged their personal acquaintance with the development team at Microsoft's Israel office to create a collaboration that convinced the customer to pick their solution, despite not being ready for market.

This approach was on display from day one of the Israeli cyberindustry. Check Point, as we have seen, had scrambled with just a week's notice to pitch its product at the Interop expo in Las Vegas, without sending a single press release, using another company's stall—and had stolen the show.

What impact has Israeli culture made on the success of Israel's cyberindustry? I posed this question to Gil Shwed, Check Point's founder. "What's really characteristic of Israeliness is its entrepreneurial and technological power," said Shwed. "Israelis are willing to leave no stone unturned and overcome every obstacle, and in the cyberindustry, that's an essential quality."

Israelis are not only ready to turn every stone and find every shortcut; they also work really long hours, far longer than in most countries. "Israeli culture is a culture of hard work," says Eyal Benishti, the CEO and founder of Ironscales, which offers sophisticated solutions to foil phishing attacks, "much more than in other places. Israelis are willing to go the extra mile." From an international comparison, it is clear that Israelis work far longer than the average in Western countries,[1] but the official data does not reflect the full picture because in the Israeli hi-tech market, employees hang around in the office long after they have officially clocked out.

The "Jewish genius"

"I've always felt that Israeli hi-tech employees have much more in common with American hi-tech employees than they do with Israeli employees in other sectors." So I heard from one industry leader, who prefers to remain anonymous. "The hi-tech community is a global community," he says. "Hi-tech culture is more of an outgrowth of Diaspora culture than of Israel's particular culture. Jews in the Diaspora excelled in doing business with non-Jews, and the cyberindustry is just one particular case of that." In his analysis, the reason for Israel's dominance in this market is mainly because it has such a big Jewish population, not because of any specifically Israeli trait.

It is impossible to ignore the impact of Jewish culture, or the "Jewish genius" as some people call it, on the growth of the Israeli cyberindustry. Cybersecurity is a field in which human capital and high levels of expertise are essential, and neither the army nor academia can provide these alone. On the contrary, the IDF's ability to place such a heavy emphasis on its technological units is thanks to the high-quality human capital in the Israeli population. Israel has produced a talented workforce to which the army and academia only give expression, but its foundations are cultural and run much deeper.

Indeed, Jews have stood out in the fields of knowledge and science in recent centuries. While in 1900, Jews amounted to 0.6% of the world's population, and in 2022 less than 0.2%, Jews account for a full 25% of Nobel Physics Prize laureates and 21% of Nobel Chemistry Prize laureates, including six Israelis. One third of the winners of the Fields Medal for mathematics, as prestigious as the Nobel Prize, have been Jews, and Jews make up a similar proportion of Wolf Prize for Science and Arts laureates. Around one quarter of winners of the Turing Award for computer science have been Jews (including 5 Israelis, out of 75), and a similar proportion of winners of the Gödel Prize for outstanding papers in the area of theoretical computer science have been Jews—and of those, most have been Israelis.

Jewish excellence is not limited to the sciences. Jews in medieval and modern times had a powerful presence in trade and business, later flourishing in many other fields. The entertainment industry, including showbiz and Hollywood, is just one example. Jews are the richest ethnic group in the United States: only 2% of Americans are Jews, but they account for around 30% of the Forbes 400 list of the richest people in America.[2]

The reasons lie partly in ancient Jewish tradition. Unlike Christianity, Judaism has never idealized poverty, nor has it viewed commerce negatively. The Bible preaches that "it is easier for a camel to go through the eye of a needle than for a rich man to enter the kingdom of God" (Matthew 19:24) because "the love of money is the root of all kinds of evil" (1 Timothy 6:10). The Jewish Sages, meanwhile, said that Rabbi Judah Hanasi, who redacted the Mishnah, the compendium of Jewish oral traditions, respected the rich (Babylonian Talmud, Eruvin 86a) and that a "pauper" is "considered dead" (Nedarim 64b). The Babylonian Talmud states that God "rests His Divine Presence only upon one who is mighty, and wealthy, and wise" (Nedarim 38), and Jewish legal tradition allowed people to do things that would otherwise be forbidden, like leaving the Land of Israel, for the purpose of doing business.

"We've got a 2,000-year-old tradition of respecting scholarship and the pursuit of excellence," says Professor Isaac Ben-Israel. "Literacy was widespread among Jews, long before it was common among other peoples. It's not a matter of genetics," he says because

Jews spent thousands of years in the Diaspora, during which there were countless mixed marriages, and of course, conversions into the faith. It's a matter of culture.

Ben-Israel goes as far back as the biblical Abraham to explain the situation. "When I was a child, my mother read me stories from the Hebrew Bible, including the story about Abraham arguing with God about the destruction of Sodom," he recalls. "Only when I was a bit older did I realize the story's hidden message: that it's possible, and sometimes even a good thing, to argue—even with God Almighty. And if you can argue with God, you can argue about anything and ask questions about anything. That's the basis of modern science: it's all built on the ability to argue and dispute things."

Some scholars have called this cultural phenomenon "religious intellectualism": a book-based culture, which keeps going back to its texts and debating them; a culture that celebrates argumentation and nitpicking about minute details, and that cultivates abstract thinking, and has always encouraged vocal arguments. These cultural characteristics were able to move relatively seamlessly into nonreligious fields, and in the worlds of science and business, they flourished with full force.[3]

Nadav Zafrir says something similar: "Israeli culture refuses to accept reality as it is. It's a culture that places an emphasis on study through argumentation." To this he adds the element of innovation: "Innovation means identifying how reality could be different, and this alertness is intensified by this cultural refusal to accept things as they are." Zafrir identifies this quality with Israeli culture, but its specifically Jewish nature is even more striking.

Does Israel's edge in the cyberworld, in terms of its human capital and culture, simply reflect some advantage that Jews have over non-Jews? Israel's culture of improvisation and shortcuts, of assuming that everything will work out somehow, seems to be characteristically Israeli and to relate to Israel's Zionist and military ethos. This culture puts Israel at a disadvantage when it comes to building large and established companies, which require organized workflows—where Israel's culture of shortcuts can end up making this unnecessarily complicated. But when it comes to startups, Israel seems to have a winning combination of a Jewish culture of business and excellence with an Israeli culture of audacity and a willingness to leap into the unknown.

The culture of mutual assistance

Even before Yevgeny Dibrov turned 20, when he was still in the army, he liked going to innovation conferences. "I remember the conference where I met Yizhar Shai. We got to know each other there and became friends," he recalls. Shai founded and sold Business Layers, later working as the CEO of V-Secure Technologies, until it got acquired. When they met, Shai was a partner in the Canaan Partners venture capital fund. "I approached him and we started talking," Dibrov recalls. "I told him, I don't have an idea or even a direction yet, but I think one day I'll want to found something. He was really friendly, spoke to me, gave me his phone number, and we've stayed in touch." The pair kept in contact for years, and even when Shai became Israel's minister of culture and technology, he continued to mentor the young entrepreneur, who soon became a successful entrepreneur in his own right when he founded Armis Security.

It was an "only in Israel" story. In any normal country, if a 24-old soldier, who has not yet started his career, walks up to a hi-tech industry leader, the most you would expect him to get is a polite smile. There is nothing obvious about the fact that Shai kept talking to him and gave him his personal cell number. "In Israel, experienced entrepreneurs are often happy to help younger ones, and that's very different from other countries," explains Kobi Samboursky. "In other places, they'll help you if they've got a clear incentive. Here, they'll help you unless they've got a good reason not to." Israel, a country surrounded by enemies and full of social and security challenges, has developed a culture of solidarity, which drives experienced and well-connected people in the industry to help those at the start of their careers.

"In Israel, there's a thing called intergenerational continuity. People are very accessible and are happy to share their experience," says Amichai Shulman from Imperva. "You've got people to give you a tailwind and advice. That makes a huge contribution to the next generation of entrepreneurs."

Shulman knows what he is talking about. When we launched IntSights, we wanted to get another investment offer, besides what we had from Glilot. We thought we should raise money from angel investors, and we quickly got introduced to Shulman. He was happy to be put in touch and invited us to meet him at his office at Imperva. For us, it was an indescribable honor to visit Imperva, one of the biggest cybercompanies in Israel, and meet one of its founders face to face. But for

Shulman, this wasn't a big deal, and he was happy to talk to us at our own level. As a veteran tech leader, he was quick to understand what we wanted to do and what value it offered companies, and he decided to invest. He became one of our main backers, who helped us with anything we needed, made connections, and gave us advice. I understood him better when I found myself in a similar position after making my own exit, when young entrepreneurs started coming to me to pick my brains: I admired them and wanted to do my best to help them because I saw them as the next generation.

Access to people who are willing to help is a priceless resource for early-stage entrepreneurs trying to break into the cyberworld. It lets them stand on the shoulders of giants, build on their experience, and enjoy their huge network of connections. That's one of the reasons why Shlomo Kramer advises Israeli entrepreneurs to start their companies in Israel: "You've got to found a startup in your own community. It's much harder for Israeli entrepreneurs who've moved to Silicon Valley." Kramer knows what he's talking about. He spent a long time living in Silicon Valley as the CEO of Imperva, but he still decided to build his latest company, Cato Networks, in Israel.

The pioneers

One of the toughest stages in the process of launching a startup is finding the first customers who will agree to use your product. Nobody knows who you are, you've got no reputation, it's hard to bank on you, and nobody wants to be the guinea pig for your new product.

Your company's first users will be critical to its future. They will help your company understand how to build the product and where to invest your efforts to give your customers the most bang for their buck. They will have to be special: they'll have to put up with the mistakes and glitches that always exist at the beginning; they'll need to have an appetite for risk because that's what makes it possible to try out new technologies; and they will need to love innovation and change. They'll need to put up with technical bugs and products that are still missing the full functionality of more established services, but they will enjoy other things instead. By getting on board early, they will be able to play an active role in shaping your product and adapting it to their needs, and they'll also take huge satisfaction in being part of your company's success.

When we moved to IntSights' new offices, we invited Danny Wish-litzky, Gett's information security manager and one of the first people to adopt our product, to talk to everyone at the company about how it was helping him. One of the things he said has remained etched in my memory: "Your product has quite a few features you can chalk up to me." He was absolutely right. Much of the feedback he gave us at the start got translated into new capabilities, which made our product a bigger success.

"There's just no competition for the early efforts that get invested in Israel," says Eyal Benishti from Ironscales. "It's a critical factor." In 2014, Benishti started sending messages through LinkedIn to security managers across Israel: "I'm an entrepreneur, working on something interesting, coffee's on me." To his surprise, lots of them got back to him and asked to meet. "Some of the top people in the cyberdefense industry helped us build our product's story and pitch it properly, and they even paid for something that wasn't totally finished," he says—and that's what drove his company forward.

Israeli entrepreneurs in other sectors will always prefer American feedback, which better reflects their target market, but in the cyberindustry, many of the key insights are universal and apply to everyone. When IntSights started selling to Europe and America, we always looked for feedback from our Israeli customers. They were not available for any questions we had, and of course, also characteristically blunt. Whenever something was not working, our Israeli customers told us loud and clear, without any awkwardness, and that was hugely valuable for our ability to improve and develop the best product out there. Contrary to what people might think, Israel's straight-talking culture—what Israelis call *dugri*—makes Israelis outstanding customers.

Our ambassadors abroad

Shira Kaplan, a promising young Israeli, decided to work for the Swiss private bank Julius Baer in 2011. After a year or two into the job, something seemed off. "I read the newspapers and asked myself, how does it make any sense that Swiss banks hold $18 trillion, a quarter of the world's capital, and none of it's going into the Israeli cybermarket? Can't they see the world's heading toward cyber and Israel's at the forefront of the industry? What can Israel see that they can't?"

Kaplan reflects another advantage of Israel's socially dense culture: its people's networks of connections around the world, which help to market Israel itself as a product. She decided to set up a venture capital fund that would invest in Israeli cybersecurity startups, but then she ran into another challenge: why would Israeli startups even want to take her money? After all, there were already so many venture capital funds investing in the cyberindustry, many of them based in Israel, closer to the entrepreneurs than she was in Switzerland.

"I asked myself, what's the biggest value I can give these entrepreneurs to make them go with me?" she tells me when we meet. Her answer was that Israeli startups needed customers, and if she could help them sell to major customers, she would become a much more attractive investor. Unlike many venture capital funds, which immediately scramble to raise money, Kaplan started by building a network of ties with Swiss industry leaders, introducing them to Israeli technologies and products in order to make business connections. "Switzerland is not an easy market to crack. In 2016, when I mentioned the words *cyber*, *startup* and *Israeli* to executives at international Swiss companies, they had no idea what I was talking about. It was like I was talking Chinese. Nowadays, it's self-explanatory." One of the companies that Kaplan connected with at the start of her journey was IntSights. She connected us to several major Swiss corporations, which became our customers, and over the next few years, she helped us close deals worth more than $3 million.

"So far, we've brought in $30 million in sales for Israeli cybercompanies," Kaplan says with satisfaction. Some five years after proving her theory worked and that she could deliver unique value for Israeli companies, she pivoted to founding Cyverse Capital, which focuses on investing in Israeli cybercompanies. The fund also helps these companies reach customers and shows Swiss investors that major Swiss companies are buying Israeli products—giving the Israeli cyberindustry a "seal of quality" and encouraging these Swiss investors, one by one, to invest their money in Kaplan's fund.

Kaplan is, as we have seen, just one example of the phenomenon of Israelis working as "outposts" in foreign countries, creating connections that help them to market Israeli cybersolutions. There aren't many of them, but there is definitely a critical mass that is especially significant for early-stage startups fighting for every customer. These "ambassadors" of course provide connections, but they can also help to bridge cultural gaps in cases of misunderstandings and messages that fail to land properly. At IntSights, we called on Israeli partners to reach our first major customers in Britain, Switzerland, Japan, and Mexico—and there were many more like us. This network of connections is another advantage of the Israeli system and part of the ecosystem in which the Israeli cyberindustry has boomed.

When I ask Kaplan what she makes of the Israeli entrepreneurs she meets and what her Swiss colleagues make of them, she doesn't hold back on superlatives: "Israelis are the best, so much better than others. You don't sleep at night. You're hungry. You're technologically savvy," she says, stressing that Israelis are insanely good at sales, while salespeople in other countries are mostly good at "selling to universities." "In every conversation with information security managers, you see Israelis' edge."

CHAPTER 20

The Cybersecurity Industry Snowball Effect—Elements of the Israeli Ecosystem

"From a historical perspective, Check Point created a giant industry. There are over 40 cybercompanies nowadays run by ex-employees," says Gil Shwed with undisguised pride. "When Check Point started out, every role had to be built from scratch. There was nowhere else from which we could take people who understood the field. Nowadays there's already a huge ecosystem. When you've got around 10,000 Check Point graduates wandering around Israel, there's a lot of knowledge that each can bring and contribute to the market."

This phenomenon is not unique to the cyberindustry, and other countries also have clusters of industries that have often emerged thanks to one successful company. Richard Stiennon, founder of the analytics company IT-Harvest, also points this out. "Israel has a booming cyberdefense ecosystem," he says in a conversation with me, "and that ecosystem was created by Check Point." Nir Zuk, who rose up the ranks of Check Point and eventually became its most powerful commercial competitor, hammers the point home: "Unit 8200 and similar

units in the army provide a talented workforce of engineers, not necessarily cyberpeople. The real reason for the power of the Israeli cybersecurity industry is the snowball effect that Check Point launched."

Good companies, Zuk explains, create chain reactions: "These
companies produce good people, who produce new companies. In Israel, Check Point started the snowball effect, just like Symantec and
McAfee did in Silicon Valley." Indeed, it would be hard to overstate
Check Point's role in nurturing entrepreneurial and engineering talent, and steering it toward the cyberindustry.

When Check Point was founded, it was just another company, one
of many, in the Israeli hi-tech world. By the late 1990s, Unit 8200 was
already considered the "startup training unit," but most Israeli startups were not involved in information security at all. The IDF's pivot to
cybersecurity in the new millennium was definitely important, but the
question is whether it was enough to direct the unit's veterans specifically to this sector. It is possible that if Shlomo Kramer had not scored
such an early success with Check Point, he wouldn't have gone on to
found Imperva and Cato Networks, and invest in dozens of cybercompanies. Check Point itself acquired many Israeli cybercompanies, and
Nir Zuk founded Palo Alto Networks, which competed with the company he had come from and reached global dominance in its own right.

Among the companies founded by ex-Check Point employees
are Tufin, launched in 2005 by Ruvi Kitov and Reuven Harrison and
sold to the U.S.-based Turn/River Capital investment firm in 2022 for
$570 million; Orca Security, founded in 2019 by eight former Check
Point employees, which skyrocketed to unicorn status in 2021 and
raised $340 million, with a market valuation of $1.8 billion; LightCyber,
headed by Gonen Fink, one of Check Point's first employees, which
Shlomo Kramer and Marius Nacht invested in, before it was acquired
by Palo Alto Networks in 2017 for $130 million; and Fireglass, founded
by Guy Guzner, another former Check Point employee, who sold it to
Symantec in 2017 for $250 million. Guzner's partner, Dan Amiga, went
on to found Island, which catapulted to unicorn status in 2022.

The snowball effect was created not only because of Check
Point employees founding their own companies, but also because of
many other factors that kept the snowball rolling and growing: these
new companies gave rise to even newer companies, and their capital got pumped into even more companies. Shlomo Kramer calls it
"community spread," explaining: "Whereas in the past, innovation
came from outside, from the security services, there's now a self-
sustaining process of mentoring in the community." Kramer knows

what he is talking about: not only did he himself leave Check Point to found new companies and invest his own capital in more companies, he also mentored many of these new entrepreneurs. A similar process of "community spread" happened at IntSights. As of writing, former IntSights employees have founded two new companies—Guardz and Anecdotes, which have raised serious capital—while others are founding more companies of their own.

Check Point's impact is not limited to talent and capital. At IntSights, we were intensely aware of the power of this massive company operating alongside us in the cybermarket. We knew that Check Point had an expansive network of connections and partners all around the world, and that if we could harness them for our benefit, we would have a great springboard. We spent many long months working on a collaboration that eventually took hold, leading to Check Point selling our product together with its own. Thanks to Check Point, we reached many new customers in Australia, which we had zero access to before, and several major customers in the United States. Such collaborations with Israeli startups are not rare, but the story of IntSights shows the importance of a company the size of Check Point to the ecosystem of Israeli cybercompanies.

For me, growing up with a dad in hi-tech, Check Point was always the standout success story of Israeli hi-tech. When people ask me what my dream is, I still say, "building the next Check Point." Its existence in the market and runaway success inspired other companies. Check Point's story—a business that three Israeli guys founded in someone's grandma's apartment, which broke into the U.S. market, signed giant deals, and enjoyed an initial public offering of tens of millions of dollars—fired up so many Israelis' imagination and appetite.

Will this snowball necessarily continue rolling forever? Nir Zuk warns that there is no guarantee. In Boston and Atlanta, there were a few cyberompanies that triggered a similar effect, but it soon fizzled out, partly because of a shortage of talent. In Israel, there is also considerable evidence of a difficulty recruiting quality manpower and finding enough talent to sustain the sector's growth. The cybersecurity industry has grown and flourished in Israel ever since the 1990s, but nobody can promise that this snowball will keep rolling.

Besides government policy and the impact of the army, which I discuss in previous chapters, there are three more important factors of huge importance to the Israeli cyberecosystem and the whole industry's future: the venture capital industry, international corporations with offices in Israel, and the booming reputation of Israeli cybersecurity resulting from the success of the industry and contributing, in turn, to its success by attracting customers and investors to Israel.

Made in Israel venture capital

Congratulations! You've decided to build a cybersecurity company in Israel. You've got an idea (or maybe you don't), you've got outstanding workers, you've got skills and maybe also experience from the army, you've got partners you met in the army or academia or maybe even in high school, and now all you need is to sit in your grandma's basement or apartment and develop the product that will take the world by storm. Oh, and you also need one more small thing: money.

Money isn't everything in life, but if you want to build a startup, you'll need quite a lot of it. You'll need to hire people, buy computers, purchase software, fly to the United States to pitch your product, and pay marketing professionals. In short, you need capital. Capital is the blood flowing through the veins of the hi-tech industry, and especially the cybersecurity sector.

Investors often understand that their role is not all about money and that they are expected to give some added value for their investments to pay off. They won't just trust your abilities, therefore, but will also actively help you, giving you advice about business or technology, opening doors and introducing you to investors and customers, and helping out in lots of other different ways. Obviously the more expertise your investors have in your specific field, the better their chances—and yours—of turning your company into a success story.

As Israelis with an idea for a new cyberstartup, you've got an advantage: the investment market in Israel is bursting with investors and specialized knowledge. Moreover, you can also meet investors much more easily than most of your counterparts around the world. You've got a pretty good chance of knowing someone who knows someone, especially if you served in one of the IDF's technological units.

Not that it's a walk in the park. You're not the only one with an idea and abilities; there are many Israelis like you, and the competition is intense. Most investors you go to will turn you down on the spot or will politely say, "That's an interesting idea, let's keep in touch," which is usually code for "that's a terrible idea, please never talk to me again."

But still, the Israeli market puts capital and experience at your disposal, so that you can build the next big cybercompany.

Slowly but surely, a system of financial support has emerged in Israel for hi-tech innovation in general and cybersecurity in particular. By the 2010s, Israel had no fewer than five venture capital funds dedicated specifically to cybersecurity, in addition to many other general funds. We will soon discuss these funds and the smart capital that has been filling Israel in recent years, but first, let's go back to the very first days of Israeli cybersecurity.

"When we founded Check Point, we had no one to raise money from," Kramer recounts. We had to create a simple solution that didn't require many resources." Check Point, as we know, raised its initial investment of 250,000 NIS from BRM, which had made a fortune selling antivirus systems. In today's terms, this sounds ridiculously low, especially considering that this capital was enough to buy half of the stock of a company that would soon be worth billions of dollars. In any case, that was one way of raising capital: through corporate venture capital.

Corporate venture capital funds will not always be willing to invest in early-stage startups with unclear futures. These companies' main investors are venture capital funds. Most startups do not end up making eye-watering exits or becoming unicorns with huge market valuations, and investments in them can often go down the drain. When investors put their money in such businesses, there's a good chance they'll never see their money again or that they will only see a meager return. On the other hand, some investments prove unbelievably profitable, and that's exactly what the whole venture capital model is based on: funds invest in companies and know that they will see little, if anything, from most of them, but their returns from some of them will be astronomically high enough to cover all their other investments, with a healthy surplus left over.

In the 1990s, there were few venture capital funds in Israel. The country had one government venture capital fund: Yozma, which we have already discussed. Yozma helped to launch Israeli startups, although its impact on the cybersecurity world was less keenly felt. There were also other funds, some privately owned and others traded on the stock market. Gili Raanan, who would later set up a specialist cybersecurity venture capital fund, secured his initial capital for Sanctum, which he founded in 1997, from Mofet Venture Capital, a publicly traded fund run by Eli Bar, a former Unit 8200 commander. All that Bar needed was to believe in Raanan and his abilities to invest in him.

Venture capital discovers the cyberindustry

In the late 1990s, the Israeli hi-tech scene started to boom and attract foreign investors. One of the world's most successful venture capital funds, Sequoia, opened an Israel office in 1999, its first outside the United States. One of the companies it invested in was Raanan's Sanctum in its second funding round. Raanan joined Sequoia as an active partner in 2009, having founded two more startups and sold them to major companies in the meanwhile.

"I got back from the U.S. in 2007 and settled down in Mikhmoret [a locality north of Tel Aviv]. Having sprinted two marathons, I was exhausted and spent nearly two years resting. I was already thinking about setting up my third startup with a friend, this time in the field of robotics. It was a personal dream of mine as an avid reader of Isaac Asimov. Then came Sequoia's offer."

Raanan accepted the offer to become a partner in Sequoia and started working at the Israel office. "At first, I avoided investing in cybersecurity," he says. "It was a field where it was easier for me to spot faults, so much harder to invest." But there were still cases where he saw fewer faults and invested. "Looking back, two of my three major successes were cybercompanies," he says, referring to Adallom and Armis. Sequoia also made an investment offer to IntSights, which was exciting for us because Sequoia is a huge fund, but its competitor made us a better offer and we had great chemistry with its team, so after weighing up both proposals we accepted the offer from Glilot, which specialized in the cybersecurity industry anyway.

Back then, we were still naïve and inexperienced. We weren't really thinking about raising capital and didn't understand how important it was for product development and customer support. We didn't have a slideshow or figures to show Glilot, but luckily for us, the company was looking to invest in a firm just like ours. Glilot was familiar with the market and all the data, and we were right up its street. Not only did Glilot give us capital for product development, support, and sales—it also connected us to our first customers in the United States, helped us build up our company and hire a sales team, and in an extremely unusual move, even gave us a couple of rooms at their office.

Before writing this book, I met up with Kobi Samboursky from Glilot and asked him to describe how the fund began. Samboursky and Arik Kleinstein founded Glilot Capital Partners in 2011. Having worked with Israeli security agencies over the previous decade, Samboursky was beginning to understand what a hot topic cybersecurity was in the market. At first he founded Lamda Communication Networks, an offensive cybercompany (or "reconnaissance cyber," as he calls it) that focused on satellites. The positive reactions that he started getting as an Israeli in the field of cybersecurity made him understand that Israel had some genuine advantages, and the growing awareness of cyberthreats made him understand that there was real demand in this sector. And thus, having sold his company in 2010, he founded Glilot Capital Partners.

It was not an easy start. "When I set up the fund, lots of people asked me: what does *cyber* mean? Others said, oh, that's just information security, what's new about that?" Others tried to talk him out of getting into this field, which they did not think was particularly profitable. Even the idea of venture capital funds was not especially popular at the time. Between the bursting of the dot-com bubble at the start of the previous decade and the 2008–2009 economic crisis, the feeling in the market was that hi-tech investments weren't worth it.

In 2012, a year after he founded Glilot Capital Partners, the Kauffman Foundation, a veteran fund that fosters innovation, published a report, provocatively titled "We Have Met the Enemy and He Is Us." The report argued that, as a rule, the asset class that venture capital funds were investing in was unprofitable and involved far too much risk and too little potential profit.

The sentiment in the Kauffman Foundation report was nothing new. Samboursky was already struggling to secure investors for his new fund, and most of those who were ultimately willing to invest in it were private entities, some of which were only investing for patriotic or ideological reasons, and not necessarily out of economic considerations. But eventually, the fund became a roaring success, and by 2022, it had produced 12 exits—including IntSights.

Nadav Zafrir's Team8, which is not a regular venture capital fund but a kind of cybercompany creation platform, entered the scene in 2013. Zafrir had founded the company that year, when he retired from his military service, together with Israel Grimberg, the outgoing commander of Unit 8200. After a shaky start, when few players in the local cybersecurity market understood the need for their new idea, Zafrir found the right partners. He told me once that one day, his wife told him that she had overheard a few people at a café in Herzliya talking about cybersecurity and that maybe he should talk to them. So he did. The person he met was the entrepreneur Yuval Shachar, who was just setting up a venture capital fund called Marker, after building and selling three companies to Cisco in the United States. Despite Zafrir and Grimberg's reservations, Shachar thought it was an interesting idea and joined them. They were then joined by more partners, and from then on, it was smooth sailing.[1]

Team8, as we recall, did not start off as a venture capital fund: it built teams to examine the needs of the cybermarket, raise ideas, and explore the feasibility of certain investments. Only after a drawn out process did the group invest in companies, in exchange for 50% of their shares. Among the companies founded through this framework were Claroty, a unicorn that provides cyberdefense for industrial facilities; Sygnia, which provides cyberattack prevention services and was sold to the Singaporean company Temasek in 2018 for $250 million; Portshift, which developed platforms to secure cloud applications and was sold to Cisco in 2020 for $100 million; and many other companies. Only later, wanting to expand its operations, did the group create its own venture capital funds focusing on cyber and fintech.

Venture capital and offensive cyber

Because of its problematic image, venture capital funds have stayed clear of the offensive cyberindustry. NSO, as we have said, raised only its initial investment from Eddy Shalev, relying on customer revenues ever since. The companies that followed it, such as Candiru, could not even raise any initial capital: they had to finance themselves and find customers as quickly as possible. This model is called "bootstrapping," as in the old story about Baron Munchausen who gets stuck in a swamp and pulls himself up by his bootstraps. These companies have to rely on their independent capital and pull themselves up to succeed. Sometimes it works, but it is not easy, and it comes at a price.

Alon Kantor, co-founder of offensive cybercompany Toka, an example of the new and "clean" wave of cybercompanies, points out that venture capital funds' refusal to invest in offensive cyber has meant that paradoxically, these businesses are hungry for customers and cannot afford to be picky when they are already predisposed to sell to dodgy customers. Toka wanted to change tack. "We wanted to set up a company like a proper startup and raise money from funds, but not to be dependent on customers or under pressure to sell as quickly as possible, and to build our product the right way," Kantor recalls. Within two months of opening, Toka had already raised $12.5 million from some of the leading funds in Silicon Valley and from Entrée Capital in Israel.

It might have also helped that Toka was pitched to the media mysteriously as a "company that helps states improve their information security."[2] Or slightly more precisely, the company's goal was to "provide a framework of cyberproducts for governments and various security agencies around the world,"[3] without mentioning "offensive cyber" even in passing. In any case, Toka proved that the offensive cyberindustry could also raise capital the normal way, perhaps even paving the way for the next companies.

The entrepreneur community's fund

In 2018, Raanan decided to launch his own cyberfund. Sequoia had just decided to close its branch office and invest in the country through its American head office. Raanan founded Cyberstarts, a cybersecurity investment fund that would operate on a totally different model from traditional funds.

In a conversation with Raanan, he tells me about the background to this fund and what makes it special. Cyberstarts has a narrow, practically niche, focus. "It's practically the antithesis of a venture capital fund that spreads out over a range of fields," he says, "but if you ask me, even cyberdefense is too broad a sector. I don't invest in hardware, or offensive cyber, or cyberfirms that sell to governments, or ones that sell to medium and small customers. I only sell SaaS," he says, referring to "software as a service," which he will only sell to chief information security officers (CISOs) at major companies. "Second, I get in as early as possible. None of the 16 companies we invested in was even registered when we got in. You can't get in any earlier."

"I went back to my 27-year-old self, fresh out of the army, who thought he knew it all but didn't even know what he didn't know," he recalls, "and I told myself, what kind of fund would he have wanted to encounter? It was easy for me to launch Cyberstarts because I knew the other side well, the side that uses these funds. And that's how I made several key decisions when launching the fund."

Raanan's first decision was not to invest in ideas or products, but in people. "I've invested in a few excellent entrepreneurs with excellent ideas, and in many excellent entrepreneurs with mediocre ideas, and I've also ended up investing in excellent entrepreneurs who don't even have an idea at all."

Raanan's second decision was to get the Israeli cybercommunity involved when he set up his fund, and the whole "Who's Who" of the Israeli cyberindustry invested: Shlomo Kramer, Marius Nacht, Mickey Boodaei, Rakesh Loonkar, Amichai Shulman, Nir Zuk, Assaf Rappaport, Yevgeny Dibrov, Nadir Izrael, Michael Shaulov, Roy Zisapel, and more.

"Despite setting out alone, I wanted to create a community around me that would support the project from the get-go," Raanan says. "Despite my background with Sequoia and my ability to raise money from basically anywhere, I decided to raise funds from successful cyberentrepreneurs. At first I went to the people I knew best: Shlomo Kramer, Marius Nacht, Nir Zuk, Mickey Boodaei. I told them my story and their answer was: *we're in.* They understood the massive opportunity here: why did we need all these outside funds that kept calling us up and wanting stock in our funding rounds when we, the cyberentrepreneurs, were the ones bringing all the value? Cyberstarts is basically the cyberentrepreneurs' fund. We'll put down the first major check. We'll bring the knowledge of how to help entrepreneurs. We'll bring the connections and ability to hire people, and the whole set of our abilities, in an undiluted way," he adds, noting that cyberentrepreneurs invested in companies directly, without giving a cut to intervening funds. In time, I too became one of the fund's investors.

This new approach, so direct and typically Israeli, proved successful. "With American funds, I was used to meetings, PowerPoints, and follow-ups. You've got five Stanford grads there asking tons of great questions, but it all takes so long. With us, in a short, half-hour conversation you get the gist of it and can shift massive sums."

Raanan's third decision was to not charge management fees, but only *success* fees. "It's partly because the people I raised money from were friends, and I felt uncomfortable drawing a salary and taking money from friends. My thought was to place myself exactly in the entrepreneurs' shoes—if they made a profit, so did I. And if they didn't, I'd just worked for free for a few years.

"It's really rare in the venture capital world, and one of the things I was critical of in the standard model is that lots of funds don't end up with huge successes, but their partners become rich because of management fees. In my model, I'm the one facing the entrepreneurs, and it's clear to them that we're on the same page and my goal is exactly the same as theirs, namely—for the project to succeed." Some of the companies that Raanan has invested in have paid back his investment, big time. Among them are unicorns such as Wiz, Island, and Noname Security.

Dan Amiga, who founded Island, tells me how significant his choice of Cyberstarts was. "I wanted an Israeli investor," he tells me. "I'm in Israel and I want someone I can talk to in Hebrew and who's got experience. I really admire Gili and the experience he gained at Sequoia is priceless. There are hundreds of venture capital funds in our industry, but Sequoia's the absolute top."

Besides the most prominent investment funds, such as Cyberstarts, Team8, and Glilot Capital, other new funds have also decided to focus on the cybermarket. One of them is the venture capital fund YL Ventures, established in 2007 without an original focus on cybersecurity, but in time, it too decided to focus on this market.

Hyperwise Ventures was founded in 2020 by three entrepreneurs: Unit 8200 veterans Aviv Gafni and Ben Omelchenko, and veteran entrepreneur Nati Shuchami. In 2015, the three entrepreneurs had sold their cyberdefense business Hyperwise Security to Check Point, just a year and a half after founding it, for $80 million. Five years after this stunning exit, the trio decided to ride the cyber venture capital trend—and open up one of their own.

The well-trodden path

Those who've been in the cyberindustry for many years now look at its huge transformation with astonishment. Mickey Boodaei, a serial entrepreneur, looks at the dramatic shift with 20 years of hindsight. "Nowadays, the cyberworld's one of the easiest places to set things up, with cybersecurity funds. When Amichai and I went knocking at the old-school Israeli funds—some of them are still active—they threw us out. They didn't even want to talk to us about ideas that nowadays, I could raise 20 or 30 million dollars with a single slide. 'What's this cyber thing? What's information security? Bring us some e-commerce'— those were the usual reactions."

Shlomo Kramer expands on this point. "There's a new generation today," he says. "There are whole systems geared toward setting up cybercompanies. There's a highly organized plan, they've got CISOs talking to them, there's a playbook for setting up a company." The CISOs Kramer is referring to—chief information security officers—are the main buyers of cyberproducts, and the firm connection between them and venture capital funds helps dramatically to develop and market products, as we saw in the case of Cyberstarts. The playbook for launching startups, which investment funds share with entrepreneurs, is also extremely important, and their accumulated experience is critical to companies' success and targeted development.

Early-stage entrepreneurs usually make lots of mistakes, and cybersecurity funds know how to help them make fewer mistakes and put them on the best footing to start their companies. Funds also know which customers to call up and which introductions to make, and they also help entrepreneurs hire professional talent abroad—not necessarily top-notch engineers, but also experienced managers and salespeople, and anyone else their companies need.

There is already a standard playbook for founding a startup. At one of the companies I invested in recently, outside the cybersecurity sector, I found they'd already hired dozens of programmers and written tons of code before even meeting any customers. If they were a cybersecurity company, they would probably have followed the playbook of the investment funds in this sector and would have understood this was a serious mistake—because their product might have been fantastic, but totally unsuited to what the market actually needed.

Emmanuel Benzaquen notes the major shift of the past decade and a half: "We started with Checkmarx in 2006 using the bootstrap method. Even when we had a product and were starting to sell, we didn't raise money. Nowadays, companies that don't even have a thought-out idea are already raising money." Indeed, the norm now is to raise capital even before you have a product. After you raise capital, your investors will help you find design partners: customers who will present you the market's needs and help you fine-tune your product. Your first sales will have to be to these customers, and all this in the United States alone: not in Israel, and hardly at all in Europe. Entrepreneurs who do things in this order will stand better chances of success, and the knowledge that venture capital funds have introduced to the market is incredibly valuable.

But investment funds do so much more than hand down knowledge. Ofer Schreiber, who manages the Israeli office of the YL Ventures fund, explains: "Even experienced entrepreneurs know a very small number of information security managers. The cybersecurity sector is noisy and crowded, and customers are bombarded with offers from startups from every direction. Being able to count on an investment fund that knows everyone in the market is invaluable, especially at the early stages of a startup's life, when it needs constant input from customers to make sure its product suits the market and addresses a genuine need. Having someone join you for the ride who can deliver a huge potential customer base gives you a real boost."

Schreiber explains that when he performs due diligence on a company that wants investment, he always deals with five information security managers from each company, giving them inputs that often make them ditch their original ideas. "The entrepreneurs were really happy with this process because it cut down the time it took them to realize their idea was a bad fit. In a week and a half, they figured out something that would have taken them several months."

It was Gili Raanan who hammered home the importance of using customers to build the specifications of a new product, using a model at Cyberstarts that aimed to help entrepreneurs design products as quickly as possible in a speedy and rigorous process. It's called Sunrise. "I didn't invent the process, and I didn't come up with the name, either," Raanan admits. "It's a concept I knew from Sequoia. I get the sense they're still angry with me for 'stealing' their concept. Their insight was that your biggest opportunity to influence a project's strategic direction is in its first 60 days. Anything you'll be able to fix later will be much smaller. During this period, you've an opportunity to have an entrepreneur's ear and fix things, if there's even a need. Sequoia tells entrepreneurs: we can reach any person on earth, so write down the 20 most important people for your business. You want Eric Schmidt from Google? Elon Musk? You've got it. Two weeks later, you go to their office in Menlo Park [in Silicon Valley], sit there for a whole day, and every half hour, someone else from your list walks in. And so as an entrepreneur, you're sitting there for a day or two, in 10 or 15 meetings with your most significant potential customers. It always makes entrepreneurs change and rethink things."

Raanan decided to improve the Sunrise process. "It was a great process," he says, "but as someone who worked with it, I could also see its shortcomings. The main drawback: it takes a whole day, but to change thinking on a strategic level, it takes time for ideas to sink in. You need a breather between meetings. You need time to process and change direction. Second, as an entrepreneur, you're static there in Menlo Park, meaning many of your customers, who are very busy people, won't come. Silicon Valley types will come, but Credit Suisse's information systems manager won't fly out especially for a half-hour meeting in Menlo Park. As good as this process is, it won't give you enough input in terms of 'market pain' and what your customers need. That's why I created a different Sunrise mechanism."

Raanan set up a group of potential customers for cyberproducts, people he knew personally. These customers would meet entrepreneurs and right in the first meeting define the major problem in the target market and the "pain" that needs to be solved, and in the second meeting, they try to find the ideal solution to that problem. "This process allowed Cyberstarts' companies to reach the market quicker and more accurately—measurably so—than other companies. It let them reach major customers and succeed more than other companies."

Cyberstarts' approach to customers helped the companies it was investing in to reach some massive customers in no time. As Assaf Rappaport of Wiz says: "Usually with startups, you start with medium and small businesses, and then you make your way up, knocking the doors of the major companies. With Gili's Cyberstarts, you can take a shortcut straight to the top."[4]

Angel capital

If you're starting a business and applying to venture capital funds, you'll need to brace for disappointment and lots of rejections. But no worries, you might be able to go to a private investor who'll put his own money on a company he believes in—an angel investor. Angels also plan to turn a profit, but from this nickname, you can already tell that their motives are not exclusively financial.

I have already mentioned how Shulman helped us as an angel investor, not just with funding but also with good advice. I kept this lesson in mind even after we made our exit, when I decided to divert some of the money I had made from the sale to becoming an angel investor. I invested in five early-stage businesses, not all in the cybersector. My reasons for investing were largely personal: I wanted to learn from the paths that other entrepreneurs were making, and I wanted to give entrepreneurs who reminded me of myself advice and connections: opportunities that they could not always find the usual way. It's not easy to raise funds from established venture capital funds, and many entrepreneurs struggle to get past the series of tests that funds put them through in order to secure investment. Angel investors offer a bypass, a quicker and more personal route. Near the end of writing this book, I learned that one of the companies I had invested in—Cider Security—had been acquired by Palo Alto for $300 million. The happiness of a successful exit is so much more than a matter of money; you get a share in the founders' happiness and a huge feeling of satisfaction that something you believed in, cultivated, and invested in turned out to be so successful and valuable.

Sometimes these introductions with investors come from inside companies themselves. Dan Amiga, who founded Fireglass in 2013 and sold it to Symantec in 2017 for $250 million (and then went on to found the unicorn Island), shares his side of the story as an investor: "At Fireglass, something incredible happened: we were less than 20 people in Israel, and 5 or 6 companies came out of it. In 5 of them, I was the first investor, even before investment funds and long before the entrepreneurs even knew they wanted to be entrepreneurs. In one case, I called up one of my employees' dads, and I told him: your kid's ace, he needs to do this and set up a company."

Angels have proven hugely valuable for entrepreneurs in times when it is hard to convince major venture capital funds of their sectors' importance. The cybersecurity sector was only just starting to heat up in 2011, and although Glilot was set up that year, the field was still a strange unknown for the older funds. That was when Michael Shaulov and three friends from Unit 8200 founded Lacoon Security, which developed security products for cell phones. "Venture capital funds told us, 'Cyber? There's no such thing. You're not getting our money,' and then I reached Shlomo," Shaulov tells me, recalling his company's beginnings. By "Shlomo," of course, he means Shlomo Kramer, who was already an angel investor and major personality in the cybersector.

How do you get to Shlomo Kramer? You leverage connections. "At first, I tried to reach him through a contact I had at NICE Systems, but he didn't get back to me. Then I asked my best friend to send a message through his best friend from Unit 81, who'd worked with Shlomo at Imperva. Shlomo got back to me and we arranged to talk." Kramer sent Shaulov to Mickey Boodaei, and a month after meeting, they had already signed an investment term sheet. Kramer invested $2.5 million in the "Check Point of cell phones," as the media called it at the time. This investment turned out to be extremely profitable in 2015, when Lacoon Security was sold to Check Point for $100 million.

Shaulov then decided to invest in young startups, one of which was Armis Security. His involvement as an angel investor went way beyond money. "There's one case I remember clearly," says Shaulov. "In 2016, Armis found a crazy information vulnerability with Bluetooth. They tried to get into Black Hat to present it, but they didn't get accepted." Black Hat Briefings, one of the biggest cyberconferences in the world, brings together cyberdefense experts from all around the world to learn about all the latest innovations in their industry. A Bluetooth vulnerability is a serious issue because it could allow hackers to break into any computer or smartphone. These are precisely the things that get lots of attention at Black Hat, but the proposal that Armis' founders sent in still got rejected. Shaulov tried to understand what exactly had happened, and Yevgeny Dibrov, its cofounder, showed him the proposal they had submitted. "I looked at their proposal and I could have fainted," he says. "The headline was extremely technical. I told Dibrov, change the heading! Write something like: 'New Bluetooth Vulnerability Exposes Every Device in the World to Hacking!'" This good advice helped: the reworded proposal was accepted and caused shockwaves at the conference. Thousands of people downloaded their app, and Armis Security reached dozens of new customers.

As we saw in Chapter 7, Lior Div, Yonatan Amit, and Yossi Naar also struggled in the beginning to find funding through the usual channels. In January 2012 they decided to start a company to deal with the cyberthreats that were starting to pop up and would develop a platform to offer a flexible response. "Lots of Israeli VC funds gave us a cold shoulder," Div says.

Sometimes entrepreneurs get sent to angel investors by the venture capital funds that refused to invest in them. Aviv Gafni, a co-founder of Hyperwise, recalls how he and his partner Ben Omelchenko reached investors in 2013: "After a few ideas for startups in different fields, we decided to go for cyberdefense. We went on vacation in Thailand and from there decided to send emails to funds. One of those that answered was Lightspeed." Lightspeed, a U.S. fund that opened an Israel office in 2006, did not specialize in cybercompanies but invited the entrepreneurs in for a meeting anyway.

"We showed up without a PowerPoint," Aviv says. "Dudu [Gossarsky, one of the two managers of the Israel office] said: 'I just met with Mickey Boodaei. I don't come from the cyberworld, but Mickey's one of the leading guys in the country. Want to talk to him?'" Boodaei, Gafni recalls, helped them narrow down their idea, and once they cracked the concept that would soon underpin their company, everything quickly fell into place. The idea was to scan computers for malware by checking the activities of their processors and whether they were operating any processes that should not have been running. "Mickey loved it, and by the next day, he sent us to Shlomo [Kramer], who also loved the idea. Rakesh [Loonkar] also got on board." Their third partner, Nati Shuchami, got to them through Shlomo Kramer, who had just met with him. "We clicked from our first conversation, and we're still working together," says Aviv. As we saw, Hyperwise made a rapid exit, and the trio soon set up their own cyber-oriented venture capital fund.

International corporations

"I didn't want to develop just another solution," I hear from Michal Braverman-Blumenstyk, explaining why she decided against founding her own company, "but to be the one who planned a comprehensive solution." In 2003, Braverman-Blumenstyk joined Cyota, founded by Naftali Bennett, who would later become Israel's prime minister, as its chief operating officer. Cyota developed solutions to combat cyberfraud and became the first company in the world to find a way to track and take down phishing sites designed to make people hand over their credit card details. After Cyota was sold to RSA, an American company, for $145 million, Braverman-Blumenstyk became the CEO of its Israel office. But Microsoft kept chasing her, and in 2013 she decided to accept its advances and fly to the United States to meet its CEO, Satya Nadella.

Back then, Microsoft was not yet involved in developing and selling cyberproducts, and most of its business was about securing its own products. When Nadella asked Braverman-Blumenstyk to move to the United States to help launch Microsoft's cyberoperations, she insisted that it should all be set up in Israel. "I explained that Israel had an edge when it came to cybersecurity. Where else in the world do so many international companies have cybercenters?" Microsoft was convinced, and Braverman-Blumenstyk was given the mission of building

Microsoft's cyberproduct development center in Israel. She is now the CTO of Microsoft Security, Corporate Vice President at Microsoft Corporation, and general manager of its Israeli R&D center.

Six of the 10 biggest non-Israeli cybercompanies in the world have R&D centers in Israel. So do several software giants, including AT&T, Dell-EMC, IBM, and Cisco, which are all developing cyberdefense solutions in Israel. These centers have become an important element of the emerging ecosystem in Israel that has cultivated its cyberindustry. Microsoft's R&D center, for example, has grown by more than 60% since Braverman-Blumenstyk entered the job, employing over 2,000 workers, including almost 1,000 in the field of cybersecurity.

Global corporations are used to opening R&D centers around the world, outside the United States, but usually for cost-saving reasons. One of their favorite places, for example, is India because they can find excellent software engineers there who are much cheaper than in the United States. In this context, their choice of Israel, and especially Tel Aviv, where most R&D centers are based, is far from obvious. It costs more than $180,000 to hire an experienced software engineer in Tel Aviv, more than in most cities in the United States, including Dallas and New York, and close to what it costs in San Francisco, the most expensive place in the United States to hire software engineers.[5] But companies are still opening R&D centers in Israel because the quality of the manpower there justifies the high costs.

From start-up nation to exit nation

Making an exit—selling your startup to a large corporation—is in many respects the dream of every Israeli entrepreneur. Most entrepreneurs don't start out planning to set up a global corporation that will push ahead independently forever, and for them, success means selling their startups for huge sums to some big international corporation. The presence of so many global corporations' R&D centers in Israel has a real effect on this "exit dream."

When RSA acquired Cyota, it effectively turned it into an R&D center—and it is not alone. When Microsoft acquired Adallom in July 2015, Assaf Rappaport became the head of its cloud security division. Just three years later, the Israeli cyberworld was shocked to learn that Rappaport would head Microsoft's R&D center in Israel, despite his youth (he was 35) and the fact he was relatively new there. In fact,

Rappaport leapfrogged over Michal Braverman-Blumenstyk, who only got the job after he left in February 2021.

"Microsoft made a strategic decision to get into the cyberdefense sector through acquisitions, and all those acquisitions are happening in Israel," Rappaport explains in a conversation with me. "Once Microsoft's got a center in Israel, it'll always be easier for it to snap up Israeli companies, even if they're a bit less good than other companies somewhere else in the world. The critical mass is key." In other words, the snowball effect exists here, too.

Corporations that have already built infrastructures in Israel—that have already acquired Israeli companies; use Israeli suppliers; and are familiar with Israel's laws, culture, and unusual calendar—will find it much easier to snap up more companies and attach them to their existing research centers. The employees of companies that get acquired will also find the transition easier because they will be greeted by fellow Israelis who can help them acclimatize. It's easier to integrate somewhere where others understand your language and culture, can identify with your difficulties, and can meet you face to face when you start working there.

What most people don't know about the "exit dream" is that around 70%–90% of acquisitions fail because merging two companies is a painful process.[6] In many cases, they fail because the corporation just can't absorb the startup without frictions emerging. Employees who chose to work for Adallom, for example, and suddenly woke up to find they worked for Microsoft without anyone asking them, found it harder to take instructions from managers they didn't know and hadn't chosen to work for. For corporations, acquiring companies in places where they already have a presence can mitigate these risks and seriously contribute to the chances of the acquisition succeeding. When acquisitions can cost anything from tens to hundreds of millions of dollars, obviously corporations prefer not to gamble such sums, and the desire to buy companies that can coexist with existing R&D centers is understandable.

One of the biggest R&D centers in Israel belongs to Palo Alto Networks, the U.S. company founded by Nir Zuk. In recent years, it has acquired no fewer than eight Israeli cybercompanies, basing its R&D center in Israel around them. But it has not stopped at this and has worked hard to expand its R&D center, taking it up to 800 employees. "You can develop cybertechnologies anywhere in the world, but in Israel, you can develop them quicker," Zuk tells me. "There are good engineers all around the world, but most of them are concentrated in Silicon Valley and Tel Aviv."

Another point about acquisitions becomes clear in my conversation with Zuk: when a corporation acquires a startup, it gains not only new products and technologies, but also opportunities to recruit talent quickly. In the Israeli hi-tech market there is intense competition for skilled workers, especially engineers, and so it is very hard to hire a large workforce in a short time. When Rapid7 acquired IntSights, it immediately added 50 Israeli R&D staff to its team. Had it tried to recruit them one by one, it would have taken it at least two years.

"In short," says Rappaport, "Microsoft will prefer Israel to San Francisco." San Francisco is its own brand in the hi-tech world, the biggest city in Silicon Valley, just a two-hour flight away and no time zone difference away from Microsoft's global HQ in Redmond; nevertheless, when it comes to cyberdefense, Microsoft will prefer to acquire a company in Israel—because of the excellent manpower there, but also because as soon as it established an R&D center in Israel, it became easier to buy and absorb new companies.

Global corporations have very deep pockets and a massive appetite for acquisitions. For many startups, which the market is unwilling to embrace as standalone products, the only way to declare success is to get acquired. Corporations are looking for good companies capable of reaching the finish line of making an exit without stagnating or failing and closing down. These acquisitions create phenomenal returns for investors and entrepreneurs, and generally contribute to the industry's success. This success draws in even more investors, entrepreneurs, and employees, who go on to found Israel's next cyberdefense companies and get bought out. Global corporations have thus become key to the success stories of the Israeli cyberindustry—and that snowball keeps rolling.

Importing knowledge

"The difference between Adallom and Wiz is Microsoft," says Rappaport confidently. Not that Adallom wasn't successful: it was acquired by Microsoft for hundreds of millions of dollars in no time, even before it had a massive customer base or revenues, but Wiz was a whole new order of success. It hit unicorn status in less than two years, and in August 2022, it smashed a world record when its annual revenues shot up from $1 million to $100 million in 18 months flat. By then, just two and a half years after launching, Wiz already had close to 500 employees. Its founders were able to build a company on such a scale largely thanks to the knowledge and experience that Rappaport amassed at Microsoft.

When startups get acquired, one of the conditions that their founders usually accept is called a "holdback." What this mechanism means is that the entrepreneurs receive a certain cut of the sale—usually 20%–40% of the sum, spread over two to four years—only on condition they stay at the acquiring company for a certain time. Its main purpose is to ensure that the startup's senior management will help out as their company gets absorbed, but founders provide even more added value by sticking around: they are usually their companies' life force and leadership, and if they quit, their employees might follow. This mechanism is supposed to ensure that startups get absorbed smoothly, and their employees integrated successfully into the acquiring corporation.

Most founders stick around for the minimum time required and quit as quickly as possible. The bureaucracy of a large corporation can be annoying and frustrating for people used to doing business quickly. Mickey Boodaei, who together with his partner Rakesh Loonkar sold Trusteer to IBM for $800 million in 2013, is an extreme case. "We managed to agree with IBM that Rakesh and I would stick around for only three months," he tells me. "They were anxious to close and agreed to this condition, and that's what happened: after three months, we just left." Boodaei, a serial and speedy entrepreneur, didn't like how things were done at the huge company that bought him out. "On our second or third day at IBM, someone came over from the IT Department and told us we had to close our Gmail accounts and switch to IBM's Lotus Notes. I told them, as far as I'm concerned, you can set up forwarding from my Gmail—I'm not touching that thing."

Rappaport took a similar approach when he started at Microsoft, but as we have seen, he soon changed tack. "We insisted on staying no more than two years," he tells me with a smile, "but in the end, I stayed for five. I got to know a different culture from what I was used to, and I got to build a business on a massive scale. Taking a business of a few million dollars and bringing it to a place of hundreds of millions of users and billions in sales in less than five years—that's a whole other kind of excitement."

Working for a global company is not only exciting, but also a formative experience that can teach entrepreneurs how to go about building a large company or running a massive sales operation and huge client base. Unlike startups, corporations have lots of employees, and therefore, need many more communication mechanisms so that everyone can know the company's strategy. Likewise, the executives at a small company know all its customers and can give them personal attention, whereas in large companies, this is simply impossible, and managers have to ensure that whoever works with customers goes through proper training to understand the company's products and how to make its customers satisfied. These are just a few examples, but these different modes of operation are clear in nearly every aspect of management. That's how an entrepreneur like Rappaport, who gained management experience at a massive corporation, could leave with new skills and go on to found a company that would break the world record of time taken to hit $100 million in revenues.

This is not just about management. When it comes to engineering, R&D centers also have an advantage because they develop whole products, instead of being responsible for developing just a small part of another product, like many startups do. "Palo Alto's center here is creating whole new products, not just parts of a product ('features') for the center in the United States. Such centers are good for the industry," Nir Zuk explains. "Once you've got to build a product that works and gets sold, and it's all on you, it's different from working at a big company and developing some small feature that doesn't affect its bottom line."

R&D centers that make their employees take responsibility for entire products teach them the full picture of product development and management, including getting to know the competition, building a long-term strategy, and pitching comprehensive products to salespeople and customers. Since corporations usually make their strategic decisions to open cybersecurity R&D centers in Israel based on an appreciation of its human capital, they trust their Israeli employees to promote their products from end to end. When they eventually leave these corporations, these employees leave with rich experience in product development—experience they take with them to any other company they work for.

Living the good life?

When you walk into the new building of Microsoft's Israel R&D center, you immediately see the innovative layout, planned by some of the best architects and interior designers. In front of the entrance is a huge cafeteria with health snacks, fruit shakes, and a free coffee bar for workers, staffed by a barista who'll make your coffee however you like it. Besides the pampering work environment, Microsoft's employees are also entitled to terms that colleagues at other Israeli companies can only dream of. Mothers, for example, receive 10 months' paid maternity leave, and fathers receive three full weeks.

International corporations come under criticism for their Israeli operations. One point of criticism is about their investments in recruiting talent, which is one of the biggest challenges for Israeli cybercompanies. Corporations are willing to pay extremely high salaries for quality manpower in Israel—paychecks that young startups simply cannot compete with. The other perks that come with working for global corporations are also extraordinary.

Barak Perelman, who along with two partners founded Indegy, which developed a cyberdefense solution for large-scale industrial systems, describes his experience of selling his startup to an American corporation: "They gave our employees benefits we didn't have at Indegy," Barak tells me, "six weeks' paid parental leave for both moms and dads, an extra vacation day as a birthday present, and eight days off in the summer. We were already in top-end offices, but I assume if that weren't the case, we'd have gotten an upgrade." Thus, by the same token that one can argue that the cyberindustry is depleting the IDF's stocks of brains and skilled manpower, the international industry, with its bottomless pockets, can also be seen as hurting local startups.

But startups have so much more to offer workers beyond money and benefits. They invite their employees to be partners in building a company from scratch. Their employees play a role in fulfilling a dream of protecting organizations from attacks that until they got involved had no solution, and in developing new technologies that did not previously exist. This all adds a deep sense of meaning that is hard to emulate at a major corporation. The intense and stressful work often creates powerful personal connections and a sense of excitement that does not exist in any other workplace. In terms of perks, startups can offer stock options, potential shares of the company, and if it succeeds, those shares will be worth so much more when the business gets acquired or has an IPO. Options, as we have seen, offer an advantage because they are taxed at just 25%, while normal shares are taxed at anywhere between 25%–50%.[7] Bottom line, startups can still compete with the local offices of international corporations in the battle for excellent manpower.

On the other hand, as Shlomo Kramer has said, there are probably too many startups in Israel, and the competition with global corporations has created a mechanism that filters out the weakest companies. The best entrepreneurs can recruit the best workers by raising even more capital or convincing candidates of the advantages of their project, and the less promising projects will naturally wilt.

From the perspective of hi-tech employees, they definitely benefit from this rise in standards, but they are not alone. These high standards are trickling down to hi-tech companies, which have to meet the same conditions in order to retain their employees, such that everyone working in the sector benefits.

The global corporations setting up R&D centers in Israel are therefore important players in the unique emergent ecosystem in Israel. Israel's human capital is what attracts these companies to Israel, and these, in turn, import specialist knowledge, boost the startup sector's prosperity as potential buyers, and create collaborations that push these startups forward, even if to some extent they also constitute competition for the same talent. No doubt, the Israeli industry would have looked completely different if Israel had not become, as Assaf Rappaport puts it, an attractive alternative to San Francisco.

When Israel gains kudos

When Check Point was still in its infancy, its founders hired a consultant from Boston to help them find the first customers who would agree to install their product. The consultant gave them a tip that Kramer has never forgotten: "Don't say you're an Israeli company. Speak English, so they'll think you're American."

That was in the 1990s, before the wave of terror attacks of the early 2000s, but also long before Israel was known as a high-quality incubator for cybercompanies. The consultant understood that Israel was perceived as a tiny country that people only ever visited to see places where Jesus walked, and not exactly as a producer of high-end cybersecurity products. He assumed that customers would feel more at ease buying from an American company. "Nowadays, when I'm in a meeting in Tokyo with a customer," Kramer tells me, "his interpreter opens with the sentence, 'They're an Israeli cybercompany, so they must be serious.' Today—Israel is a brand name."

Mickey Boodaei also points out this huge shift, in such a short timeframe: "When we set up Trusteer in 2006, our Israeli identity was a problem we had to deal with. The fact we were an Israeli company, not an American one, was considered a disadvantage. With Transmit Security, which was set up in 2014, it was the complete opposite: being Israeli was suddenly an advantage."

I have already charted Israel's transformation from a country that entrepreneurs tried to avoid mentioning to a strong global brand, in Chapter 7. Nowadays, many customers understand the unique advantage of the Israeli ecosystem and prefer products from Israel. In most target markets for Israeli companies—including North America, South America, Western Europe, Southeast Asia, and Australia—Israel is a brand that opens doors. The exceptions are states that have not normalized relations with Israel, although even there, Israelis sell their products through intermediaries. We sold IntSights' product to a bank in a Gulf state that has no relations in Israel at all, through an Indian partner. They probably knew that the product they'd bought was from Israel, but as long as they weren't in direct contact with us, they had no problem protecting their company with a Made in Israel product. It is possible that the Israeli brand name was an advantage, even indirectly, without the customer admitting it.

The strength of the Israeli brand plays to the benefit of offensive cybercompanies as much as cyberdefense entrepreneurs. Even though Israeli companies are routinely slandered by the media and human rights organizations, their dominance in the field is undisputed, as we saw in previous chapters. Customers around the world see Israel as the ultimate center for the development of offensive cybersolutions, letting Israeli companies overcome the hurdles for massive sales even in countries that do not have diplomatic relations with Israel, such as Saudi Arabia and other Gulf nations.

Before founding his offensive cybercompany, Toka, Alon Kantor was high up at Check Point. "I saw that everyone wanted to be like Israel," he says, and he decided to hit the road with this trump card. That was his cue to go and found an offensive cybercompany that would bring Israeli capabilities to more states. "There are very few countries with cybercapabilities," he says. "It's the future, and there are hardly any players in this market."

Customers and investors are not the only believers in the Made in Israel brand. Global distributors of cybersecurity solutions also admire Israeli technology and are happy to sell it. When we set out with IntSights, it was clear to us that we would focus on the U.S. market first and then expand to Western Europe. Asian states were not our top priority; we knew the languages and cultures were completely different, so we preferred to leave them to later. Around two years after we set up the company, we got a call from the Israeli representative of Asgent, one of the biggest cyberdefense product distributors in Japan, which has been working with Check Point for years and is one of its most powerful Japanese partners. "The CEO of Asgent is planning to visit Check Point's HQ in Israel," the representative told us, "and he wants to meet you too and explore options to work together." We were not thinking about selling to Japan at the time, but this would be an opportunity to learn about the Japanese market and to explore the possibility of having a distributor sell our product in the Land of the Rising Sun.

The Japanese executive, Takahiro Sugimoto, came to our offices after visiting Check Point's sprawling headquarters. He is a highly respected businessman in Japan, with an impressive demeanor, and he came escorted by someone whose every twitch and glance showed his huge respect for him. I was a little embarrassed when I took them to our tiny offices in Herzliya and we all squeezed into a boardroom that could barely fit six people, around a table from Ikea. None of this put Takahiro off. "We have been working with Check Point since they started and we know what it means to work with Israeli startups," he explained. "We are one of the biggest distributors in Japan, and we would be happy to start a process of considering your product." I was struck by the serious look on his face when he said this, and it made me understand even more the power of the Made in Israel brand.

You'd struggle to find a wider cultural chasm than between Israel and Japan. The Japanese are calculated, introverted, self-disciplined perfectionists. Israelis are blunt, trust their intuitions, and are always cutting corners to reach their goals quickly. You might think that these differences would deter the Japanese from doing business with Israeli startups, but they have learned through experience how to work with Israelis and even to prefer collaborating with them over cyberprofessionals from other countries. Asgent's representatives persuaded us that they could work with Israelis easily and led us into a partnership that culminated with IntSights entering the Japanese market.

"Israel is one of our advantages"

The story that perhaps best illustrates best the synergy between Israel's global reputation, venture capital funds, and the desire of international corporations to open centers in Israel, as well as the importance of connecting all these to the ecosystem of the Israeli cyberindustry, is the story of UST Global. This giant U.S. corporation has operations in 30 countries and 30,000 employees around the world. UST Global provided IT services to companies using manpower based mainly in India. With rising demand for cyberdefense products and services, its executives decided to expand into the cyberdefense business and to set up a subsidiary to provide cyberdefense services to customers. The mission fell to one of UST's executives, by the name of Tony Velleca.

Tony was friendly with David Blumberg, the founder and managing partner of Blumberg Capital in San Francisco. Blumberg was personally familiar with the Israeli cyberindustry and its latent potential, ever since he invested in Check Point in its early stages and effectively led its commercial development for a while. Later on, he had invested in even more Israeli cybercompanies, including Cyvera, and IntSights. "David taught me that the best of the best in the security field come from Israel and from Unit 8200," Velleca tells me. Blumberg took him on a visit to Israel, to learn more about cybertechnology. "I was really surprised by the number of startups," he recalls. "Everyone was so full of passion and really well funded. Everyone was looking to do something different." He imagined that many people were having similar thoughts about Israel, and that is exactly what soon became clear.

This visit pushed Velleca to decide to set up his company's global headquarters in Israel, of all places. It was a highly unusual decision. Manpower is much cheaper in India than in Israel, and the obvious move would have been to expand the Indian operations and supply cybersecurity services from there. But Velleca was captivated by the Israeli ecosystem and believed that its added value would compensate for the high employment costs. The new center—CyberProof—was founded in Israel, but Velleca did not stop there. Knowing the unique character and talents of Israelis, he decided that his company's services would be based mainly on the products of Israeli cybercompanies. This offered a twofold advantage: both connections to groundbreaking products and technologies, and also physical proximity between CyberProof's employees and counterparts at Israeli companies. This proximity allowed CyberProof to maintain close relations with these companies and quickly communicate their requests for product upgrades. CyberProof opened an office in the Azrieli Towers, within a two-mile radius of the leading cyber startups and companies in Israel. One of the companies that started collaborating with CyberProof was IntSights. Even after IntSights got acquired by Rapid7, CyberProof still remains in close contact with the company's R&D workers, selling IntSights' product for hundreds of thousands of dollars a year.

"We chose Israel because we wanted to do something different, innovative, and disruptive," says Velleca. "The fact we're in Israel is one of our advantages against competitors, and it boosts our chances of selling services." CyberProof came to Israel because of its reputation and because of the connections of a certain venture capital fund manager, and it is leveraging Israel as a brand to boost its own sales. There are many other partners like it around the world, which recognize the uniqueness of Israeli companies and cyberdefense products and give them priority over others. For their part, Israeli startups are leveraging this to create collaborations at record speed, which translates into even quicker access to customers, including in markets where they have no physical presence. That's the snowball effect in operation.

Cybertourism

Since time immemorial, the Holy Land has attracted visitors from overseas. Every year, Israel welcomes planeloads of pilgrims and tourists, along with relatives from overseas coming to visit their families. But with the rise of the Israeli cyberindustry, a new form of incoming tourism emerged: cybertourism.

When I speak with Mickey Boodaei, it is clear that, for him, this phenomenon epitomizes the evolution of the Israeli cyberbrand: "Who even heard of CISOs coming to the Holy Land to learn about cybersecurity 10 years ago?" he asks. CISOs (chief information security officers) at major companies are the cybersecurity industry's main customers. Basically anyone who develops a cyberproduct will aim to sell to them. But instead of having to knock on their doors, the opposite is happening in Israel because CISOs from all over the world are now going there to learn about the latest developments in the field and find new products that can answer their organizations' challenges.

Israel plays host to popular conferences that attract cyberexperts from all over the planet. One of them is Cyber Week, an annual conference at Tel Aviv University with around 9,000 attendees. Cybertech, also in Tel Aviv, is even bigger and attracts close to 20,000 participants, showcasing over 200 companies. These events are attended by industry leaders from all levels and roles, from Israel and abroad, and even the prime minister of Israel plays a starring role, with a keynote speech. During these conferences, it is normal to see information security officers from the world's biggest companies taking turns to sit and talk with Israeli entrepreneurs, offering them products and deals.

There are bigger and more important conferences around the world than those in Israel—by way of comparison, the biggest cyber gathering is the RSA Conference, which attracts over 40,000 people— but these are still major events, attracting huge audiences and global industry leaders. Especially relative to Israel's size and distance from the massive U.S. market, these events are huge.

Perhaps even more important than what happens at these conferences is what happens on their sidelines. Information security managers take advantage of their stay in Israel to visit Israeli startups that pique their interest. Meanwhile, their evenings become filled with networking events, where they're able to meet local entrepreneurs and explore opportunities for working together. It's a win-win for everyone involved: information security managers can glimpse the most cutting-edge technologies and learn how to protect their organizations from the latest kinds of attacks. Israeli entrepreneurs and companies, meanwhile, can meet new potential customers, who have come all the way to their front door in huge numbers, and create opportunities for lucrative deals.

This kind of tourism opened significant doors for us at IntSights. Besides Asgent's CEO visiting Israel from Japan on a targeted business trip, we also met a representative of a global company who visited Israel with the aim of meeting as many entrepreneurs and discovering as many solutions as possible.

In October 2019, I received an email from Nofar Amikam at Glilot Capital Partners, our first investors: "Ford Israel wants to hear about IntSights." Ford is a massive company, which any entrepreneur would be thrilled to add to their customer base, and I arranged a meeting with Gilad Barzilay from its Israel office. Barzilay had just finished working at Argus, an Israeli cybercompany that focused on automotive cybersecurity, and he had moved to Ford in order to help them find innovative cybertechnologies that would help them protect their organization and components from cyberattacks. "Ford's global information security manager is coming to Israel," he told me, "and we want him to hear about IntSights. We believe he'll be interested in your product, and this is your chance to highlight your unique value and convince him he needs it." Barzilay and I started talking and exchanging messages on a daily basis, prepping for the visit.

About a month later, Ford's global information security manager landed in Israel. The trip's coordinators had set up a "speed-dating" session for him with Israeli entrepreneurs, who were each allocated 15 minutes. I walked into the room all excited, humbled by the occasion. He was sitting on a sofa next to his deputy, and after a quick get-to-know-you, he told me, "Please begin." I started telling him about the unique intelligence alerts we could provide and about how we not only detected threats but also knew how to deal with them. When I was done, he asked me a few questions and then turned to his deputy and said, "When we get back from this trip, reach out to IntSights and look into whether this could fit." I couldn't have hoped for a better ending. With this executive interested in our company, and with some help from Barzilay, we managed to move ahead with Ford. The company loved our unique advantage and eventually became one of IntSights' biggest customers.

This visit by Ford's global information security manager to Israel was nothing unusual. Information security managers from all over the world visit Israel regularly to check out interesting startups and think about how they can use them to boost their organizations' information security. "Speed dating" is one model that lets them meet and be introduced to tons of companies. Other visitors prefer to go to companies' offices because that lets them have longer meetings with each company and to get down to details about their products, and it also lets them get a feel for the workforce and atmosphere in the office.

In the cyberworld, customers and suppliers see each other as partners and share a goal of creating the best possible cyberdefense product together. The hi-tech company remains open to listening and improving its product, while the customer is able to enjoy a high-quality product that keeps improving in line with its needs. By visiting their potential partners' offices, customers can get to know them better before deciding to make a commitment and buy their product.

This influx of visiting cybersecurity leaders is a huge asset for Israeli companies. Israel is at an inherent disadvantage as a small market, a fact that forces its companies to focus on bigger, faraway markets. Cybertourism brings these distant markets closer to Israel and gives Israelis opportunities to meet their customers face to face. This direct communication improves Israelis' abilities to compete with massive companies in their target markets and to rope in major customers and partners who would otherwise be very hard to reach. And international visitors catch an unmediated glimpse of Israel's strong points: a crowded market where everyone knows everyone, companies that are all close to each other, excellent human capital, the presence of global corporations, high-quality venture capital funds, and technological developments that justify Israel's incredible global reputation.

The cyberstate: The secret sauce

Let's imagine you're a state or an island somewhere in the world, watching in astonishment as Israel plants its flag at the top of the global cyberindustry. You want to gauge the reasons for Israel's success, either because you want to emulate it or simply out of curiosity. What have we learned so far?

We have learned that the military's technological units, which pump skilled and talented workers into the private sector, play a pivotal role in the Israeli cyberindustry. Their work is based on conscript soldiers performing time-limited service because only thus can the army both select the best candidates and also release them into the private sector in a few short years. Civilian spy agencies that have to compete with the rest of the market, without conscription, and then retain their staff are less useful for building an industry.

The state can help with a beneficial tax regime, encouragement for new sources of capital, and political support, but any more active attempt to steer the industry is unlikely to succeed. The role of academia in fostering cyberinnovation is limited, but it does play a key role in educating participants in the army's advanced programs and training engineers for work in the industry.

We have learned that Israeli culture and the "Jewish genius" have made a significant contribution to the industry's success. The emphasis on education and challenging conventional wisdom, the appetite for hard work, and the blunt and straight-talking approach have only helped.

But none of this is enough. Something needs to trigger a snowball effect: one company that makes it big and sweeps the whole market along with it. A company whose employees will go on to set up their own businesses and pump more and more capital into the industry. Combined, these factors will attract capital (both local and international) and encourage international companies to flood your market with even more knowledge and contacts with foreign customers and investors. This positive feedback loop will intensify even more when your country's reputation for excellence gives your emerging cyberindustry an even bigger boost.

If you can put all these conditions in place, you will probably be on the right track to developing one the most advanced cyberindustries in the world.

Conclusion: Where Is Everything Going?

One of the best engineers who worked for us at IntSights was a brilliant and promising guy, whom I hoped would one day join the company's management. He was earning around 30,000 NIS ($8,700) a month and seemed to be satisfied. One day he walked up to his manager, Amir Hozez, and said he was quitting because a rival company had offered him 42,000 NIS ($12,200). "I know I'm not worth that much," he admitted, "but if they're offering, why shouldn't I take it?"

"This story illustrates what employers were going through during the times of plenty in 2021," Hozez tells me. "Cheap money and competition for talent sent the whole industry into a frenzy."

Bring me people: The challenge of human capital

The future of the Israeli cyberindustry looks promising, but just as it can continue soaring, it can also lose altitude. Throughout this book, we have discussed the many factors that have pushed the Israeli cyberindustry ahead. The most important and fundamental factor behind Israel's success appears to be the high-quality human capital in the country.

Israeli culture and the IDF's technological units produce a large share of the talented entrepreneurs we have seen here, and they also provide a springboard for the engineers and other highly capable workers who have become the backbone of the industry. It is this human capital that attracts investors and gives them the confidence to invest in Israeli companies; it is this human capital that pushes international corporations to decide to acquire Israeli companies or set up their own global R&D centers in Israel despite the high cost of manpower. The people working in this industry are the ambassadors who build its reputation, and ultimately, lead the development of the products and innovation coming out of Israel. "What feeds an ecosystem? Human capital. You've got to invest hard in human capital because that's what everything gets built on," emphasizes Michal Braverman-Blumenstyk, the general manager of Microsoft's research and development center in Israel.

When I ask serial cyberentrepreneur Shlomo Kramer about threats to the industry's future, the first thing he notes is the need for quality people. "That's the glass ceiling of Israeli hi-tech," he says. "There's plenty of money. In 2021, more money was poured into here than the whole of the previous decade, but you need people." Nir Zuk, founder of the successful Palo Alto Networks, agrees with Kramer's insight. It was Zuk, as we recall, who pointed out that Check Point triggered the snowball effect that has produced a whole booming industry. "This snowball will stop rolling only if we run out of talent here," he says. "Even now, it's hard to hire manpower. There's a shortage of talent." This concern about Israel's limited supply of people gets raised by many of the people I interviewed for this book, and it is hard to find anyone who would dispute that this is the main danger to the continued growth of the Israeli cybersecurity sector—but not just this sector of the industry.

In my six years at IntSights, as someone who ran recruitment and managed a workforce of over 200 people, I personally experienced the huge difficulty that everyone is talking about. Hiring a top-level engineer can take months; for every candidate there is intense competition, and recruiters have to launch whole campaigns to persuade them that they are the best place to work. In those six years, paychecks just kept getting bigger. Employees who were on a certain salary at the start felt within a year or two that they were getting much less than they could fetch elsewhere. The employees themselves are, of course, happy when their salaries keep rising, and the state is also happy to rake in more taxes, but this is a clear symptom of a manpower shortage that is only getting worse. "The most painful thing is the shortage of quality Israeli manpower," says Assaf Rappaport, founder of Wiz and Adallom. "The supply of talent isn't growing relative to the amount of money getting poured in."

Gil Shwed, co-founder of Check Point, agrees. "The amount of talent is limiting our ability to succeed," he admits, but emphasizes that there are two sides to this coin: "This ceiling, this limitation, is also an advantage. It would be a huge mistake to think that if we chuck more resources at the problem, it'll solve itself. The trick is to find the right balance. When you've got limited resources, you've got to use them wisely; you've got to be creative." As we saw earlier, a crisis can also create a competitive advantage. Israel's advanced army and successful defense and technology industries emerged because of a tangible threat to the country's existence.

The fact that Israel's local cybermarket is so small has become an advantage in that it has forced Israeli entrepreneurs to think globally from day one. Shwed believes that it is exactly this manpower shortage that is forcing Israelis to be more creative in recruiting and managing manpower, squeezing maximum productivity and efficiency out of the existing labor supply.

Another positive side effect is the element of natural selection. As we shall soon see, many in the industry believe that there is no justification for the huge number of Israeli cybercompanies. One extreme example is the field of cloud security: Israeli cyberentrepreneurs have founded no fewer than eight separate companies, and that's even before we count the non-Israeli companies. This is not a particularly big niche, with space for no more than three major companies. The rest will probably all disappear or get acquired by bigger players, but this process also takes time. Employees, talented as they may be, cannot know in advance what the future holds for their companies and whether they are on a firm footing. They do not have access to all their data, nor do they have any efficient way of comparing companies' performances. Therefore, even if this process is inevitable, it can take a long time, and in this time, the best companies, which need manpower in order to grow, will get slowed down.

As we have seen, one of the main sources of talent in Israel's cyberindustry is the IDF's technological units. These units, of which Unit 8200 is the largest and most important, produce a constant stream of military veterans who can then find work in the industry. This stream has intensified as these units have grown, but it simply cannot catch up with the growth of the market. In theory, it might be possible to recruit more soldiers into these units, thus helping more people find work in the industry, but the technological units do not exist to serve the growth of the Israeli hi-tech market. They have a mission: to defend the State of Israel. They have a duty to fulfill this mission, and to do so in the best way possible.

Israel Grimberg, a former high-ranking commander in Unit 8200 and founding partner of Team8, which founds and invests in cyber-companies, is blunt about the situation: "We [in the unit] get judged by whether we win or lose a war, not whether we influence the industry. That's 100% a side effect" he makes clear to me when we meet to discuss the issue. Grimberg is also referring to Unit 8200's plans that highlight its social role and seek to integrate more sections of the population into the IDF's technological units, which he sees as hugely important, but emphasizes that it's important not to flip the pyramid. These units require manpower to meet their operational needs; they do not exist to serve as cyber-training schools for the private sector. If the military loses focus, it can end up wasting vital resources and damaging its supreme mission: national security.

These manpower problems are not unique to Israel. Silicon Valley addresses its own shortage through immigration: the United States lets tech companies bring in workers from around the world on special visas. Many of them eventually receive a green card, giving them permanent residency rights and a pathway to citizenship. Thanks to its global reputation and ecosystem, which provides fertile ground for new, groundbreaking tech companies, Silicon Valley is able to attract talented immigrants from all over the world to join its established hi-tech industry. A report from 2017 showed that over 50% of R&D workers in Silicon Valley were born outside of the United States,[1] and 55% of unicorns have at least one immigrant on their founding teams. If we count also the children of immigrants, that number jumps to two-thirds of unicorns. Around half of unicorns founded by immigrants in the United States are based in Silicon Valley. In short, Silicon Valley relies, in large part, on foreign manpower, and it is hard to see how it could have reached its present status as the world's most hi-tech center without immigrants.[2] It is not surprising that when the Trump administration pushed to limit immigration to the United States, many Silicon Valley executives denounced this policy.[3]

Israel has more limitations in this respect because any immigration policy that might undermine its Jewish majority would run into stiff political opposition. The Israeli government is aware of the need to boost the labor supply and has passed various measures to make it easier to employ foreigners in the hi-tech sector,[4] but cybercompanies hardly use them, and the bureaucratic and operational hurdles are so high anyway, with no pathway to citizenship for those with work permits, that Israel's ability to attract manpower in large numbers is severely restricted.

Another option is to do things the other way around: instead of bringing in foreign workers, companies can outsource work to people abroad. Many Israeli cybercompanies already outsource their development work, usually through Eastern European or Indian companies. But geographic distance and cultural differences are obstacles to the transmission of knowledge and expertise to workers in another country, and therefore, companies do not task their outsourced workers with the parts of their products that require the highest levels of technology or an in-depth understanding of cybersecurity. At IntSights, too, when we outsourced work to people abroad, it was usually to develop applications that would be in dialogue with our product; we didn't let them touch the heart of our product's technology, so outsourcing only addressed our manpower problems at the margins. In other words, Israel's advantage lies in its possession of human capital with a deep understanding of technology and cybersecurity; outsourcing services that do not necessarily have these capabilities, and are available to any other company in the world, cannot give Israel the comparative advantage that has made it a world leader. At most, it can play a supporting role.

The only reasonable solution to Israel's manpower crisis is to move more Israelis into the hi-tech sector. But where will they come from? If we look at the percentage of salaried workers employed in the hi-tech sector, we find that the participation rate in Israel is exceptionally high. Of all salaried workers, 10%–11% work in hi-tech, and if we take into account R&D workers in other fields outside the hi-tech sector, that number reaches 14%, representing 447,000 workers.[5] This makes Israel the country with the highest proportion of citizens employed in hi-tech in the world. As it stands, the hi-tech sector already enjoys excellent PR, attracting more and more talent, so it is hard to see how Israel could significantly boost the proportion of citizens in this industry.

What's *cyber* in Yiddish?

"When I returned to Israel after seven years in San Francisco, the gaps between those involved in the hi-tech industry and those outside it were very noticeable to me," says Idan Tendler, a serial hi-tech entrepreneur, in an interview to *Calcalist*. "The momentum of high-tech does not reach everyone, and if we want it not to be just a locomotive, but also the engine of the entire Israeli economy, the reality must change."[6]

Twenty-three percent of Israeli men (outside the ultra-Orthodox community) already work in hi-tech. For most of the population, hi-tech is presumably an unsuitable career path because of their personality types, abilities, or interests, and there seems to be little room for this to grow. By way of comparison, only 11% of Jewish women outside the ultra-Orthodox community work in hi-tech; only 5% of ultra-Orthodox men and 6% of ultra-Orthodox women are in hi-tech; and among Arab men and women, those numbers are just 3% and 1%, respectively.[7]

These figures can be seen as reflecting a societal problem and discrimination against population groups that are not currently enjoying the excellent conditions of the Israeli hi-tech sector, but industry leaders see this also as an opportunity: if they can smash the entry barriers in the way of these population groups, they will be able to dramatically boost the labor supply for the industry.

An Israeli government committee formed in 2022 to find a solution to the problem of manpower shortages in hi-tech reached a similar conclusion.[8] The committee submitted its interim findings in September 2022, and the Israeli government approved several policies to try to boost participation in the hi-tech workforce among underrepresented groups, specifically women, Arabs, ultra-Orthodox Jews, and members of the Ethiopian community.[9] These policies include steps to foster academic excellence in fields relative to hi-tech, training programs, gender equality, and support for human capital from abroad to enter Israel, but first and foremost, they focus on education.

The main policy is about investment in English and science—essential skills in the hi-tech world—"with an emphasis on introducing children to hi-tech, shaping their image of the future, and giving each pupil a sense of competence," from elementary school through to high school. "It is no wonder that the Human Capital Committee specified the education system, in general, and the 'hi-tech matriculation certificate', in particular [five units in math and physics or in computer science and English] as the foundation whose importance to Israel's economy cannot be understated," says Dadi Perlmutter, chairman of the committee. "The committee places great emphasis on the quality and growing quantity that's coming out of students from all parts of Israeli society."[10]

In any case, even if these government resolutions are fully implemented, it will take years for their impact on the industry to be felt. It takes around 15 years for a child starting elementary school to reach the job market in Israel, and around 9 years from the start of middle school, so the program will only start to bear fruit in a decade at the earliest.

In earlier chapters, I mentioned the conclusions of the national cybernetic taskforce, headed by Professor Isaac Ben-Israel, whose recommendations included scientific and technical education in formal schooling and the creation of informal education frameworks, such as the "Cyber Scouts." Israel became the first country in the world to decide that every research university would establish its own cybersecurity center and teach the subject.

Meanwhile, a grassroots initiative to teach cybersecurity to children started emerging. After over 20 years of service in R&D roles in the IDF Intelligence Corps' technological units, Sagi Bar had begun a new position as the head of the cybersecurity human capital division in Unit 8200. In his role, he noticed something interesting and worrying: only 3% of soldiers in the IDF's technological units came from Israel's social and geographic periphery. Ultra-Orthodox Jews and Arabs do not usually enlist in the IDF, so it was unsurprising that they were not represented, but why were almost all these units' soldiers from the greater Tel Aviv area? There was a whole swath of the population that the Intelligence Corps could benefit from; these people could leverage the knowledge they gained from their military service when they entered the lucrative cyberindustry. Bar decided to set himself the mission of fixing this and set up a variety of programs to encourage Israeli students to aim for cybersecurity studies.

The most important program was Magshimim, which started out as a pilot program in Beersheba in 2010. The idea was to create an afterschool club for high school students in the country's geographic periphery, which would give them knowledge and important skills in the field of cybersecurity, thus giving them a leg up into the IDF's technological units. Success was quick, and within three years, it was adopted as a national program. Nowadays, graduates of this program already line the ranks of the IDF's cyber units and the industry; on a personal note, I too have already invested in a startup founded by a Magshimim graduate.

The private sector is also making an effort to bring underrepresented population groups into the industry. In all our years running IntSights, we always aimed to integrate these groups without lowering our standards. In practice, despite serious commitment on our part, we were only able to recruit a handful of people from outside the non-ultra-Orthodox Jewish mainstream. I was very surprised by how few good candidates we received from other sections of the population. I knew there were lots of courses and training programs for under-represented groups to gain knowledge and be hired in the industry, so how come hardly any of these people were coming our way? After investigating the issue, we realized that even if they received the right training, they were still struggling to fit in. There are very few junior entry positions in the hi-tech industry, and they usually are filled through the grapevine: you need someone on the inside to recommend you. Those without friends in the hi-tech sector, therefore, find themselves at a disadvantage. Moreover, many of them are unfamiliar with the hi-tech world's jargon, and they find it hard to overcome this language barrier and pass job interviews. Together with two partners, I decided to take action and address this glaring gulf.

Mohammed, a young Arab man from the village of Kafr Kanna in the Galilee, had been to a coding boot camp and applied for interviews but wasn't managing to find a job anywhere. He had the sense that because of language and cultural gaps, he wasn't managing to communicate his knowledge and personality to interviewers. My partners and I founded Step2Tech precisely for people like Mohammed: it aimed to help young people, especially ultra-Orthodox Jews, Arabs, and Ethiopian immigrants, get to know the hi-tech world from the inside and make connections that would help them blend in. The idea is to pair up young people with hi-tech workers and let them shadow them at work for a day. This way, they can learn about the industry and its day-to-day work and can make useful connections. Mohammed joined the project, and after he had spent a whole day with a programmer at JFrog, the programmer came to know him and recommended him to the company's recruitment department. About a month later, Mohammed signed an employment contract at JFrog.

September 2022 saw the launch of the Place-IL platform, a large-scale project created to train 10,000 hi-tech workers from underrepresented population groups within two years. It was the initiative of Idan Tendler, who co-founded Bridgecrew in 2019 with two partners and sold it to Palo Alto Networks within just two years for $200 million. A year and a half later, as a high-level Palo Alto employee, he decided to set up this new initiative in collaboration with his workplace and a range of companies, personalities, and investment funds.

Tendler also noticed that there were many organizations training and running courses for these population groups, but people were still struggling to fit into the industry. He realized that the industry itself would have to be brought on board and made to take responsibility and commit itself to this mission. The idea behind his initiative is to create a platform for training providers to pool the details of young people who had been through training, while at the same time giving companies access to all these candidates and examining them in a way that would let them give expression to their abilities. These companies also help with the funding side and have already raised millions of shekels for the project. They also commit to take in young people for internships. The initiative does not focus only on cybersecurity, but its cyber side is keenly felt, both because its founder came from the cybersecurity world and because cybersecurity companies are amply represented among the businesses supporting the program.

Bottom line, the Israeli cybersecurity world seems to be looking at the population groups that are not yet filling its ranks and it sees a reason for optimism with the biggest challenge being how to give expression to the talent, wisdom, and creativity that can be found by the bucket load there too.

Where are the women?

You might have noticed that most of the people interviewed for this book have been men, and unfortunately, this is no coincidence. Even before I drew up my list of interviewees, it was impossible not to see that among industry leaders, and especially entrepreneurs, there are very few women. Unlike other underrepresented groups, whose children get no exposure to the hi-tech or cybersecurity worlds, in the case of women, this discrepancy is more surprising. After all, they grow up in the same homes as boys and go to the same schools, so why aren't they seen?

It would be pointless trying to elaborate on all the research and the whole discussion about the interplay between gender and employment. Instead, I decided to pose this question to the women I interviewed for this book, and the first was Michal Braverman-Blumenstyk, one of the most powerful women in the industry. She believes that everything begins very early on, and she points to a U.S. study that shows that one typical characteristic of entrepreneurs and successful people is a willingness to take risks. On this matter, there is a huge gulf between boys and girls at a very early age, which she says is caused by gender conditioning: society encourages boys to take risks, while at the same time urging girls to be cautious.

"There was a study that checked how far parents let their toddlers wander from a park bench before calling out to them to come back because it's dangerous, and as early as one and a half, there's already a statistically significant difference showing they let boys go farther away," she says.

The solution, she argues, is early-childhood education. "As parents, we need to educate our daughters to take risks from the age of zero." But the question of whether this is all about education is controversial. In her book *The Sexual Paradox*, the Canadian psychologist Susan Pinker outlines several studies showing a natural tendency among men to taking risks, even extreme risks. From the studies that Pinker presents, this seems to be an innate tendency, not only a question of culture and education.[11]

But whichever homes girls grow up in, the education system has immense power to create change, especially when it comes to scientific and technological subjects. "You've got to start at a young age encouraging girls to play technological games and investing in amazing math teachers," says Braverman-Blumenstyk. "Girls tend to make less of an effort to excel in math or to choose to focus on science and technology. If we expose them to these subjects at a very young age, it's possible that more of them will fall in love with them and might naturally want to find their way into hi-tech when they grow up.

"When I was a young girl, I thought that since I couldn't feel the glass ceiling, it didn't exist, and that any woman who wanted to succeed, could. But that's just not true. I was lucky to have a dad who encouraged me to go in this direction and was a major figure in my life, but many women aren't as lucky, and they need obstacles to be removed for them." But Braverman-Blumenstyk adds a warning: "Affirmative action can end up hurting women. If we teach girls and young women to take risks and love science, and make them believe they can do anything they want, they'll grow up to be women who realize their full potential and can change the global tech industry, and there'll be no need for affirmative action."

What about the "masculine" environment that everyone talks about? Numerous reports have called out a culture of "toxic masculinity" in the hi-tech industry. Is this a culture that turns off women to the cybersecurity industry? One of the entrepreneurs I interviewed was Noa Zilberman. Together with her husband, Or, and his childhood friend, Gilad Steinberg, she founded Odo Security in 2018. Odo Security, which raised $5 million, was sold to Check Point in 2020 for $30 million, making a handsome profit. When I ask Zilberman and other women about their experiences as female entrepreneurs in the cybersecurity sector, I hear answers that might surprise some readers. "I had a great experience," she says. "I felt there were only advantages for me as a woman. There's no doubt it helped us raise money. It's partly because there are so few female entrepreneurs nowadays, so I was more 'memorable.' When 10 startups are trying to raise money, we're going to be remembered more." It's not that she never had people making false assumptions about her because she was a woman, but it never bothered her. "I kind of ignore these things," she says. "Sometimes when I talk to investment candidates, they ask to speak with 'someone in the know' because they assume I'm from human resources or I'm a secretary, but I just correct them and move on."

Today, says Zilberman, she is slightly more level-headed and conscious of the existing problems. "I see that in a high proportion of situations, I'm the only woman in the room, definitely in the tech world. The company recently held an event with 100 people, and I realized I was the only woman. It doesn't bother me in terms of confidence or career progression, but I'm more aware of the reality. Whereas in the past I tended to avoid discussions about gender, I'm leaning into it more now because I see the results, and I'm aware that the fact I'm a woman, at this point in time, is actually a plus. I'm here because of so many strong and brave women before me who opened the door for me."

Zilberman says that as an investor, she regularly advises entrepreneurs to include women on their teams. "When I'm facing two Unit 8200 vets who've founded a startup and randomly start dividing up the jobs, and one of them will be the CEO and the other will be the CTO, I strongly advise them to bring a female entrepreneur on board. I usually suggest that she cover the product side, both based on my personal experience in the field and also because it is really the most important role, I think, after the two others have been divided. That was an advantage we had, that we were diverse both in terms of gender and also personalities. We were three completely different people, who covered as many of the fields that had to be dealt with as possible. We each brought our own strengths to the table." In her view, this is the main advantage of integrating women. "I don't know whether it's a popular opinion, but men and women aren't the same, neither physically nor mentally, and that shouldn't be an insult or a compliment to either gender. That's exactly why social diversity is important."

Cybersecurity investor Gili Raanan, who founded the Cyberstarts investment fund, also highlights the advantage of having a woman on your team. Raanan tells me about Noname Security, which he invested in, founded by two entrepreneurs who brought in a female partner, Hila. The founders wanted to go for an application programming interface (API), and with Raanan's guidance, they went to potential customers and asked them to describe the most important qualities of their ideal product. "One customer said, 'I want it to be simple.' You might think that's a trivial statement: every entrepreneur will tell you his product is simple. But here's where the credit really goes to the entrepreneurs, and especially Hila, who really listened closely to the customers. She asked herself what they actually mean by a 'simple product,' and based on the insights she drew, they built a product that you can just install and forget about. That's how Noname became one of the leading companies in the field."

Like Braverman-Blumenstyk, Zilberman also mentions early-childhood education as a critical factor, but notes that change is already underway. "When I studied physics in high school, we were two girls in the class. By my cousin's time, a quarter of the class were girls. So I don't know what exactly we're doing, but it's working."

You can already see the change in the makeup of hi-tech work-forces, which is no mean feat considering how few women go for engineering or programming careers in the first place.

Some roles have always been done by women, such as human resources and operations, while R&D roles were traditionally staffed by men. In recent years, there has been growing awareness of the contribution that women make to workplace environments and cultures, and an honest desire to bring talented women into these roles. Women are increasingly entering software engineering jobs and senior management positions in successful companies.

Armis Security is one of them: "Of the five most senior R&D managers in the company, three are women," says Nadir Izrael, who co-founded Armis Security. "In the field of cyberinnovation, you can also gradually see change. There are already quite a few startups in the cybersecurity field with women on their founding teams. Besides Odo Security, there's also Dazz, Suridata, Eureka Security, and SAM. These companies have already raised significant sums, with Dazz raising the most: no less than $60 million. We can only assume and hope this positive trend will intensify with time."

The Israeli offensive cyberindustry: Beginning of the end?

The offensive cyberindustry entered an especially difficult crunch in 2022. In late 2021, the United States added NSO Group and Candiru to its blacklist of companies to which U.S. firms are banned from selling without special permission. It was a serious blow to Israel and the industry, as these businesses stood accused of assisting human rights abuses around the world. The move came as a thinly veiled warning to Israel to regulate its offensive cyber-industry more strictly. Indeed, Israel was quick to fall in line and started restricting the export of offensive cybertools to any states outside a closed list of democracies. Many industry leaders suspect that it is impossible for the industry to survive under such restrictions. "There isn't a big enough market," Shalev Hulio, founder of NSO, tells me. "Unless something drastic changes, the market will die," agrees an executive at another company. "Some of the countries on the list are small and irrelevant, regardless of whether or not they're Israel's allies. This restriction has basically strangled the industry because countries are going to buy less from Israel. All the Five Eyes nations [the intelligence alliance comprising Australia, New Zealand, Canada, Britain, and the United States] are developing their own offensive cybercapabilities together."

In 2022, the industry underwent a sharp shift and seemed to be sinking. NSO Group was in advanced talks with L3Harris about getting acquired, but they did not lead to a deal, and NSO soon announced 100 layoffs and Shalev Hulio's resignation as CEO. Cognyte decided to shut down its offensive cyber subsidiary, Ace Labs. Nemesis Security, which had tried to challenge NSO with its own cell phone spyware, also closed its doors. Industry insiders speak of other firms looking to get acquired or in financial straits. Paragon and Toka have not been directly impacted by these new restrictions because they were already selling only to democracies. At the time of writing, all eyes are on these companies to see whether they can hit sufficient revenues from such a restrictive list of democratic customers and achieve long-term profitability.

The feeling in the industry is that while the Israeli state backs these companies, it is not doing so strongly enough. In effect, Israel changed the rules of the game after these domestic companies were already established and had gotten used to a different reality. "It was a sensation," I hear from the CEO of one of the companies. "They panicked because of the Americans. Out of 19 Israeli companies under supervision, 40% have shut down. The industry in Israel is being wiped out. Israelis are either moving to Cyprus, Malta, and Macedonia, or they're moving to different fields. Lots of security researchers are leaving the country, and some have moved to Singapore because vulnerability researchers get paid really well there."

These restrictions govern not only which countries can buy Israeli offensive cyberproducts, but what use they can make of these technologies. According to a new law, customers may only use Israeli technologies within their own national borders. This created a massive rift with customers that are trying to defend themselves from Iran, for example, because now they are forbidden from scooping up intelligence from inside Iran or Lebanon. If customers in the UAE want to work out whether missiles are being aimed at Dubai, they can no longer use Israeli systems to look into it.

The bad news is, there's no such thing as a vacuum. When Israel restricts offensive cyberweapons sales, other actors enter the picture. China, for example, has started selling to Oman and Saudi Arabia, raising concerns with the United States, which is competing with it for global dominance. But even in the United States itself, there is a battle raging between spy agencies and zealous defenders of privacy rights in Congress. The U.S. intelligence community understands that busting crime and counterterrorism require offensive cybercapabilities, but cell phone and computer giants are not holding back and sometimes even bankroll politicians' campaigns to get them to resist.

An Israeli working in the offensive cyberindustry told me about an example he heard from a high-ranking U.S. intelligence official: in January 2022, a gunman stormed the Congregation Beth Israel synagogue in Texas during the Sabbath prayers. He locked himself inside for eight hours and was in touch with his brother in Britain this whole time, but U.S. intelligence agencies had no way of retrieving information from his cell phone, and none of them dared trying to buy such abilities from any of the companies on the blacklist.

The Israeli public might not be concerned and might even believe that this new policy is not so terrible. This is an industry that has, after all, supposedly given Israel a bad name, so perhaps it might be better to shift resources to the cyberdefense industry, which has a much bigger economic impact and is a source of pride for the country. But unless this policy changes, we will see more offensive cybercompanies closing shop or rolling back operations, and the State of Israel's immense knowledge in the field will recede along with them. The geopolitical and diplomatic rewards produced by this industry will disappear, and it is safe to assume that the vacuum will be filled either by Israeli companies that have relocated abroad, by competitors from Europe or the United States, or alternatively—by China and Russia.

When I ask an offensive cybersecurity industry leader what he thinks of the subject, he agrees with my short-term forecast, but is optimistic about the long run: "In the short run, the outlook's quite gloomy," he says. "Regulators always move slowly and toward extremes, and it takes them time to return to some kind of balance. The next few years are going to be really tough, but I think in 15 years, the pendulum will swing back to somewhere normal. It's going to be an incredible industry and I'm convinced Israel will be a major player in this industry because of the high-quality manpower here."

A few weeks before I finished writing this book, Shalev Hulio rocked the Israeli offensive cybersecurity market by announcing that he and former Austrian chancellor Sebastian Kurz were founding Dream Security, which would focus on cyberdefense for critical infrastructure. Hulio's misgivings about the future of the offensive cybersecurity industry in general, and about his own future, were already clear in our first conversation, months before he announced this move. After his announcement about Dream Security, we met up again and I asked him to explain what stood behind his decision.

"I left [NSO] even before the announcement that the company was going on the U.S. export controls list," says Hulio. "After what happened, I decided to go back for a limited one-year period to get the business back on track. I brought in potential buyers, we streamlined things, and I felt it was time for me to move on. I'm still very connected, and I advise them on anything they need—I haven't disappeared." Hulio completely rejects the theory that his departure is linked to a sense that the industry is being choked off. "I wanted to set up a company, and what, I'm gonna compete with NSO? I'd never do that.

"I went into cyberdefense because I think I founded maybe the best offensive cybersecurity company in the world. I didn't want to do the same thing again; I wanted to do something different," he says. Even after switching to cyberdefense, Hulio did not stick to the same field of cell phone devices like NSO, but pivoted to critical infrastructure. "I did it because I saw what the impact of a cyberattack on critical infrastructure could look like. I 100% believe we'll see a 9/11-style event in the cyberworld in the next few years, some explosion or attack caused by cyber, and the world will understand how important it is to protect this infrastructure.

"The situation can't stay the way it is today, with everything being up in the air," Hulio stresses. He believes there needs to be a kind of offensive cyber Geneva Convention, with clear rules about ethical conduct in the field, so that companies can sell to states that sign this treaty. "Meanwhile, we're at a watershed moment: the field might open up or completely shut down, but it can't stay like this. Most crime-busting and counterterrorism activities in Israel are made possible by cybertools, whether it's in Unit 8200, the Shin Bet, or Mossad, or whether it's thanks to Israeli cybercompanies. It's a strategic technological capacity and also a strategic diplomatic one. The state must protect them at all costs."

One point that Hulio is keen to emphasize is that he expects Israel's government to fight for Israeli companies. "At the end of the day, the State of Israel is neck-deep in this field: it grants permits and licenses, and there's never been a single sale, by any company, that it didn't give its full approval to. That's why the state's got to fight the U.S. decision [to blacklist Israeli offensive cybersecurity companies] and throw its full weight against it. I'm saying this as an ordinary citizen, not as the founder of NSO. The state uses lots of these cyberintelligence companies' capabilities, and it could have acted differently and helped the businesses that had helped it out. I know the state is fighting and speaking with the Americans, but it could have taken a much firmer stance and protected these companies much better. It's not too late to fix things."

The future of the Israeli cyberindustry depends not only on regulation, but also on technology: cyberdefense capabilities keep getting better every year, making it increasingly hard for would-be hackers. Ehud Schneerson, founder of Paragon, draws a distinction between the short term and long term, and says, "Is it possible that one day we'll reach a point where people give up and say it's just too hard? Maybe, but systems are becoming increasingly complex and interconnected. So cyberdefense will also get harder. It might get more difficult to hack things, but it'll still be possible. The good news is that it'll become more expensive with time, but you'll still be able to sell to a more exclusive clientele. When will these abilities get shut down, without a doubt? In the quantum computing age. The little problems we're dealing with today will all look completely ridiculous once we've got quantum computers. Many of the cyberworld's problems will get solved when quantum capabilities become relevant." Quantum computers are set to possess extraordinary computing power, of the sort that might rewrite the rules of the game when it comes to encryption. Quantum computers might be able to easily crack ciphers that are now considered impenetrable.

Schneerson is convinced that quantum computing must be the Israeli government's main focus. "During the Cyber Revolution, as a result of our national security problems, we became world leaders. The artificial intelligence (AI) revolution was led by other players— Facebook, Google, Chinese actors. They played the most exciting role in this revolution, and we were only bit-players. But with the quantum computing revolution, it can be just like what happened with cyber, especially in terms of external threats, with China and Russia now posing much bigger challenges than Iran and terrorists. We've got to be in the first group of states to achieve such capabilities.

"There's a letter from U.S. President John F. Kennedy that I like showing people," says Schneerson. "He wrote it in April 1961, after Yuri Gagarin took off into space, which was a huge reputational victory for the Soviets. It's a short letter to the Vice President, with five paragraphs and main questions about the space race: 'Do we have a chance of beating the Soviets by putting a laboratory in space, or by a trip around the moon, or by a rocket to land on the moon? . . . How much additional would it cost? . . . Are we making maximum effort? Are we achieving the necessary results?' That's the kind of letter that's got to come out of Jerusalem and propel the whole country to the next stage."

Schneerson emphasizes that this is not just a question of national security. "The issue is the future of the Israeli industry in a generation or two. It's about whether Israel will be one of the first states doing quantum computing, quantum algorithmics, not just for decryption, but also for finding gas and petroleum, financial management, and more. It'll give us incredible power with which we can build the next generation of the industry. Cyber as we know it will no longer exist, but we've got to think ahead toward the new challenges the future holds."

What's next? From small companies to major corporations

The offensive cyberindustry may be in dire straits, but cyberdefense industry leaders agree on one thing: the demand for their services is going nowhere. To quote Amichai Shulman, co-founder of Imperva:

"At the end of the day, the sector's got a growth engine that hasn't shut down: cyberattacks. There are constant innovations there, and that's why there's a need for dynamic, self-reinventing defense. I'm not worried we'll end up unemployed." Kobi Samboursky from Glilot Capital is also chilled: "Since it's all a game of cat and mouse in the cyberworld, I don't see this ending." And given the constant need to monitor attackers and devise solutions against new attacks, no one can afford to remain idle. Organizations have got to keep constantly updated and find new solutions, and so hostile actors will continue to drive the evolution of the cybermarket into the future.

Hackers are not the only ones making progress; technological advances in the field of computing are also pushing innovation forward. Every new piece of computer technology requires its own tailor-made protective outfit, as has always happened: when PCs took off, antivirus solutions were invented. When the internet started to spread, along came Check Point with its firewall to block remote access to internal networks. When websites, and especially e-commerce sites, were suddenly everywhere, along came Imperva with its own firewall to defend them. In recent years, with the rise of cloud computing, cloud protection companies popped up, including Wiz. "The biggest waves in the cybermarket have been connected to changes in the IT world, like the move to the cloud," explains Samboursky. "As the technological infrastructure changes, cyber is adapting." As long as innovation in the computing world continues, therefore, cyberentrepreneurs will have to catch up with innovation on their own turf.

"When you're in lockstep with the future, whatever happens will only make you stronger," Samboursky summarizes. But there are still a few risks to the industry's future growth. The existing model, in which computer infrastructure is so vulnerable to begin with, is not ideal. "The fact that the world is so vulnerable on the cyberfront is a problem," says Esti Peshin, who manages the Israel Aerospace Industries' cyberdivision. "The arms race can be shrunk if we make a few global regulatory steps." Peshin cites online anonymity as one example: "If we attached to every piece of information sent over the internet another piece of information pointing out its origin, that would prevent a lot of attacks," she explains. "Hackers find it convenient that it's hard to detect them, and such a move would deter cybercriminals." But even so, as Peshin notes, this would not completely solve the problem because it would not necessarily deter state actors like China or North Korea from launching attacks.

In practice, there has been very little progress in reducing the scope of cyberattacks on a systems level. In any case, it will take many years for us to enter such a world, and even then, we can assume that hackers, and especially state actors, will find ways to skirt these defenses and do as they want, as they have been to date. Cyberdefense entrepreneurs still have lots of work to do.

"There are too many cybercompanies"

In one of my conversations with an information security manager at one of the world's largest food companies, I casually asked him how many cyberdefense products he was using. "Over 60," he replied. His answer left me speechless. How could he possibly be running so many systems? How could anyone manage an efficient operation with so many tools? How could he justify spending tens of millions of dollars on cyberdefense? Seeing the surprised look on my face, he laughed and said: "Yeah, it's crazy, but we don't really have a choice."

Why was there no alternative? Because large organizations use many different systems: PCs and servers, cloud services and smartphones, and a host of other internet-compatible devices. Each system is based on a different kind of technology, and each is vulnerable to cyberattacks from multiple directions. There is no such thing as a single, comprehensive protective solution for all these many systems, and this leaves large organizations to deal with dozens of different suppliers, each working on professional solutions in its own field.

The proliferation of systems and threats meant that every year, more and more protective solutions were developed. Every time hackers developed a new mode of attack, another tool was added to the protective toolkit. This created a new kind of burden: not only did organizations have to deal with attackers; they now had to manage a whole raft of security tools. The market is suffering an acute shortage of manpower—especially manpower with the knowledge to deal with the latest technologies—and this makes the whole problem worse because there will always be a need to find people who can operate all these different systems. It is no surprise that according to polls, information security managers consider managing this growing toolkit to be one of their biggest challenges.[12]

One of the people fighting this proliferation of products is Nir Zuk. "It's illogical that every time there's a new cyberchallenge, a whole new company gets set up to deal with it. Palo Alto's fighting this," he explains. "Lots of organizations need dozens of different products and producers to achieve their information security needs. Palo Alto's idea is to take everything that's being done in the cyberindustry, and over time, to add them to a single platform." When Palo Alto started out, it focused on securing organizational networks. Its main product was its firewall, but there were other companies in the market providing targeted solutions for network security challenges. Palo Alto's original vision was to merge all these solutions into a single product, which would soon become the company's flagship product: a next-generation firewall. Later, through acquisitions and in-house inventions, Palo Alto broadened its product basket in order to provide a comprehensive organizational security solution and to spare customers from managing a huge array of security solutions and suppliers by themselves. This strategy proved itself, and Palo Alto is now the biggest cybersecurity company in the world. Other companies taking a similar approach, such as Check Point and Fortinet, are also among the world's biggest cybersecurity companies.

We also did the same thing at IntSights and offered customers technology to replace a large number of products that offered pinpoint solutions. The CEO of one of our customers, Blackstone, which soon also became an investor, noted this explicitly as the reason why he took us on. IntSights let him replace three different solutions with a single comprehensive solution, thus streamlining his whole operation and saving money. Another company that joined this trend was Cato Networks, founded by Shlomo Kramer, based on the same understanding of what the main problem is in today's cyberdefense world. "We understood that the problem is one of simplicity," says Kramer. "Cato replaces lots of different partial solutions and provides a single end-to-end solution."

Any company that develops a single solution has a serious advantage. This focus lets it dive deeper and develop the best possible product more efficiently than a company trying to span the whole security field. That said, customers will settle for products that are slightly less good but good enough for their needs if this saves them the bureaucracy of dealing with yet another supplier and the hassle of installing and running a product from a new supplier. This situation creates incredible pressure for startups to create much better products than those offered by the major manufacturers, which naturally have a competitive edge. Startups that create pinpoint solutions that customers will prefer to receive as part of a bigger product will therefore struggle to take off and survive as independent companies. These startups will almost always follow a strategy of trying to get acquired and will struggle to secure customers and grow. They will need to develop truly unique technologies to justify getting acquired—and that's no mean feat.

The 2010s were a decade of rapid growth for cybercompanies, many of which focused on different products from each other. Whereas in the preceding decade, 10 new cybercompanies on average were established in Israel every year,[13] this decade saw an average of 50 new Israeli cybercompanies every year, with the trend intensifying until the middle of the decade. The peak came in 2016, when over 70 such companies were founded, but this trend could not continue forever. Over time, it became clear to entrepreneurs that it was unsustainable to keep founding new companies to specialize in small solutions: even if the founders are aiming for an exit, for solutions that can ultimately be incorporated into bigger companies, they still need to sell to enough customers to prove the demand for their products and technology. Over time, however, customers have grown fed up with the proliferation of solutions and suppliers, making life difficult for the countless new companies popping up. Investors have also understood that it is problematic to have so many niche companies, and so the available capital for developing such companies has shrunk.

"I hope there'll be fewer feature companies," says Emmanuel Benzaquen, CEO of Checkmarx, referring to companies that develop single niche products. "These companies will always exist, but people have gotten confused between the ability to raise money and what these businesses actually produce. There have been feature companies that have raised investments based on valuations as if they were product companies or platforms. In the end, they're good for a certain industry and get acquired for $50 million or $200 million, and it all ends there. That's not a unicorn. We've seen lots of feature companies sprouting up here based on a promise of being the next unicorn, but unicorns are no longer a big deal. Multicorns [companies worth *billions* of dollars] are the latest thing. The next multicorns will be companies providing full platforms, not small features. There used to be lots of money in the market going to all sorts of different places, but now, money will be smarter and will focus on what the market really needs."

The market got the hint. Since 2016, the number of new cyberompanies founded in Israel has been dropping, and in 2021, Israel saw only 44 new cybercompanies. This downward turn does not point to a decline in the industry, but to a process of consolidation.

"Cyberentrepreneurs used to aim for exits of $100–$300 million," says Ofer Schreiber, a partner at YL Ventures. He sees this shift as a sign of the industry growing up. "Funding rounds have become even bigger, and everyone's starting to think big, to aim to become a unicorn and not to sell quickly. That's a good and positive development for the industry. We're no longer tech suppliers; we want to be category leaders." Investors and entrepreneurs no longer want to develop technologies in order to get bought out by major companies; instead, they are searching for major problems that justify building huge companies. Ofer says that as a consequence, it has become more complicated to launch a startup: it requires more friction with the market and a deeper understanding of business and not just technology, and even the process of finding a new idea takes longer than it used to. If this is the reason for the drop in new startups, Schreiber is undoubtedly right to say that this is a positive and healthy development for the industry.

At the time of writing, we are in the grips of a global financial crisis that began in January 2022 with sharp drops in global stocks, spiraling inflation, and a general slowdown in investments and economic activity. Many cybercompanies have started slimming down and laying off workers, and many have plummeted in value. Since the 2008 financial crisis, the world economy has experienced mainly growth. In this period, the S&P 500 grew by no less than 530%. The Israeli cyberindustry rode this wave, enjoying a massive bump in 2010, which launched a decade that saw hundreds of new startups and several major companies, including SentinelOne, Cato Networks, and Transmit Security. This was such a big jump that many wonder whether this is simply a "cyberbubble" based on overvaluations. In January 2023, venture capital fund Viola published a report arguing that only half of Israeli unicorns can justify their price tags and are actually worth at least $1 billion. The researchers noted, for example, that many unicorns had not raised any funds at all in ages, ever since the original funding rounds that gave them unicorn status.[14]

After the 2008 crisis, central banks in the United States and most of the Western world introduced extremely low interest rates, which encouraged financial institutions to invest in venture capital. During this time, the industry was flooded with money, driving up demand for investments in cybercompanies. As a result, many entrepreneurs turned their attention to founding cybersecurity companies, and even the less brilliant companies managed to secure investments. "There's inflation in cybersolutions nowadays," Amichai Shulman tells me, reflecting what many in the industry are feeling. "There's no room for so many startups all doing similar things."

Cybersecurity companies will probably struggle to justify their pre-crisis valuations and raise investments on such favorable terms like they used to. It also seems likely that less money will flow into venture capital, and fewer companies will emerge in the near future. That said, the cybersecurity industry has survived crises before, and Israeli companies, which enjoy a global reputation and a powerful ecosystem, are relatively well placed to weather the storm. Looking ahead, therefore, it is possible that the crisis in the Israeli cyberindustry is just a bump in the road or an adjustment away from the full-on rush in previous years, but not something that will stop it in the long run.

Will there ever be another Check Point?

"You're claiming the Israeli cybermarket is a success," Nir Zuk tells me, "but the question is, how are you measuring success? The right question isn't how many cybercompanies there are, but how many are making money. You could also measure how many companies have reached $1 billion in sales. If you check using these criteria, you'll see a different picture. There aren't many Israeli cybercompanies generating positive cash flows. There aren't many Israeli businesses hitting $1 billion in revenues. We've built great technologies, but not big companies."

There is a good reason why Zuk is choosing to stick a small pin in the Israeli cybersecurity industry's overinflated sense of self-importance. To understand where the industry can keep developing, it is important to understand its current condition and where it is running into trouble. One possible metric for the state to measure companies' success, according to Zuk, is whether they are paying taxes: "Businesses that don't make profits don't pay taxes. Their employees pay taxes, but they'd still be paying taxes even if they were working for another company. So it's important for the state that companies make profits, and if they aren't making serious profits, it's unclear how much the industry is really contributing to the State of Israel, compared to other hi-tech sectors."

The only cybersecurity company in Israel that meets these criteria of large revenues and sales is Check Point. After 30 years of unprecedented growth in the volume of business, investment, and innovation in the market, Check Point is still the only Israeli member of the top tier of global cyberfirms. Internationally, there are around 10 cybercompanies with a similar turnover as Check Point, which is the only non-U.S. firm on this list. Nir Zuk's Palo Alto Networks, which is a U.S. company, also stars on this list. Israel is definitely overrepresented, therefore, in terms of its relative population, but the question remains: is it still producing the next global industry leaders?

The Israeli market has traditionally grown around strong tech people who have understood how attackers work. As we have seen throughout this book, very many Israeli cyberentrepreneurs are veterans of the IDF's technological units, where they received a rich background in technology and a top-notch understanding of cyberattacks. What they did not receive there, however, was an understanding of business or of how to build global companies. In the military, there are no companies, no markets, and no sales. "It's hard to build a big company in Israel because you don't have people who know how to do it," says Zuk. "There's no one here who's ever run a company the size of Palo Alto. These sorts of companies have simply never existed in Israel."

Israel has always been far from its primary target market in the United States, and so it has always been at a disadvantage in understanding its customers, both culturally and commercially. In the previous section, we saw how Israeli entrepreneurs have found ways to bypass this problem and turn it to their advantage, but it is still an obstacle to founding major companies. Palo Alto's CEO, for example, reached his role after 10 years' experience in the number two job at Google. It is impossible to find people with such experience in Israel. The country has given rise to many companies that have produced good products, but only rarely have they managed to become truly excellent commercial giants, which has naturally led to Israeli companies getting sold to globally dominant businesses. "I don't think in the foreseeable future we'll see a company the size of Palo Alto getting established here," Zuk says in summary.

But however confident Zuk is in this belief, others completely disagree. "In the future, we'll see more companies the size of Check Point and CyberArk," Ofer Schreiber of venture capital fund YL Ventures tells me. "I'm sure there'll be another Check Point," declares Israel Grimberg from Team8.

Why are they so confident? What's going to change? The answer might have something to do with the personality types of Israel's tech entrepreneurs.

The startup wave of the 2010s produced several success stories, including IntSights, Adallom, Fireglass, and Lacoon. For many entrepreneurs, including me, this was their first hi-tech experience and many mistakes were made along the way, from pursuing bad ideas to chasing insufficiently big markets to other commercial management errors. Most entrepreneurs were aware that there was a gap between technological savvy and their business know-how. They all sent one partner to live in the United States to be closer to the market, and employed professional salespeople and managers overseas, but they were still plagued by cultural differences and misunderstandings with customers.

Exits have made some entrepreneurs extremely wealthy, but hardly any of them retire early or decide to spend the rest of their lives traveling around the world. Being a successful entrepreneur requires a very specific kind of personality, which includes a mixture of ambition, an urge to do and create, and a fierce desire to crack major challenges. Entrepreneurs get absorbed into the companies that buy them out, but sooner or later, they all want to quit for a new adventure. We have already seen this with Mickey Boodaei and Rakesh Loonkar, who managed to wriggle out of IBM after it acquired the company they had founded, Trusteer, in just three months.

Most entrepreneurs stick around for a certain period in their new companies in order to help incorporate their product and enjoy a less stressful period after a couple of years of intensive work, when they carried the whole responsibility for their startups. But most of them, while still working for the companies that have bought them out, get bitten by the entrepreneurial bug again and start pursuing their next idea. After little more than a year at Rapid7, which had acquired IntSights, I too understood that working at a large company was not for me, and I decided to take a break, after which I'd start to work on my own next project.

Outside observers might think that these entrepreneurs are working on "just another project," but these entrepreneurs cannot allow the final result to be anything like their first project. The next stage has always got to be much bigger. If they've already made an exit of hundreds of millions of dollars, the next stage must be a business that is worth billions and will stay independent. Entrepreneurs hitting the road for a second time start with significant experience, but more importantly, also a much bigger appetite. For most, another exit of a few hundred million dollars would be considered a failure. You can see the difference in their funding rounds. When I set out in 2015, it was normal for early-stage cybersecurity startups to raise between $1.5 and $3 million, but nowadays, experienced entrepreneurs are raising between $10 and $20 million.

The market itself is starting to see some unprecedented sights. Companies such as Assaf Rapaport's Wiz and Michael Shaulov's Fireblocks reached massive turnovers in record time. "People talked about us like we were a cybersuperpower, but we were a kind of tech production workshop, where large companies came to buy things," Gili Raanan tells me. "In recent years, the major companies in the cybersecurity sector have for the most part been Israeli firms. I believe there's no going back. Israeli entrepreneurs' dreams have gotten bigger."

Ambitions have changed across the whole market. "Today, even first-time entrepreneurs aren't looking for an exit," Assaf Rapaport tells me, sharing his thinking with me. "They've got other dreams, very ambitious ones, of building real businesses and big companies." Seasoned entrepreneurs are not the only ones hoping to build major companies instead of making quick exits. The change in the industry has also fired up the imagination of first-time entrepreneurs, who are looking left and right and seeing others building businesses with massive revenue streams, and they're saying to themselves, *I want to get there too.* "There are even more ambitious entrepreneurs nowadays who are taking on even bigger problems than in the past," agrees Shlomo Kramer.

Let's loop back to Nir Zuk's question: how is all this supposed to happen in a country with hardly anyone who already knows how to build a major company with billions of dollars of revenues and profits? The answer has to do with the fact that both the entrepreneurs and their companies have grown up. There's more money, more knowledge, more experience, and more connections, but what everyone points to now as the most important factor is the entrepreneurs' dreams. Since they're determined to build major companies, and some have come with an "it's all up to me" attitude from Unit 8200 and Unit 81, at least some of them will presumably overcome the obstacles.

Twenty years ago, nobody could have imagined that Israel would produce so many startups, which would make so many exits. A decade ago, no one could have imagined that Israel would have so many unicorns or companies with over $100 million in annual sales. So in the future, why shouldn't Israel produce massive cybersecurity companies on the scale of Check Point and Palo Alto? The learning curve will be steep, and there will no doubt be bumps along the way, but there are many good reasons to be optimistic.

With all due humility

One of the most interesting conversations I had in the course of writing this book was with Mickey Boodaei, who has lived and breathed the industry for the past 30 years. When we spoke, he drew my attention to what I now consider the biggest threat to the future of the industry: "Be careful of hubris. It's a disease we've got as Israelis. The Yom Kippur War didn't teach us anything. Success leads to hubris, and hubris means you get thumped and have to reorganize. I don't think we've been thumped yet, but the hubris here is growing. There are good people around the world, and many countries can give us a stiff fight in the cyberindustry. If we slip into complacency and start to think we're the best just because we're Israeli, we'll get thumped in the future."

All of us in the Israeli hi-tech industry have got to take Boodaei's message to heart. We mustn't get dazzled by success, and we must always be on our guard, so that the industry can prosper for many years to come. I too, as an entrepreneur, committed the crime of hubris. In my company's first few years, I belittled one of our rivals. Their product struck me as too complicated, and I couldn't understand why any customer would pick them over us. So I took them less seriously and kept less of an eye on them. Only at a later stage did I understand the genius behind their product, which suited a more sophisticated clientele and was easier to introduce to new fields. That allowed them to run ahead more quickly and become a major company in our sector. If I'd seen them as strong competitors whose strategy I had to delve into all along, we might have overtaken them in the competition for customers. That's a lesson I learned the hard way, and which no one in the industry can afford to forget.

"We should all be proud of the fact that cyber is such a critical field in the world and that this sliver of real estate in the Middle East has produced such huge and important companies—in terms of business, not just technology," says Gili Raanan. "We could also be paranoid, and

I can talk to you about the dangers, but I'm mostly very optimistic and very proud."

It's hard not to agree with these sentiments, which are also shared by the large majority of Israeli cyberindustry leaders. This has been an amazing success story, against all the odds, and it's a real source of national pride.

But while remaining optimistic, we must also pay attention to the threats and challenges, such as limited manpower, distance from target markets, tectonic shifts in the world of computing, the lowering of expectations, and pressure on companies to consolidate, which are all threatening the industry's continued prosperity. Industry insiders are aware of the dangers, and together with state authorities, are determined to overcome them, and that's why, like Raanan, I am very optimistic. The Israeli people's entrepreneurial spirit has brought the industry this far, and there's no reason why it shouldn't continue pushing it forward into the latest challenges. If only we can learn from others, work hard, and not sit on our hands—the Israeli cyberindustry can look ahead to many more years of plenty.

Notes

Chapter 1

1. Kim Zetter, "Inside the Cunning, Unprecedented Hack of Ukraine's Power Grid," *Wired*, March 6, 2016, available at **https://www.wired.com/2016/03/inside-cunning-unprecedented-hack-ukraines-power-grid/**
2. John Markoff, "An Internet Pioneer Ponders the Next Revolution," *The New York Times*, December 20, 1999, available at **https://archive.nytimes.com/www.nytimes.com/library/tech/99/12/biztech/articles/122099outlook-bobb.html**
3. "Computer and Internet Use in the United States: 2018," *Census.gov*, April 21, 2021, available at **https://www.census.gov/newsroom/press-releases/2021/computer-internet-use.html**
4. Jon Ying, "Meet the Team! (Part I)," *blog.dropbox.com*, February 5, 2009, available at **https://blog.dropbox.com/topics/company/meet-the-team-part-1**
5. Pete Townshend, "The 5 Biggest GDPR Fines and Why They Were Issued," *Smartframe*, September 23, 2022, available at **https://smartframe.io/blog/the-5-biggest-gdpr-fines-and-why-they-were-issued/**
6. Data Protection Commission, "Data Protection Commission Announces Decision in WhatsApp Inquiry," September 2, 2021, available at **https://www.dataprotection.ie/en/news-media/press-releases/data-protection-commission-announces-decision-whatsapp-inquiry**
7. Andy Greenberg, "Hackers Remotely Kill a Jeep on the Highway—With Me in It," *Wired*, July 21, 2015, available at **https://www.wired.com/2015/07/hackers-remotely-kill-jeep-highway/**; see also YouTube report: **https://youtu.be/MK0SrxBC1xs**

Chapter 2

1. Choe Sang-Hun, "South Korea Blames North for June Cyberattacks," *The New York Times*, July 16, 2013, available at **https://www.nytimes.com/2013/07/17/world/asia/south-korea-blames-north-for-june-cyberattacks.html**
2. Carol Morello, "Crimeans Vote to Break Away from Ukraine, Join Russia," *The Washington Post*, March 16, 2014, available at **https://www.washingtonpost.com/world/2014/03/16/ccec2132-acd4-11e3-a06a-e3230a43d6cb_story.html**; "Ukraine crisis: Timeline," *BBC News*, 13 November 2014, available at **https://www.bbc.com/news/world-middle-east-26248275**
3. "Crimea without Power after Pylons Blown Up," *BBC News*, November 22, 2015, available at **https://www.bbc.com/news/world-europe-34893493**
4. "When the Lights Went Out," Booz Allen, available at **https://www.boozallen.com/content/dam/boozallen/documents/2016/09/ukraine-report-when-the-lights-went-out.pdf**

5. Nicole Perlroth, *This Is How They Tell Me The World Ends: The Cyberweapons Arms Race* (New York: Bloomsbury, 2021), 26.

6. Julia Voo, et al., "National Cyber Power Index 2022," Belfer Center, September 2022, available at **https://www.belfercenter.org/publication/national-cyber-power-index-2022**

7. *List of Cyber Warfare Forces*, **Wikipedia.org**

8. U.S. Cyber Command PAO, "Mission and Vision," **cybercom.mil**, October 18, 2022, available at **https://www.cybercom.mil/Media/News/Article/3192016/cyber-101-us-cyber-command-mission**

9. "Iran Vows Revenge after Assassination of Top Nuclear scientist," *The Jerusalem Post*, November 29, 2020, available at **https://www.jpost.com/breaking-news/iranian-nuclear-scientist-assassinated-near-tehran-report-650457**

10. Daniel Nasaw, "Hackers Breach Defences of Joint Strike Fighter Jet Programme," *The Guardian*, April 21, 2009, available at **https://www.theguardian.com/world/2009/apr/21/hackers-us-fighter-jet-strike**

11. Franz-Stefan Gady, "New Snowden Documents Reveal Chinese Behind F-35 Hack," *The Diplomat*, January 27, 2015, available at **https://thediplomat.com/2015/01/new-snowden-documents-reveal-chinese-behind-f-35-hack/**

12. "GRIZZLY STEPPE—Russian Malicious Cyber Activity," *cisa.gov*, December 29, 2016, available at **https://www.cisa.gov/uscert/GRIZZLY-STEPPE-Russian-Malicious-Cyber-Activity**

13. "Background to 'Assessing Russian Activities and Intentions in Recent US Elections': The Analytic Process and Cyber Incident," *dni.gov*, January 6, 2017, available at **https://www.dni.gov/files/documents/ICA_2017_01.pdf**

Chapter 3

1. Albert Gonzalez, Part 1, *Malicious Life Podcast*, **https://youtu.be/sdFK-hBb8Po**

2. "Retail Hacking Ring Charged for Stealing and Distributing Credit and Debit Card Numbers from Major US Retailers," *justice.gov*, 5 August 2008, available at **https://www.justice.gov/archive/opa/pr/2008/August/08-ag-689.html**

3. From the indictment, available at **https://tinyurl.com/zasrydce**

4. "Visa, MasterCard, UnionPay Transaction Volume," *statista.com*, November 30, 2020, available at **https://www.statista.com/statistics/261327/number-of-per-card-credit-card-transactions-worldwide-by-brand-as-of-2011**; Michael Keenan, "Global Ecommerce Explained: Stats and Trends to Watch in 2023," *shopify.com*, 24 November 2022, **https://www.shopify.com/enterprise/global-ecommerce-statistics**

5. "Lithuanian Man Sentenced to 5 Years in Prison for Theft of Over $120 Million in Fraudulent Business Email Compromise Scheme," *justice.gov*, 19 December 2019, available at **https://www.justice.gov/usao-sdny/pr/lithuanian-man-sentenced-5-years-prison-theft-over-120-million-fraudulent-business**; "Five Years in the Clink for Super-Crook Who Scammed Google, Facebook out of $120m with Fake Tech Invoices," *theregister.com*, December 20, 2019.

6. For a list of other phishing attacks: **https://www.teiss.co.uk/rimasauskas-jailed-phishing**.

7. Jonathan Berr, "'WannaCry' Ransomware Attack Losses Could Reach $4 Billion," *CBS News*, May 16, 2017, available at **https://www.cbsnews.com/news/ wannacry-ransomware-attacks-wannacry-virus-losses/**

8. "How Much Money Did WannaCry Make?" *webtitan.com*, July 20, 2020, available at **https://www.webtitan.com/blog/how-much-money-did-wannacry-make**

9. Catalin Cimpanu, "How US Authorities Tracked Down the North Korean Hacker behind WannaCry," *ZDNET*, September 8, 2018, available at **https://www.zdnet .com/article/how-us-authorities-tracked-down-the-north-korean-hacker-behind-wannacry/**

10. Brittany Chang, "CNA Financial Paid Hackers $40 Million in Ransom after Cyberattack," *businessinsider.com*, May 22, 2021, available at **https://www.business insider.com/cna-financial-hackers-40-million-ransom-cyberattack-2021-5**

11. Anat Georgy and Ronny Linder, "It Came Out of Nowhere. Suddenly All the Patients' Information Just Disappeared," *The Marker*, October 29, 2021 [Hebrew], available at **https://www.themarker.com/news/health/2021-10-29/ty-article-magazine/.highlight/0000017f-f109-da6f-a77f-f90f887c0000**

12. Yaron Doron, "Two Weeks after the Cyberattack: Hillel Yaffe Hospital Starts to Recover," *Israel Hayom*, October 27, 2021 [Hebrew], available **https://www .israelhayom.co.il/health/article/5331698**

13. Jason Hill, "Good for Evil: DeepBlueMagic Ransomware Group Abuses Legit Encryption Tools," *varonis.com*, October 19, 2021, available at **https://www .varonis.com/blog/deepbluemagic-ransomware**

14. Swati Khandelwal, "Feedly and Evernote Hit by DDoS Attacks, Extortion Demands," *Thehackernews.com*, June 12, 2014, available at **https://thehackernews .com/2014/06/feedly-and-evernote-hit-by-ddos-attacks.html**

15. Yasmine Ryan, "Anonymous and the Arab Uprisings," *Al Jazeera*, May 19, 2011, available at **https://www.aljazeera.com/news/2011/5/19/anonymous-and-the-arab-uprisings**

16. **https://www.dailymail.co.uk/tvshowbiz/article-508807/Profile-Church-Scientologys-efforts-block-Tom-Cruise-video-rant-backfire.html**

Chapter 4

1. "617 Million Hacked Accounts Put on Sale on the Dark Web," *digit.in*, February 13, 2019, **https://www.digit.in/news/general/617-million-hacked-accounts-put-on-sale-on-the-dark-web-46437.html**

2. "The Dark Overlord: Cyber Investigation Report Written by Vinny Troia," *nightlion .com*, available at **https://nightlion.com/wp-content/uploads/2020/12/The-Dark-Overlord-Investigation-Report-Night-Lion_v1.01.pdf**

3. Daniel Moore and Thomas Rid, "Cryptopolitik and the Darknet," *Survival*, 58, no. 1 (2016): 7–38.

4. Lorenzo Franceschi-Bicchierai, "Another Day, Another Hack: 117 Million LinkedIn Emails and Passwords," *Vice*, May 18, 2016, available at **https://www .vice.com/en/article/78kk4z/another-day-another-hack-117-million-linkedin-emails-and-password**

Chapter 5

1. Yuval Dror, "Aladdin Leaves Private Market and Cuts Workforce," *Haaretz*, June 26, 2022 [Hebrew], available at **https://www.haaretz.co.il/misc/2002-06-26/ ty-article/0000017f-e1d7-df7c-a5ff-e3ff75ed0000**
2. Ella Jacoby, "CA Acquires Iris Anti-Virus for $4 Mln," *Globes*, July 5, 1999, available at **https://en.globes.co.il/en/article-376204**
3. Ella Jacoby, "CA Continues Shopping Spree; In Advanced Negotiations to Buy Carmel Software Engineering Anti-Virus for $4–5 Mln," *Globes*, June 28, 1999, available at **https://en.globes.co.il/en/article-376047**
4. Shlomo Kramer, "Check Point Software and Cato Networks Co-Founder Shlomo Kramer Shares His Journey: From 'Firewall-1' Software to Today's Firewall as a Service," *firewall.cx*, available at **https://www.firewall.cx/general-topics-reviews/ sd-wan/1212-shlomo-kramer-check-point-firewall-1-to-cato-networks- cloud-based-security.html**
5. Ibid.
6. "Exclusive Interview with the Founder of a $1.9 Billion Dollar Cyber Security Company," *Business Podcast for Startups*, September 27, 2019, available at **https:// mixergy.com/interviews/check-point-with-gil-shwed/**
7. W.R. Cheswick and S.M. Bellovin, *Firewalls and Internet Security: Repelling* the *Wily Hacker* (Boston, MA: Addison Wesley, 1994). Sections of this book were reproduced in Vol. 16 of *Computer World* in May 1994. In an interview a few years later, Cheswick recalled the surprise success of the book, which had sold 10,000 copies in a week, alongside the noise that Check Point's firewall was making at the time, saying: "It came at just the right time." Roger Grimes, *Hacking the Hacker* (Indianapolis, IN: Wiley, 2017, 96).
8. InfoWorld, May 2, 1994.

Chapter 6

1. Dudi Goldman, "We'll Strike Check Point," *ynet*, November 9, 2004 [Hebrew], available at **https://www.ynet.co.il/articles/0,7340,L-3001873,00.html**
2. Dan Blacharski, "How I Got Here: Nir Zuk, CTO, Palo Alto Networks," *Computerworld*, April 5, 2010, available at **https://www.computerworld.com/article/ 2756415/how-i-got-here--nir-zuk--cto--palo-alto-networks.html?page=2**
3. Neta Yaacobi, "Check Point Grows—Now the Competition," Haaretz, August 29, 2002 [Hebrew], available at **https://www.haaretz.co.il/misc/2002-08-29/ty- article/0000017f-e3a4-d568-ad7f-f3ef84870000**; Ofer Levi, "I Believe Our Tech Is More Advanced than Check Point's," *Globes*, August 3, 2004 [Hebrew], available at **https://www.globes.co.il/news/article.aspx?did=821005**; Dudi Goldman, "We'll Strike Check Point," *ynet*, November 9, 2004 [Hebrew], available at **https:// www.ynet.co.il/articles/0,7340,L-3001873,00.html**
4. Sophie Shulman, "You've Got to Understand, the Whole Internet Economy Is in Danger," *Calcalist*, November 28, 2019 [Hebrew], available at **https://newmedia .calcalist.co.il/magazine-281119/m01.html**

5. Inbal Orpaz and Orr Hirschauge, "Antivirus for Banks Worth $800 Million," *The Marker*, August 16, 2013 [Hebrew], available at **https://www.themarker.com/ markerweek/2013-08-16/ty-article/0000017f-f62e-d47e-a37f-ff3ed74c0000**

6. Oren Freund, "Check Point Killer: See the Palo Alto Billboard Denigrating Check Point," *TheMarker*, March 20, 2013 [Hebrew], available at **https://www .themarker.com/markets/2013-03-20/ty-article/0000017f-e124-d38f-a57f- e7766ac10000**

Chapter 7

1. Eric M. Hutchins et al., "Intelligence-Driven Computer Network Defense Informed by Analysis of Adversary Campaigns and Intrusion Kill Chains," *Leading Issues in Information Warfare & Security Research* 1, no. 1 (2011): 80.

2. "40/40: Promising Young People of 2017," *TheMarker* [Hebrew], available at **https://www.themarker.com/magazine/2017-11-09/ty-article-static/ 0000017f-f051-d487-abff-f3ff8eb80000**

Chapter 9

1. Amitai Ziv, "Give Gili Raanan a Spoon, and He'll Tell You a Few Things the Guys at Unit 8200 Don't Understand," *TheMarker*, April 3, 2019 [Hebrew], available at **https://www.themarker.com/technation/2019-04-03/ty-article/.premium/ 0000017f-dff3-d3ff-a7ff-fff3fd430000**

2. "Gartner Says Worldwide IaaS Public Cloud Services Market Grew 40.7% in 2020," *Gartner*, June 28, 2021, available at **https://www.gartner.com/en/newsroom/ press-releases/2021-06-28-gartner-says-worldwide-iaas-public-cloud- services-market-grew-40-7-percent-in-2020**; "Gartner Says Worldwide IaaS Public Cloud Services Market Grew 41.4% in 2021," *Gartner*, June 2, 2022, avail- able at **https://www.gartner.com/en/newsroom/press-releases/2022-06-02- gartner-says-worldwide-iaas-public-cloud-services-market-grew-41- percent-in-2021**

3. Assaf Gilead, "The Valuation Bubble of Israeli Cyber Firms Is Exposed," *Globes*, June 8, 2022 [Hebrew], available at **https://www.globes.co.il/news/article .aspx?did=1001414575**

Chapter 10

1. Zack Whittaker, "NSA Finally Admits Why It Couldn't Hack San Bernardino Shooter's iPhone," *ZDNet*, June 10, 2016, available at: **https://www.zdnet.com/ article/nsa-comes-clean-on-why-it-couldnt-hack-san-bernardino- shooters-iphone/**

2. "A Message to Our Customers," February 16, 2016, available at: **https://www.apple.com/customer-letter/**
3. Ian Beer and Samuel Groß of Google Project Zero, "A Deep Dive into an NSO zero-click iMessage Exploit: Remote Code Execution," December 15, 2021, available at **https://googleprojectzero.blogspot.com/2021/12/a-deep-dive-into-nso-zero-click.html**; Oded Yaron, "Analysis: Their Own Processor in an iPhone: Pegasus Managed to Astonish Even Google's Researchers," *Haaretz*, December 16, 2021 [Hebrew], available at: **https://www.haaretz.co.il/captain/software/.premium-1.10473423**

Chapter 11

1. Cyrus Farivar, "Hacking Team Goes to War against Former Employees, Suspects Some Helped Hackers," *arstechnica.com*, May 20, 2015, available at: **https://arstechnica.com/information-technology/2015/07/italian-prosecutors-investigate-former-hacking-team-employees-for-role-in-hack/**
2. Based on an internal corporate document leaked to WikiLeaks, titled: "Finfisher™: Governmental It Intrusion and Remote Monitoring Solutions."
3. Available on WikiLeaks, under "SpyFiles4," **https://wikileaks.org/spyfiles4/**
4. Gur Megiddo, "'We're on the U.S. Blacklist Because of You': The Dirty Clash between Israeli Cyberarms Makers," *Haaretz*, December 17, 2021, available at **https://www.haaretz.com/israel-news/2021-12-17/ty-article-magazine/.highlight/were-on-the-u-s-blacklist-because-of-you-the-clash-of-israeli-cyberarms-firms/0000017f-f195-dc28-a17f-fdb72e9a0000**
5. Bill Marczak et al., "Hooking Candiru: Another Mercenary Spyware Vendor Comes into Focus," *The Citizen Lab*, Report #139, July 15, 2021, available at: **https://citizenlab.ca/2021/07/hooking-candiru-another-mercenary-spyware-vendor-comes-into-focus/**
6. **https://www.themarker.com/embeds/pdf_upload/2020/20200902-161742.pdf**
7. Amitai Ziv, "Deals Worth Millions, Contracts in the Persian Gulf: A Rare Peek into one of Israel's Most Secretive Companies," *TheMarker*, July 30, 2020 [Hebrew], available at **https://www.themarker.com/technation/2020-07-30/ty-article/.premium/0000017f-e256-d568-ad7f-f37f2a4b0000.**
8. Sagi Cohen, "'We Don't Want These Kinds of People': NSO Employees Pay the Price for Pegasus Spyware Scandal," *Haaretz*, February 6, 2022, available at **https://www.haaretz.com/israel-news/tech-news/2022-02-06/ty-article/.premium/we-dont-want-these-kind-of-people-is-nso-a-cv-stain/0000017f-e8e8-d62c-a1ff-fcfb60330000**
9. Thomas Brewster, "A Multimillionaire Surveillance Dealer Steps Out of the Shadows . . . And His $9 Million WhatsApp Hacking Van," *Forbes*, August 5, 2019, available at **https://www.forbes.com/sites/thomasbrewster/2019/08/05/a--multimillionaire-surveillance-dealer-steps-out-of-the-shadows-and-his-9-million-whatsapp-hacking-van/**

10. Reuters and Omer Benjakob, "Greek Intel Chief and Top PM Aide Quit Over Israeli Spyware Scandal," *Haaretz*, September 7, 2002, available at **https://www.haaretz.com/israel-news/security-aviation/2022-08-07/ty-article/greek-intelligence-service-boss-quits-amid-allegations-of-misusing-israeli-made-spyware/00000182-73aa-d9c2-afa6-ffbaca5f0000**

11. Crofton Black et al., "Flight of the Predator: Jet Linked to Israeli Spyware Tycoon Brings Surveillance Tech From EU to Notorious Sudanese Militia," *Haaretz*, November 30, 2022, available at **https://www.haaretz.com/israel-news/security-aviation/2022-11-30/ty-article-magazine/.premium/jet-linked-to-israeli-spyware-tycoon-brings-spy-tech-from-eu-to-notorious-sudanese-militia/00000184-a9f4-dd96-ad8c-ebfcd8330000**

12. Thomas Brewster, "A Multimillionaire Surveillance Dealer Steps Out of the Shadows . . . And His $9 Million WhatsApp Hacking Van," *Forbes*, August 5, 2019, available at **https://www.forbes.com/sites/thomasbrewster/2019/08/05/a-multimillionaire-surveillance-dealer-steps-out-of-the-shadows-and-his-9-million-whatsapp-hacking-van/**

Chapter 12

1. Violet Blue, "Top Gov't Spyware Company Hacked; Gamma's FinFisher Leaked," *zdnet.com*, August 6, 2014, available at **https://www.zdnet.com/article/top-govt-spyware-company-hacked-gammas-finfisher-leaked/**

2. **https://www.reddit.com/r/Anarchism/comments/2cjlop/gamma_international_leaked**

3. David Pegg, "Bahraini Arab Spring Dissidents Sue UK Spyware Maker," *The Guardian*, October 11, 2018, available at **https://www.theguardian.com/world/2018/oct/11/bahraini-arab-spring-dissidents-sue-uk-spyware-maker**

4. "New FinSpy iOS and Android implants revealed ITW," *securelist.com*, July 10, 2019, available at: **https://securelist.com/new-finspy-ios-and-android-implants-revealed-itw/91685/**

5. Oded Yaron, "The Developer of FinFisher Spyware Is Closed and Will Remain Closed," *Haaretz*, March 28, 2022 [Hebrew], available at **https://www.haaretz.co.il/captain/software/2022-03-28/ty-article/.premium/00000180-5bad-db1e-a1d4-dfed16720000**; Ryan Gallagher, "German Spyware Vendor FinFisher Claims Insolvency Amid Investigation," *Bloomberg*, March 28, 2022, available at **https://www.bloomberg.com/news/articles/2022-03-28/spyware-vendor-finfisher-claims-insolvency-amid-investigation**

6. Alex Hern, "Hacking Team Hacked: Firm Sold Spying Tools to Repressive Regimes, Documents Claim," *The Guardian*, July 6, 2015, available at **https://www.theguardian.com/technology/2015/jul/06/hacking-team-hacked-firm-sold-spying-tools-to-repressive-regimes-documents-claim**

7. Amir Barnea, "Citizen Lab vs. NSO: The Small Canadian Institute Taking Down Israel's 'Mercenary Spyware' Firms," *Haaretz*, January 13, 2022, available at **https://www.haaretz.com/israel-news/tech-news/2022-01-13/ty-article-magazine/.highlight/citizen-lab-vs-nso-the-institute-taking-down-israels-mercenary-spyware-firms/0000017f-e971-d62c-a1ff-fd7b32710000**

8. **https://citizenlab.ca/about/**

9. Bill Marczak et al., "The Great iPwn: Journalists Hacked with Suspected NSO Group iMessage 'Zero-Click' Exploit," The Citizen Lab, Report #135, December 20, 2020, available at **https://citizenlab.ca/2020/12/the-great-ipwn-journalists-hacked-with-suspected-nso-group-imessage-zero-click-exploit/**

10. Zack Whittaker, "Citizen Lab Discovers iMessage Vulnerability Exploited to Infect Saudi Activist's Phone with Pegasus; Apple Releases Patch," *Business & Human Rights Resource Center*, September 13, 2021, available at **https://www.business-humanrights.org/en/latest-news/citizen-lab-discovers-imessage-vulnerability-on-saudi-activists-phone-infected-with-pegasus-apple-releases-patch/**

11. **https://citizenlab.ca/about/**

12. **https://forbiddenstories.org/about-the-pegasus-project/**

13. Roman Loyola, "Apple Patches Critical Security Flaw with MacOS Big Sur 11.5.1," *macworld.com*, July 27, 2021, available at **https://www.macworld.com/article/351641/macos-big-sur-11-5-1-security-updates-pegasus-spyware.html**

14. David E. Singer et al., "U.S. Blacklists Israeli Firm NSO Group over Spyware," *The New York Times*, November 3, 2021, **https://www.nytimes.com/2021/11/03/business/nso-group-spyware-blacklist.html**

15. Assaf Gilead, "Export Controls Strangling Israel's Cyberattack Industry," *Globes*, April 25, 2022, available at **https://en.globes.co.il/en/article-tighter-export-controls-strangling-israels-cyberattack-sector-1001410066**

16. "Mossi Raz Attacks NSO: 'A Company that Shames Us around the World," *ice*, November 3, 2021 [Hebrew], available at **https://www.ice.co.il/media/news/article/834253**

17. Haim Gelfund, "Throwing the Baby Out with the Bathwater," April 24. 2021 [Hebrew], available at **https://www.the7eye.org.il/414106**

18. In Hobbes's words: "The finall Cause, End, or Designe of men, (who naturally love Liberty, and Dominion over others,) in the introduction of that restraint upon themselves (in which wee see them live in Common-wealths) is the foresight of their own preservation, and of a more contented life thereby; that is to say, of getting themselves out from that miserable condition of Warre, which is necessarily consequent (as hath been shewn) to the naturall Passions of men, when there is no visible Power to keep them in awe." (*Leviathan* Part II).

19. Alan Rusbridger and Ewen MacAskill, "I, Spy: Edward Snowden in Exile," *The Guardian*, July 19, 2014, available at **https://www.theguardian.com/world/2014/jul/18/-sp-edward-snowden-interview-rusbridger-macaskill**

20. Jack Nicas et al., "Censorship, Surveillance and Profits: A Hard Bargain for Apple in China," *The New York Times*, May 17, 2021, available at **https://www.nytimes.com/2021/05/17/technology/apple-china-censorship-data.html**

21. Avishai Grinzaig, "Probe Clears Israel Police of Unlawful NSO Spyware Phone Hacking," *Globes*, August 2. 2022, available at **https://en.globes.co.il/en/article-probe-clears-israel-police-of-unlawful-nso-spyware-phone-hacking-1001420165**

22. Josh Breiner, "Pegasus Scandal: NSO Threatens to Sue Israeli Newspaper," *Haaretz*, February 10, 2022, available at **https://www.haaretz.com/israel-news/2022-02-10/ty-article/pegasus-scandal-nso-threatens-to-sue-israeli-newspaper/0000017f-e660-d97e-a37f-f76553830000**

Chapter 14

1. Talk Hatuka and Erran Carmel, *The Dynamics of the Largest Cybersecurity Industrial Clusters: San Francisco Bay Area, Washington D.C. and Israel* (Tel Aviv: Tel Aviv University, January 2021), available at **https://icrc.tau.ac.il/sites/cyberstudies-english.tau.ac.il/files/media_server/all-units/Cyber%20DIGITAL%20Final%20unlocked-1.pdf**
2. Interview with Jay Leek, Managing Partner at venture capital fund SYN Ventures.
3. IT Harvest, Security Yearbook 2022. The data suggest that the rate is 7%, but this includes companies that supply information security services and do not develop their own technology. As a proportion of companies that produce technology and products, there are many more Israeli companies because Israeli companies tend to focus on technology. Moreover, many Israeli companies that opened offices in the United States are classified as American despite having been founded in Israel and having very large offices in Israel, so in practice, the proportion is far higher. The percentages cited are based on calculations I ran, with the range depending on how companies are classified as cybertechnology companies and as Israeli entities.
4. See footnote 3. Data based on total cybersecurity firms, including service companies.
5. CBInsights, The Complete List of Unicorn Companies available at https://www.cbinsights.com/research-unicorn-companies; see also Douglas Blakey, "Ranked: The 59 Cybersecurity Unicorns You Need to Know About," *retailbanker international.com*, November 7, 2022, available at **https://www.retailbanker international.com/features/cybersecurity-unicorns-ranked/**
6. Canada: eSentire, Trulioo, and 1Password. Switzerland: Acronis, which was founded in Singapore in 2003, entered Switzerland in 2008—and opened an R&D center in Israel in 2021. Lithuania: NordVPN, with its flagship product Nord Security. China: Tongdun Technology.
7. Start-Up Nation Central reports $6.6 billion in investments in security companies, of which $6.25 billion were for cybersecurity. See IT-Harvest, Security Yearbook 2022.
8. According to the most conservative estimates. According to rival estimates, the rate of investments in Israeli cyber companies is over 30%.
9. According to Start-Up Nation Central. According to end-of-year data about 2021 published by the Israeli National Cyber Directorate, the sum stands at $3.5 billion. Concerning the whole industry, see: Momentum Cyber, Cybersecurity Almanac 2022. This analysis is based also on information that does not appear in the report, but was given to me directly by its writers, about the level of investment in product and technology companies in 2021.

Chapter 15

1. Yasmin Yablonko, "The Hunt for Talent, Hi-Tech Style: Cyber Company Places Recruitment Sign in Front of Glilot Base," *Globes*, December 22, 2019 [Hebrew].
2. Hagar Ravet, "Unit 8200 Commander Attacks Cybersecurity Startup that Tried to Poach Soldiers," *Calcalist*, December 30, 2019, available at **https://www.calcalistech.com/ctech/articles/0,7340,L-3776723,00.html**
3. Hagar Ravet and Meir Orbach, "'We Are Not Part of the Israeli Cyber Clique, Which Is Our Strength,'" *Calcalist*, September 12, 2021, available at **https://www.calcalistech.com/ctech/articles/0,7340,L-3917654,00.html**
4. Menachem Bentov, "Who Will Save My House?" *Mabat Malam* 37 (June 2004), 34–35 [Hebrew].
5. "Shai-Haganah" entry on the website of the Israel Intelligence Heritage and Commemoration Center, **https://www.intelligence.org.il/?module=articles&item_id=17&article_id=49&art_category_id=11**
6. One such example is the Shafan Unit, which operated from Jerusalem.
7. "History of the establishment of the IDF Intelligence Directorate," on the website of the Israel Intelligence Heritage and Commemoration Center [Hebrew].
8. "In a Small Apartment on Moshe Sneh Street, a Company Worth $1.2 Billion Was Born," *Globes*, May 1, 2016 [Hebrew], available at **https://www.globes.co.il/news/article.aspx?did=1000087600**
9. As journalists Dan Margalit and Ronen Bergman exposed in their book, the title of which refers to bunker under the IDF's main base: Dan Margalit and Ronen Bergman, *The Pit: The Dark Secrets Behind the Most Serious Leadership Crisis in the IDF's History* (Or Yehuda: Kinneret Zemora Bitan, 2011) [Hebrew]. This was the context of the military police investigation into Tal Dilian, the unit's commander at the time, leading to his retirement from the army (although he was acquitted a few years later).
10. Gili Cohen, "Israeli Army Plans to Create Separate Cybercorps, Similar to Air Force or Navy," *Haaretz*, June 16, 2015, available at **https://www.haaretz.com/2015-06-16/ty-article/.premium/idf-plans-to-create-new-cyberwarfare-branch/0000017f-deea-df62-a9ff-defff3c80000**
11. Momentum Cyber, *Cybersecurity Almanac 2022*.
12. Momentum Cyber, *Cybersecurity Almanac 2022*.
13. Sophie Shulman, "Unit 81: The Elite Military Unit that Caused a Big Bang in the Israeli Tech Scene," *Calcalist*, January 8, 2021, available at **https://www.calcalistech.com/ctech/articles/0,7340,L-3886512,00.html**
14. Amir Teig, "How to Turn a Bad Idea Into a $320-million Startup," *Haaretz*, November 6, 2015, available at **https://www.haaretz.com/israel-news/business/2015-11-06/ty-article/.premium/how-to-turn-a-bad-idea-into-a-320-million-startup/0000017f-f05c-d8a1-a5ff-f0debc810000**
15. Liat Ron, "I Won't Be the First Hi-Tech Guy to Enter Politics," *Walla!* September 9, 2021 [Hebrew], available at **https://finance.walla.co.il/item/3459007**

16. Attila Somfalvi, "The Warriors for Hi-Tech Scheme: '900 Trained, Most Already in the Industry," *ynet*, July 12, 2022 [Hebrew], **https://www.ynet.co.il/news/article/bjpajc9j5**

17. Scale-Up Velocity is one example of an organization that helps soldiers who have performed combat service make it into the hi-tech world.

Chapter 17

1. Dan Senor and Saul Singer, *Start-Up Nation* (New York: Twelve, 2009), 161.

2. Gilai Dolev, "The Risk Paid Off, Big Time," *ynet*, November 3, 2004 [Hebrew], available at **https://www.ynet.co.il/articles/1,7340,L-2998709,00.html**

3. In a blog post available at: **https://davidmcwilliams.ie/ireland-inc-gets-innovative/**

4. Gil Avnimelech and Morris Teubal, *Evolutionary Innovation and High Tech Policy: What can We Learn from Israel's Targeting of Venture Capital?* (Haifa: Samuel Neaman Institute, 2005), available at **https://www.neaman.org.il/Files/ste-25.pdf**

5. "Netanyahu: Beersheba Will Be the Cyber Capital of the Eastern Hemisphere," *ynet*, March 25, 2014 [Hebrew], available at **https://www.ynet.co.il/articles/0,7340,L-4503102,00.html**

6. Israeli Government Resolution 3976, Higher Steering Committee for the Relocation of IDF Bases to the Negev, August 24, 2008.

7. "The State Will Invest 25 Million NIS in Developing Hi-Tech in Beersheba," *N12*, January 11, 2022 [Hebrew], available at **https://www.mako.co.il/news-money/2022_q1/Article-bb8d43523394e71026.htm**

8. Amitai Ziv, "The State Is Launching a New Plan to Encourage Hi-Tech in Beersheba for 25 Million NIS," *TheMarker*, April 11, 2021 [Hebrew], available at **https://www.themarker.com/technation/2021-04-11/ty-article/.premium/0000017f-e1c9-df7c-a5ff-e3fbb93e0000**

9. Irad Atzmon Schmayer and Amitai Ziv, "They Dreamed of a Silicon Valley in the South—The Start-Ups Stayed in the Center," *TheMarker*, July 11, 2019 [Hebrew], available at **https://www.themarker.com/technation/2019-07-11/ty-article/.premium/0000017f-f57a-d318-afff-f77b97d40000**

10. According to Start-Up Nation Central data.

11. Omri Zerachovitz, "The Promise of Beersheba as a Hi-Tech City Is Stuck: 'Losing Money Every Day the IDF Doesn't Move South,'" *Globes*, November 27, 2017 [Hebrew], available at **https://www.themarker.com/technation/2017-11-27/ty-article/0000017f-ed47-d4a6-af7f-ffc7e2690000**

12. Government Resolution 3976.

13. Daniel Einhorn, "Beersheba, The Cyber Capital? Not If It Depends on the IDF," *TheMarker*, April 15, 2019 [Hebrew], available at **https://www.themarker.com/technation/2019-04-15/ty-article-opinion/0000017f-e109-d9aa-afff-f9598ca40000**

14. Omri Zerachovitz, "Israel Tax Authority Targets Tech Development Centers," *Globes*, October 29, 2020, available at **https://en.globes.co.il/en/article-israel-tax-authority-targets-tech-development-centers-1001347504**

Chapter 18

1. Erez Livne, "The Space Race: This Is How Israel Surprised the World on Its Way to Launching the First Made in Israel Satellite," *tech12*, October 4, 2022 [Hebrew], available at **https://www.tech12.co.il/index-technology_first/Article-e3555 a32dc79381026.htm**
2. Senor and Singer, *Start-Up Nation*, 67.

Chapter 19

1. OECD (2022), Hours worked (indicator). doi:10.1787/47be1c78-en.
2. "How Many of the Forbes 400 Are Jewish?" *CJNews*, available at **https://www .chicagojewishnews.com/how-many-of-the-forbes-400-are-jewish/**
3. Jerry Z. Muller, *Capitalism and the Jews* (Princeton, NJ: Princeton University Press, 2010), 87.

Chapter 20

1. Hagar Ravet and Meir Orbach, "Co-Founder of Team8: 'Success Requires that the Stars Align for You. We Know How to Align Them,'" *Calcalist*, September 20, 2020, available at **https://www.calcalistech.com/ctech/articles/0,7340,L-3850759 ,00.html**
2. Yasmin Yablonko, "Ehud Barak-Founded Cybersecurity Co Toka Raises $12.5m," *Globes*, July 16, 2018, available at **https://en.globes.co.il/en/article-ehud-barak-founded-cybersecurity-co-toka-raises-125m-1001246322**
3. Eliran Rubin, "Startup Cofounded by Ehud Barak Raises $12.5 Million for Cybersecurity," *Haaretz*, July 16, 2018, available at **https://www.haaretz .com/israel-news/business/2018-07-16/ty-article/startup-cofounded-by-ehud-barak-raises-12-5-million-for-cybersecurity/0000017f-db1f-df9c-a17f-ff1fbc0d0000**
4. Aaron Holmes, "How a Former Sequoia Capital Partner Cornered the Israeli Security Startup Market," *TheInformation.com*, August 16, 2022.
5. Based on average salary data from **Glassdoor.com** and taking into account other employment costs, such as pensions contributions, and healthcare, based on the premise that, in Israel, these top-ups are equivalent to 35% of a worker's salary, and in the United, States, that number is 25%. For a comparison of the most expensive

U.S. cities to employ software engineers: **https://leapscholar.com/blog/guide-on-software-engineer-annual-salaries-in-america**

6. Clayton M. Christensen et al, "The New M&A Playbook," *Harvard Business Review* 89, no. 3 (March 2011).

7. According to Israeli tax law, a tax must paid on the value of shares, in addition to capital gains tax of 25% on the profit from the rise in the share price.

Conclusion

1. Chantal da Silva, "H-1B Visa Row: Foreign Workers Make Up More than Half of Silicon Valley's Tech Industry, Reports Say," *Newsweek*, January 18, 2018, available at **https://www.newsweek.com/h-1b-visa-row-foreign-workers-make-more-half-silicon-valleys-tech-industry-784272**

2. Henrique Dubugras, "Why Silicon Valley Needs More Visas," *TechCrunch*, January 13, 2019, available at **https://techcrunch.com/2019/01/13/why-silicon-valley-needs-more-visas/**

3. Farhad Manjoo, "Why Silicon Valley Wouldn't Work without Immigrants," *The New York Times*, February 8, 2017, available at **https://www.nytimes.com/2017/02/08/technology/personaltech/why-silicon-valley-wouldnt-work-without-immigrants.html**

4. Foreign Workers Administration, Protocol 5.3.0043, "Foreign Experts—Hi-Tech and Cyber."

5. Israel Innovation Authority, "Annual Report: Hi-Tech Situation 2022." Shahar Ilan, "Hi-Tech Fever: One in Nine Employees Works in Hi-Tech," *Calcalist*, January 24, 2022 [Hebrew], available at **https://www.calcalist.co.il/calcalistech/article/bymukbhak;** Hagar Ravet, "It Turns Out that 14% of Israelis Work in Tech, But It Will Probably Stop There," *tech12*, July 6, 2022 [Hebrew], available at **https://www.tech12.co.il/index-startups/Article-739b9d0862ec181027.htm**

6. Sophie Shulman, "Tech Leaders Launch Initiative to Train 10,000 Employees from Under-Represented Populations," *Calcalist*, September 22, 2022, available at **https://www.calcalistech.com/ctechnews/article/h2n3fk303**

7. "Findings and Interim Targets of the National Committee for Increasing Human Capital in Hi-Tech Ahead of the 2023 Economic Plan," July 3, 2022 [Hebrew].

8. "Interim Findings of the Committee for Human Capital in Hi-Tech," Israeli Ministry of Innovation, Science, and Technology, July 6, 2022 [Hebrew]. Hagar Ravet, "It Turns Out that 14% of Israelis Work in Tech, But It Will Probably Stop There," *tech12*, July 6, 2022 [Hebrew], available at **https://www.tech12.co.il/index-startups/Article-739b9d0862ec181027.htm**

9. Israeli Government Resolution 1852, National Plan to Increase and Develop Skilled Human Capital for the Hi-Tech and Innovation Industry and Integration of Underrepresented Groups, September 11, 2022.

10. Talia Levin, "Matriculation Certificate in Hi-Tech? The Change in the Education System that Would Foster Technological Excellence," *Maariv*, September 24, 2022 [Hebrew], available at **https://www.maariv.co.il/news/Education/Article-947734**

11. Susan Pinker, *The Sexual Paradox* (Atlantic, London: 2008).
12. A survey from YL Ventures in 2019 shows that this is one of the three major challenges reported by information security managers. The CISO Circuit Report, Q3, 2019.
13. According to data from Start-Up Nation Central.
14. Sophie Shulman, "Only Half of Israel's Unicorns Are Still Worth $1 Billion," *Calcalist*, January 2, 2023, available at **https://www.calcalistech.com/ctechnews/article/hyxyymgqi**

The Ten Commandments of the Budding Entrepreneur

1. Thou Shalt Get Going.

Big ideas don't fall out of the sky while you're lying on the sofa waiting for a eureka moment.

If you want to be an entrepreneur and launch a startup, choose the field you want to focus on and get stuck into, get to know the existing technologies in depth, explore your customers' problems inside out—and innovation will follow. Once you put your finger on the problem you want to solve and have a direction for a potential solution, don't be tempted to think that everyone shares the same problem as you or that the solution that suits you will necessarily suit other customers. You've got to conduct in-depth research, including conversations with dozens of potential clients. It's not always easy because sometimes you'll have to find someone who can make an introduction, but it's essential. In the end, 95% of successful startups address existing needs or take existing solutions up a level, or in other words—it's all about evolution, not revolution.

2. Thou Shalt Not Underestimate the Importance of Your Sector.

Your idea for a product is not the only important thing; so is the sector where it is meant to provide a solution. There are some sectors in which it is relatively easy to get a project going because investors are already familiar with it and find it easier gauging whether your company will succeed and there's a supportive ecosystem. If you're an Israeli entrepreneur, the cyberindustry is a good place to start, precisely for these reasons. Moreover, the Israeli market is small, and in order to succeed on a global scale, it is usually advisable to start with the massive U.S. market, which operates in English, a language understood by most Israelis.

Israelis and Americans have very similar needs in the cybersector, which makes it easier for Israelis to build suitable products for the U.S. market.

In contrast, in a field like health tech, which is much more location-specific (the U.S. and Israel use totally different systems, and their markets have different needs), your experience as an Israeli is irrelevant to the experience of the U.S. healthcare system. Nowadays, as an angel investor, sometimes I see great entrepreneurs with good ideas—but they have chosen sectors that don't have supportive ecosystems to push them toward customers and investors. If I invest in a cybercompany, I know that it's got a much better shot at rapid growth. Companies in other sectors, no matter how great their teams, will grow more slowly: it is harder to raise investment and much harder to create connections with customers and partners. That doesn't mean that it's impossible, only that if you're going for something that exists in a different market, make sure you study the market well and the associated risks.

3. **Thou Shalt Not Stop Building Yourself Up through Knowledge and Experience.**

There's a disproportionate number of entrepreneurs whose stories start with "I've been interested in computers since I was four, and I wrote my first line of code when I was six." It's valuable to have your eyes opened to a field that interests you as early as possible because then it becomes like a mother tongue. You'll feel comfortable with it and know how things work. If you're interested in cyberinnovation, start digging deeper as early as you can. For Israelis who are still in high school, it's a great springboard into the army's technological units. And if you're already "grown up"—no sweat. You can still make it big, if you just plug any gaps in your knowledge and experience.

4. **Thou Shalt Choose the Right Partner.**

Your partner is someone who'll have your back and hold you tight in your company's toughest moments. I remember well the moments of crisis, when I was convinced we'd never get our product off the ground, technologically, while sales and new customers kept pouring in. I remember talking to Guy Nizan, who was living in New York at the time, and saying, "I'm not sure we'll manage to get this running." Those were the moments, and he knew it, when he needed to hold me and tell me, "You know, I'm actually in the field and the customers are pleased—just wait and see, it'll all work out."

Sometimes it was Nizan who called me, inundated with complaints from customers, and it was my turn to encourage him and tell him that we were on the brink of a breakthrough, and that in three months' time, it'd all work out. What helped us most was that we never took anything personally. Even if there were times we didn't agree with each other or got angry at each other, by the following morning, we'd given each other a call, and it was business as usual. You've got to be able to give everyone the space to get angry and let off steam, but to understand that, ultimately, it's nothing compared to the project you're running together. The right partners will be able to adopt these practices, and they'll make all the difference between success and failure.

5. **Thou Shalt Be Daring and Believe in Yourself.**

I mean, be polite and gentle and attentive, but . . . don't be afraid, for example, of demanding a big price tag from investors or customers. You know all your product's faults and know what's missing and which problems might devalue you and your product. But don't forget that the same thing is true of your rivals, and there's a good chance that what you're offering is better than what they have.

Do some crazy things. At one stage of our company's life, we received a message from a massive company saying the CEO wanted to meet us. We immediately assumed that the company was interested in a strategic collaboration or in acquiring IntSights. Nizan called me the day before the meeting in New York and said, "Get on a plane, come for the meeting, and fly back." That same day, I landed in the States, went to the meeting, and boarded a flight back to Israel. It was totally crazy, but just about doable. In the end, it turned out the company was just interested in what we were doing, and it had no intention of pursuing a strategic collaboration. Nevertheless, I was happy to get this totally illogical request because I understood it was the only route to amazing achievements in the startup world. Jump at opportunities, even if they require extreme efforts. Many of your efforts might go to waste, but in the end, you'll hit the jackpot.

Sometimes you'll have to be daring with yourself, too. We started IntSights without a moment's experience in hi-tech. True, I'd served in Unit 8200, but we had no clue about customers, building products, or sales. You'll run into many problems along the way, and you'll have to tell yourselves: I've never done this before, but I trust myself to work out how to solve this, and I trust my common sense when it comes to making decisions.

The first time I sold a teaching program at Cyberschool, I went to my old high school principal and told him, "Here's the syllabus, and I want to sell this course." It was scary. I had no sales experience and I was afraid of sounding like an idiot and I didn't know how he'd respond. A few years later, my partners and I went to Glilot Capital and told the company we wanted $2 million. It's scary to get these words out of your mouth: "Give me $2 million, and it'll all work out." It's a huge sum. But if you don't trust yourselves, nobody else is going to trust you, invest in you, or buy your (excellent) product.

6. **Thou Shalt Develop Connections.**

Dave Johnson, an advisor at Glilot Capital, used to be high up at Blackstone, one of the world's biggest private equity companies (which buy companies, build them up, and sell them). We wanted to rope in Blackstone as a client, and so when Johnson visited Israel, we met up with him. At one event, he said he liked wine. The following morning, Nizan asked Noga Ginzburg, our head of operations, to send him wine from the Golan Heights. That's how we made a connection; Blackstone soon became one of our customers, and Johnson became the chairman of our board of directors and helped us enormously in building our company's strategy.

One of the times I screwed up was when I turned away an investor in a way that wasn't quite polite enough. A while later, a friend wanted to introduce him to us as a future investor, but he didn't want to work with me. It's a small world. Today you might have no idea how someone in the industry can help you, but in a few years they might just be the investor or customer you need. Being nice to people and investing in connections might feel like a waste of time because you've got a product to develop and sell, but these connections are vital for startups in the long run.

7. **Thou Shalt Begin with the Customer.**

It is said that Henry Ford once said, "If I had asked people what they wanted, they would have said faster horses." Entrepreneurs often say that "customers don't know what they want," or that "you've got to think what's best for them, or else there'll never be innovation." But innovation comes from customers and from listening to their problems, not from an approach that says, "I know better than the customer." The thing to learn from Ford is that you don't have to ask the customer what the solution is, but you do need to ask them about the *problem*. Be modest, open, and willing to hear them out.

One of the most important stories in this context is about Quibi, a company that raised a fortune and was supposed to compete with Netflix on mobile devices: it created short-form content suitable for watching while traveling, raised $2 billion, $1 billion of which was invested in content, and entered the market . . . only to discover there was no demand. Its would-be customers preferred watching TikTok, YouTube, or just shorter bursts of Netflix.

As an investor, when I hear a company's pitch, the first thing I do is pick up the phone to a potential customer to hear what they think. There was a company that wanted to build a search engine for studies and medical diagnoses in order to help doctors interpret imaging scans. When I spoke to a potential customer—in this case, a doctor—he said this wouldn't solve his main problem, which wasn't about interpreting imaging scans, but about prioritizing the most important scans to read out of the pile on his desk. In a small proportion of cases, when he wasn't sure how to read results, he went to the most senior doctor on the ward—an interaction that he wasn't willing to do without because he trusted the experience and judgment of a specialist doctor more than any app, and along the way, he also learned a thing or two. I told the entrepreneurs, *this isn't for me.*

8. Thou Shalt Take Everything in Proportion.

Lots of things can happen to beginner entrepreneurs to make them feel it's all over. I still clearly remember the first customer who left us. It was the first time I felt I wasn't a top priority for customers in the cyberdefense world and that I was at a high risk of getting laid off the moment my customers decided to cut costs. In practice, and especially when the coronavirus crisis hit and many organizations started tightening their belts, it became clear to me that there were lots of things businesses would cut if they had to, but it would take ages for them to get around to cybersecurity, and even if they did, there was no guarantee they'd cut us. And still, after our first customer left us, I was downbeat and feared for my company's future.

Entrepreneurship is a marathon, and you always have to look at the bigger picture. There'll be lots of headaches, but they're a feature, not a bug. You have to be able to pick yourself up, shake off the dust, focus on solving problems, and remember that everything you solve will have an exponential effect. Let's say five customers left you because you were missing a certain feature. The moment you plug that gap, a problem facing hundreds of other customers will be solved. In many other fields, sometimes you'll have a specific problem with a customer, so you solve that specific problem and move to solving the next customer's problems. But tech products are constantly improving. If you keep in mind the exponential effect of every problem you solve, they'll assume totally different proportions.

9. **Thou Shalt Find the Right Work-Life Balance.**

Let's be honest: it's really hard to nail the two most important parts of life, especially when you're starting out. It's really hard to be both a good entrepreneur and the good parent and partner you've dreamed of being. Being an entrepreneur will keep you busy day and night, especially since you're working with the U.S. market. You'll need tons of flexibility to deal with things that go wrong, sudden flights, urgent crises—lots of things that don't suit the timetable of a family with kids. Your family will have to be ready for this lifestyle, and it's undoubtedly a tough balance to strike, especially at the start, when you're still learning to work out what really matters and what you can give a miss.

But in time, your company will stabilize, and you'll have a management layer of people you trust and can delegate some of your tasks to. I called this chapter "The Ten Commandments of the Budding Entrepreneur," and as a religious Jew, the commandment to "remember the Sabbath day and keep it holy" has obviously become an important anchor in my life. Shabbat is a day for quiet, rest, and investing in your family. Sometimes I felt my partners had to make up for my lack of availability on Saturdays, but I always made up for it by working even more intensely overnight in the middle of the week. That was the balance that suited me, and it worked great. The more experience you get and the farther you go, try to keep tilting the balance in favor of your family. When you're at home, be at home; when you're on a family trip, try to avoid work calls; and most importantly, remember that being an entrepreneur is an exciting, important, and life-changing experience—but family still always comes first.

10.   Thou Shalt Dream Big.

Go out and grab the biggest customers in the world. Go meet the best investors out there. Always aim to provide the most ambitious solution. And most importantly, never compromise on excellent employees. Sometimes it might be scary, even paralyzingly scary, to aim so high. You might think to yourself, "How are we going to build a product that serves 500 customers and employs 200 people?" But like hiking up a steep mountain, you always have to concentrate only on your next step. It's essential to combine dreams and aspirations with experience to keep moving forward just one more step. Enjoy the ride!

Index

Page numbers followed by *f* refer to figures.